Refugee Empowerment and Organizational Change

A Systems Perspective

Edited by Peter W. Van Arsdale

A publication of the Committee on Refugee Issues, a committee of
the General Anthropology Division, a unit of the American
Anthropological Asssociation

Library of Congress Cataloging-in-Publication Data

Refugee empowerment and organizational change : a systems perspective
/ edited by Peter W. Van Arsdale.
    p.   cm.
    Includes bibliographical references
    ISBN 0-913167-53-3
    1. Refugees—Services for. 2. Refugees—International relief. I. Van
Arsdale, Peter W. II. American Anthropological Association. Committee
on Refugee Issues.
HV640.R418   1993   92-36236
362.87—dc20   CIP

TABLE OF CONTENTS

Dedicated to Dr. Gottfried O. Lang
Professor Emeritus, University of Colorado
who consistently has helped empower those around him

PREFACE

Since the late 1970s, a surge in refugee activity has been experienced worldwide. Just as this period might be tabbed the "modern refugee era," the same period research/writing-wise might be tabbed the "era of modern refugee scholarship." Because the U.S. public's attention initially was focused on S.E. Asia, research and writing in this era initially emphasized Vietnamese, Cambodian, Laotian, and Hmong refugee issues. Socio-economic, psycho-social, and political studies were numerous. Among the most important scholars of the late 1970s and early 1980s were Darrell Montero, Stanley Sue, and David Haines.

During the mid to late 1980s the scope of refugee studies broadened considerably. Attention came to be turned toward the plights of Ethiopians, Angolans, Afghans, Russians, Cubans, and Haitians (to name but a few). More synthetic and conceptually rich studies began to appear. Susan Forbes-Martin, Robert Bach, and Barry Stein were among those who contributed to the detailed analytic studies that emerged.

Within the last five years increasing attention has been turned to the conduct of innovative field studies, particularly in countries of first asylum. Economic and political issues have continued to be emphasized, with demographic and human rights issues gaining much greater attention. Exemplary in this regard is the book by Mekuria Bulcha, Flight and Integration: Causes of Mass Exodus from Ethiopia and Problems of Integration in the Sudan (Scandinavian Institute of African Studies, 1988). Also exemplary are the series of issue papers being published by the U.S. Committee for Refugees (e.g., Peace or Terror: A Crossroads for Southern Africa's Uprooted), as well as articles appearing in the Journal of Refugee Studies and Global Justice. Not enough attention yet has been turned to regional studies, although S.E. Asia, the Middle East, and the Horn of Africa have been dealt with successfully. Still needed are comprehensive syntheses of refugee developments within Central America, S.W. Asia, and E. Europe (the latter to include the former Yugoslavia).

Taking a somewhat different approach to field research, and producing a book of far-reaching importance, is Barbara Harrell-Bond. Her volume Imposing Aid: Emergency Assistance to Refugees (Oxford University Press, 1986) effectively critiques the entire aid delivery process, and places the findings within the context of a "sub-set" of dependency theory. The volume edited by Gil Loescher and Laila Monahan, Refugees and International Relations (Oxford University Press, 1989) strongly complements this.

i

Surprisingly, in studies conducted both here and abroad, relatively little attention has been focused on the ecological underpinnings of refugee displacement and subsequent acculturation. John Berry, the Dyson-Hudsons, and I are among those who (independently) have worked to apply what variously might be termed "psycho-ecological" and "cultural-ecological" perspectives. G. Ainsworth Harrison also has addressed this, albeit tangentially, in his work on famine.

Also within the last five years, greater attention has been turned to the legal ramifications of international human displacement of all types, and to the interplay of law and policy. Some of this information has been covered in the book edited by Ved Nanda, Refugee Law and Policy (Greenwood Press, 1989), as well as in the International Journal of Refugee Law. During this same period, the study of refugee mental health has reached fruition, building upon the psycho-social foundations laid from 1975 to 1987 (which in turn relied upon earlier studies of U.S. minorities). Among the most important books in this regard is that edited by Wayne Holtzman and Thomas Bornemann, Mental Health of Immigrants and Refugees (Hogg Foundation for Mental Health, 1990). Experiencing a resurgence during this same five-year period are studies of ethnicity and nationalism as these pertain to refugees and immigrants. John Sorenson and Howard Adelman are among the leaders in this research. Such efforts can be expected to expand during the 1990s as the fall-out of events in the former Soviet Union and former Yugoslavia, plus reunited Germany and dissolving Somalia, continue to exert their impacts.

Historians have played a smaller but nonetheless significant role during the era of modern refugee scholarship. A recent book by Keith Quincy, Hmong: History of a People (Eastern Washington University Press, 1987) is noteworthy in this regard. Also noteworthy is the fact than increasing numbers of anthropologists have come to incorporate increasing amounts of substantive historical information into their studies of refugee and immigrant communities. Beatrice Hackett's work in Germany exemplifies this.

*   *   *   *   *

My own thinking, as well as that of many of the authors who have contributed to the present volume, has been shaped by the above research. Of equal importance have been my contacts with those "in the trenches," the service providers and refugees themselves with whom I am privileged to work. Standing out among my refugee colleagues are Tsegaye Hailu, Banchay Sourivong, Anwar Necko, and Maysee Moua Yang.

Special thanks are extended to Prof. George Shepherd and Prof. MaryCarol Hopkins who served as manuscript reviewers. Their thoughtful comments went a long way toward improving the quality of the finished product. The secretarial assistance of Sarah Van Arsdale was most appreciated, as was the computer-related assistance rendered by Mark Brady and Sharon Walthen. Capturing the spirit of the refugee experience through a number of drawings, one of which was selected for the book cover, was former University of Denver student Robert Weil. The patience and support of my wife, Kathy Van Arsdale, made the ultimate completion of Refugee Empowerment and Organizational Change possible, as did the encouragement of the Committee On Refugee Issues (CORI).

Peter W. Van Arsdale
Englewood, Colorado

iii

PART I
INTRODUCTION

EMPOWERMENT: A SYSTEMS PERSPECTIVE

Peter W. Van Arsdale
Colorado Division of Mental Health
and
University of Denver

A Laotian refugee colleague of mine, long a resident of the United States, recently posed one of the most difficult questions that can be asked of another refugee. "My friends and I have been working for nearly five years to help you. We've had some successes and some failures. When will you be able to help yourself?" To me, this strikes at the heart of the issue, for indeed empowerment is about helping others while ultimately enabling them to help themselves.

This chapter and this book are about the empowerment of refugees. As will become apparent, empowerment takes many forms. One way to frame the diverse approaches taken, and to better understand the various models employed, is by utilizing a systems perspective.

A SYSTEMS PERSPECTIVE

Perhaps surprisingly, my initial interest in empowerment sprang from my involvement with general systems analysis. Having taught a graduate course on the topic for nearly a decade, I had increasingly become interested in the roles that individuals play in "triggering" systems change. With a few notable exceptions such as Geoffrey Vickers, systems authorities seemed consistently to bypass the roles individuals play. Eminent scholars like Kenneth Boulding wrote of the interplay of economic, cultural, biological, and other forces, but did little to address the roles played by individuals.[1] While a function of the system, empowerment occurs at the level of the actor.

Apart from empowerment, my interest in systems dates back still further, to the early 1970s. It was spurred from three directions--the general work of Ludwig von Bertalanffy, the anthropological work of Edmund Leach, and the graduate anthropology seminars I attended at the University of Colorado. The seminars were hosted by Gottfried Lang, to whom the present book is dedicated. Von Bertalanffy's writings triggered animated discussions in our seminars. What constituted a system? What were the sources of change? Were external or internal forces (i.e., inputs or throughputs) more important? How could outputs be measured? How were systems controlled and regulated?

Von Bertalanffy laid out the systems-analytic framework in masterful fashion so as to capture the imaginations of a broad range of scientists and scholars.[2] His first "formal" proposal of general system theory came in 1947; in the next decade and a half he fine-tuned and expanded upon his initial propositions. In brief, he built upon both multi- and inter-disciplinary sources to generate a hybrid discipline. He believed that both explanatory and predictive laws needed to be expanded, with the biological, behavioral, and social sciences "coming into their own," as it were. While not to be eschewed entirely, he believed it essential to move beyond more traditional, mechanistic explanations to multi-causal explanations. Unilinear, cause-effect models, while useful in some contexts, were demonstrated to be inferior to multi-variate models. Building in particular upon the work of biologists, medical researchers, engineers, and social scientists of the 1930s and 1940s, von Bertalanffy succeeded in synthesizing an extremely useful framework for scientific analysis.

While his quest for systems laws per se encountered barriers, his work did go on to demonstrate (albeit incompletely) that application could follow theory.

Leach laid out a specific case so as to capture the imagination of the cultural anthropologist.[3] In studying the Kachin of highland Burma he demonstrated that flux exists in their socio-political system. While attributable in part to variable ecological and economic forces at play in the tropical environment, it also is attributable to a certain ambiguity in Kachin ideology and social structure. While patterns exist, he was able to demonstrate that their very existence is characterized by a degree of cognitive ambiguity, an ambiguity that is adaptive. Of even greater importance, he demonstrated why the synchronic structural-functional models so prevalent to that time were of little use.

The concept of flux subsequently has proven of great importance in understanding systems variation and sustainability, and in assessing how individuals "fit" and "maneuver" within organizations.

For the understanding of empowerment as presented by the authors represented in this volume, the impact of the work of von Bertalanffy and Leach is less in terms of theory, than in terms of guideposts for "framing" the analyses--particularly those which focus on institutions and organizations.

DEVELOPMENT AND SUSTAINABILITY

Much of what has informed my thinking on empowerment has come from my work in the field of overseas development. Having had the opportunity to work on water resource projects in Southeast Asia, the Horn of Africa, the Caribbean, South America, Central America, and North America, I came to believe that indigenous peoples had a great deal of specific knowledge that could be shared with outsiders--including engineers--as to the ways water systems work. Although mechanisms and institutions often were not in place to take advantage of their knowledge, it seemed especially applicable to issues of sustainable development. It is tied directly to a systems perspective because success in projects of this type requires an understanding of the interplay of ecosystems and institutional systems.

As noted by Albertson, sustainable development has two aspects: One deals with resource renewal rather than depletion, and is usually used to refer to environmental impact and usage. The other deals with what is termed internal sustainability. Where external support systems are involved, successful development at the local level occurs when external influence has been removed and the intended beneficiaries carry on by themselves.[4]

The work of Swantz complements that of Albertson. In her consideration of labor issues in the global economy, she links sustainable development to the empowerment of workers. A particular concern is that of labor exploitation of guest workers and migrant laborers, overseas as well as in the U.S. She believes that systems change and individual empowerment will occur as principles of economics and democracy are better understood. The three most important principles are: (a) economic theorizing which starts with practice, not theory, (b) paying greater attention to issues of scale, and (c) managing economic affairs and businesses in multiple, culturally connected ways.[5]

Scott-Stevens work, in turn, complements that of Swantz and brings us full circle in terms of development. She considers sustainability from the perspective of the interplay of foreign consultants and the indigenous counterparts who work with them on specific development projects. Her own work, conducted on water resource projects in Java to which I also was assigned, illustrates the importance of empowering one's colleagues. The transfer of technology is tied to the transfer of knowledge to one's counterparts-in-training.[6]

MODELS OF EMPOWERMENT

A number of models of empowerment have been developed, either formally or informally, over the last several decades. Some literally have come "from the grassroots up," whereas others have been based upon empirical research and fieldwork. Still others are what might be termed experiential or advocacy-oriented. Among those individuals most influential in this regard have been social workers such as Ruth Parsons and community development specialists such as Lawrence Salmen. The contributions of anthropologists have been important, but usually indirect and based upon related studies of social networks, community organizations, and leadership patterns.

Based upon the analyses I have conducted, which include information from each of the chapters in the present volume, I believe that the following types of models can be identified:

* Emically-defined, grassroots models: These are models which rely primarily or exclusively upon the experiences of potential/actual project beneficiaries or community members themselves. They rarely are based on formal research upon the populations in question, but rather rely upon self-reports by members of these groups as to what has worked (and what has not) as changes have been attempted. In this volume, the chapter by Vang Pobzeb serves as a case in point.

* Etically-defined, grassroots models: These are models which rely primarily upon the observations and experiences of human services professionals, social workers, practicing anthropologists, educators, or community developers working in community settings in the U.S. or abroad. Although research data may be used to round out the models, they rarely are formulated initially owing to formal research upon the populations in question. The information on grassroots empowerment usually emanates from project-based experiences. Although not reported in detail in this volume, some of my own empowerment work with refugee Mutual Assistance Associations in Colorado is of this type.

* Empirically-based research models: These models are based upon field research conducted in community settings in the U.S. or abroad. Qualitative research is the primary method used, with material on empowerment per se often coming about as a "spin-off" from investigations into other, related topics. In this volume, the chapters by Tanya Basok, Pauletta Otis, and Art Hansen provide good examples from overseas. The chapter by Lucia Ann ("Shan") McSpadden provides a useful example of research relying upon psychological data in concert with other, qualitative data to ascertain stress, status, and aspirations.

* Institutional models: Models of this sort rely upon institutional analyses of the incentives and constraints to effecting change. Empowerment is analyzed in the context of corporations, agencies, and organizations such as NGOs (non-governmental organizations). If not explicitly, the issues of "organizational culture" often are at least implicitly addressed. The chapter by Pamela DeVoe and that by Patricia Campbell, Debra Kreisberg-Voss, and Joy Sobrepeña take this approach.

* Training and technical assistance models: These are models which are based upon the experiences and observations of professional educators and trainers working with members of the communities in question. In most instances the focus of the training has been upon skill-building, in such areas as language and employment, with links to empowerment emerging through subsequent discussions and debates. The chapter by Myrna Ann Adkins and Barbara Sample illustrates this.

* Advocacy models: These are models based upon the work of community advocates, political activists, applied researchers, and (in some instances) policymakers, each of whom has taken it upon him- or herself to speak out and pursue "the cause." The defining feature of such models is that empowerment advocacy becomes the central focus of a planned, concerted effort. In the present volume, certain of the Mutual Assistance Associations and patron - client systems discussed by Carol Mortland represent this thrust.

Clearly, the above categories are not meant to be exhaustive. For example, models derived from psychology studies have not been included (although McSpadden's work integrates some of this information). Neither are the above categories meant to be mutually exclusive. Elements of the emically-defined, grassroots models also will be found in the advocacy models, for example.

New Possibilities: In addition to the possibility of building upon the concept of flux (discussed previously), which has yet to be explored in depth, other new possibilities for empowerment models are emerging. One that is very pragmatic involves what are known as peer lending groups. These build upon collaborative linkages between small groups of refugees and "culturally attuned" lenders. For example, in the state of Washington groups to six to eight Hmong refugees are banding together along traditional clan lines for social and fiscal support. Aided by the Cascadia Development Group, loans average about $2000, and are intended for so-called micro-enterprise projects. One man used his loan to expand his 13-acre garden. Refugees are hopeful that the number of peer lending groups will increase under the Clinton administration, since microenterprise development is being touted as one method of revitalizing the economy.[7]

One other possibility needs to be discussed, since it involves coalition building. It is exemplified in the work of PrairieFire Rural Action. This non-profit, rural organizing and training organization works with diverse constituencies of farm, labor, religious, minority, and other community-based groups to build what they term a "progressive rural agenda" in the American Mid-West. Among the issues addressed have been those of ethnic tensions and economic development confronting refugees and other immigrants employed in the meatpacking industry in Kansas, Nebraska, and Iowa.[8]

Facilitated Empowerment: Each of the above complements and informs what I refer to as the process of facilitated empowerment. Coalition building is especially important. Facilitated empowerment is defined as empowerment which is couched in an institutional setting and relies upon the non-directive opportunities provided by those with greater power for those with less power. In true systems fashion, it depends upon the interplay of external and internal actors and organizations.

Those persons more familiar with the objectives at hand assist those less familiar. Ongoing training and followup occur. The internal actors (i.e., the refugees being empowered) set the general goals, the external actors (i.e., the facilitators) help fine-tune them in light of known political, economic, and American multicultural realities. The facilitators assure access to needed resources, especially information.

Interactive Approaches: The authors represented in the present volume cover concepts, processes, problems, and models of empowerment from several complementary perspectives. Each approach interacts with one or more of the others.

Five of the chapters employ what might be termed explicit systems-analytic frameworks. That by DeVoe analyzes employment systems, building directly upon the pioneering work of Immanuel Wallerstein. Her analysis of Southeast Asian refugees includes the interactive process of cultural discourse. That by McSpadden analyzes socio-economic systems, in a manner which complements that of DeVoe. McSpadden focuses on the interplay between sponsors and both Ethiopian and Eritrean refugees.

Basok's research on Salvadorean refugees in Costa Rica includes an explicit systems analysis of institutional systems. The role of inputs (e.g., from church-based organizations and lenders) are key to her interpretations. In analyzing the Kurdish refugee problem, Otis analyzes state systems. Boundary maintenance is one systems issue of concern to her. The chapter on the work of the office of the United Nations High Commissioner for Refugees (UNHCR) by Campbell, Kreisberg-Voss, and Sobrepeña focuses on the international refugee system. Information access is one systems issues that receives their attention.

While not employing an explicit systems-analytic framework, Adkins and Sample's chapter on training programs for refugees also focuses on information access. A major concern of Vang Pobzeb in his work through the Hmong Council Education Committee is information access, and the need for government agencies to be more responsive.

8

Information access and resource access go hand-in-hand. Problems of resource access are covered by Campbell et al., Basok, DeVoe, and McSpadden, as well as by Hansen in his study of Angolan refugees in Zambia. Regarding the core concept of empowerment, he stresses that it is a misconception to believe that becoming a refugee causes one to lose all power. Loss of power is a variable, not an absolute. Mortland's analysis of the evolution of Mutual Assistance Associations also is concerned with power, especially as this is manifested in patron - client (including sub-rosa) relationships and community activities.

Durable solutions to refugee displacement are detailed by Campbell et al., and touched on by Basok, Hansen, and Otis. I would anticipate that still more of the refugee studies to be conducted during the 1990s will use systems-analytic frameworks as researchers address durable solutions. In the concluding chapter, Daramola and Mozia stress that theories, policies, and practical solutions must be closely intertwined if refugees really are to be empowered.

Cautions: In considering concepts and models of empowerment, cautions also must be taken. Since the mid 1980s the term empowerment has come to be used widely, by representatives of many disciplines and diverse types of human service organization. While this book makes it clear that empowerment is not a unitary process or concept, and that no single model need be chosen to the exclusion of others, there is potential for misuse--even abuse--of the term.

By way of illustrating the diversity of usage, three brief examples from the field of Native American activity have been selected. In considering the Indian Self-Determination and Education Assistance Act of 1975, Fleming notes that it established mechanisms whereby federally recognized American Indian tribes are "empowered with freedom" to plan and implement various health, educational, and social services.[9] Another example involving Native Americans covers an HIV education program being developed in North Dakota. Initiated by the Department of Family Practice at the University of North Dakota, it is stated that it stresses empowerment through a culturally sensitive education program emphasizing traditional family values and prevention education.[10] In yet another involving Native Americans, my colleagues at the Institute of Cultural Affairs are covering empowerment of leaders through the "technology of participation."

EMPOWERMENT AND IMMIGRATION

Finally, and providing a link to the concluding chapter by Daramola and Mozia, we must consider models of immigration. Schmitter Heisler has summarized this best.[11] Couching her overall analysis in world systems terms,

Schmitter Heisler stresses that we still lack what she terms a formal theory of immigration and immigrant incorporation, but we now are much better able to understand the processes. She considers three periods, each producing models still prevalent:

1) The classic (1900 - 1969), represented by push/pull and assimilation models
2) The modern (1970 - 1989), reflecting neo-Marxist and structured inequality perspectives
3) The emergent (1990 - present), focusing on multiculturalism, social movements, and citizenship acquisition processes.[12]

Appropriately, she notes that a variety of models can be useful; no single one need dominate. The present volume reflects this diversity, but taken more from the perspective of empowerment of immigrants rather than immigration processes per se. I also agree with her that the newest, "emergent" models seem promising, if not yet fully developed. For example, at the University of Denver through the Consortium On Rights Development (CORD), we have begun pursuing models involving social movements. We are finding a great deal of enthusiasm among faculty and students for this, but as yet, relatively little substantive background research to draw upon. Further, systematic links to refugee studies have yet to be made.

*   *   *   *   *

Refugees are tremendously resilient people. Time and again they demonstrate the ability to bounce back from adversity, to adapt to strange circumstances, to smile in the face of sorrow, to help one another. As they become empowered, all of us become enriched.

NOTES

[1]G. Vickers, "Control, Stability and Choice" and K.E. Boulding, "Towards a General Theory of Growth," both in The General Theory of Systems Applied to Management and Organization, Vol. 1, D.M Jamieson et al., eds. (Seaside, CA: Intersystems, 1980).

[2]Among the numerous publications of L. von Bertalanffy, the one that synthesizes his earlier work best is "General System Theory--A Critical Review," in Modern Systems Research for the Behavioral Scientist: A Sourcebook, W. Buckley, ed. (Chicago: Aldine, 1968; article originally published in 1962).

[3]E. Leach, Political Systems of Highland Burma (Boston: Beacon, 1954). On this, also see M. Harris, The Rise of

Anthropological Theory: A History of Theories of Culture
(New York: Thomas Y. Crowell, 1968, p. 584).

[4]M. Albertson's comments on sustainable development are
derived from a presentation made at the annual meeting of
the Colorado Council of International Organizations, held in
Denver, Colorado, in October of 1992; and from his "Prospec-
tus for an International Conference on Village-Based
Sustainable Development," which is unpublished and also
dated October, 1992.

[5]M.-L. Swantz, "Patterns of Empowerment: Cultural Identity
and Global Integration," Development (1992: 3), pp. 46-49.

[6]S. Scott-Stevens, Foreign Consultants and Counterparts:
Problems in Technology Transfer (Boulder, CO: Westview,
1987).

[7]This information is excerpted from a radio feature entitled
"Peer Lending Groups," broadcast on National Public Radio,
December 21, 1992.

[8]D.L. Ostendorf, "PrairieFire Rural Action: A Force for
Empowerment in Rural America," C&A/Culture and Agriculture
Bulletin (Fall 1992), No. 44, pp. 16-19.

[9]C.M. Fleming, "American Indians and Alaska Natives: Chang-
ing Societies Past and Present," in Cultural Competence for
Evaluators: A Guide for Alcohol and Other Drug Abuse
Prevention Practitioners Working with Ethnic/Racial
Communities, M.A. Orlandi, R. Weston, and L.G. Epstein, eds.
(Washington, DC: U.S. Department of Health and Human
Services/Public Health Service, 1992, p. 157).

[10]"Indian HIV Education," The AIDS Review (Denver, CO:
Colorado AIDS Project, October 5, 1992, p. 2).

[11]B. Schmitter Heisler, "The Future of Immigrant Incorporation: Which Models?   Which Concepts?" International
Migration Review 26:   623-645, 1992.

[12]I have assigned dates which I believe are appropriate to
the latter two periods described by Schmitter Heisler.

PART II

ORGANIZATIONAL CHANGE: THE INTERNAL DYNAMIC

PATRON - CLIENT RELATIONS AND THE EVOLUTION OF MUTUAL ASSISTANCE ASSOCIATIONS

Carol A. Mortland
Dowling College

INTRODUCTION[1]

The arrival of Southeast Asian refugees to the United States since mid-1975 has been accompanied by the development of refugee self-help groups exhibiting multiple structures and goals. Over time, many of these self-help groups have adjusted their organizational structures, goals, and activities to American policy and procedures in order to obtain legitimacy and public funding, as has occurred for non-Southeast Asian refugees as well. Consequently, and in cooperation with Americans, refugees have developed what are termed Mutual Assistance Associations (MAAs) out of existing self-help groups and as new organizations intended to achieve a number of ends, including the provision of social services to refugees. In so doing, both Americans and refugees operating in the American refugee social service network have come to utilize multiple definitions of "mutual assistance associations," depending on actor and context.

This chapter discusses the development of Mutual Assistance Associations, primarily among Southeast Asian refugees (SEAR). It covers the development of an alternative social service model used by some of them, and goes on to illustrate how this differs from one "standard" American model of social service. It will be shown how a common definition of "mutual assistance association" for Americans and refugees benefits both groups, although often in different ways to meet different goals.

DEVELOPMENT OF A MUTUALLY-DEFINED MODEL OF SOCIAL SERVICES DELIVERY: THE MUTUAL ASSISTANCE ASSOCIATION

The arrival of each new wave of immigrants to the United States has been greeted by a plethora of official and unofficial modes of assistance. But no particular immigration has received as much governmental and private assistance as has that of Southeast Asian refugees, who have been accepted as refugees and transplanted in large numbers--over one million as of 1992--to this country since the overthrow of the American-supported governments of South Vietnam, Laos, and Cambodia in the mid-1970s.

The bulk of this public and private assistance has been funneled through federal programs and national voluntary agencies via state public assistance programs, local agencies, churches, and philanthropic organizations to individual refugees dispersed throughout the country.

The arrival of Southeast Asian refugees in the United States after mid-1975 saw the establishment of refugee organizations, most created by Vietnamese, by far the largest number of SEAR arriving in the country. Many were devoted to redressing the political situation in Vietnam. Resistance groups were formed, some with the goal of sending soldiers and supplies to Southeast Asia to fight against the new Communist government, others to pressure the American government either to assist in re-establishing an anti-Communist government in Southeast Asia or to protest activities of Communist governments in the international arena.[2] In addition, religious organizations began to be formed in response to refugees' desires to find familiarity in religious practice. For example, Vietnamese Catholic services became available in various local parishes, and Vietnamese Catholic priests set up services in Vietnamese communities.

At the same time, the United States government was exploring alternative ways to assist this influx of Southeast Asian refugees in integrating into American society. In addition to providing public assistance benefits through state welfare offices and contracting with national voluntary agencies (VOLAGs) for initial resettlement help and funding, the United States began exploring the possibility of funding Southeast Asian refugee organizations, whatever their original agendas, for the additional purpose of providing social services to refugees. Specifically, these services were to include employment, English language instruction, vocational training, skills recertification, general information and referral, and interpretation and translation.

Meanwhile, SEAR leaders began to see the possibility of themselves providing services that had been heretofore provided by American social service agencies. Some Southeast Asian refugee organizations were already doing this kind of work: Religious organizations, such as Vietnamese Catholic priests working in American parishes, and various Vietnamese leaders with sufficient resources, contacts, and inclination to assist their fellow refugees. These often highly educated Vietnamese, many already familiar with Western conceptions of social service and bureaucracy, also were familiar with Southeast Asian cultural ideas about "helping" and with the actual resettlement experiences and needs of refugees.

Whatever the agendas of infant Southeast Asian refugee groups, some Americans and refugee leaders themselves began to agree that social services could be provided as well, if not better, to such refugees by SEAR organizations. Refugee leaders who understood American social services and in addition the language and conceptual orientations of refugees were thought to be in a position to offer valuable services to their fellow countrymen.

And so it began: Refugee organizations turned their attention to social services and American government funding. Some organizations remained focused on their original agendas (building and/or supporting a resistance army in Southeast Asia, providing religious services, or preserving their culture), while adding social services. Others stuck to the original agendas informally (and invisibly),[3] while switching their public attention to the provision of social services to refugees. Other leaders began to see the possibility of obtaining federal and state funds for providing social services, and thus began setting up organizations which came to be called Mutual Assistance Associations (MAAs).[4]

Now, seventeen years later, the American government continues to fund MAAs, the creations of numerous and diverse refugee groups: Cambodian, Lao, Afghan, Polish, Iranian, and Haitian, to name a few. American government and state government personnel, those in policy positions, view these mutual assistance associations as community-based groups providing services to refugees with public funding, supplemented with private resources and knowledge. Private knowledge and resources are assumed to include awareness of refugee experiences, problems, and needs, as well as staff familiar with clients' language and cultural conceptions because they themselves are members of the client ethnic, national, or religious group.

However, the ethnic providers of social services and the clients who receive them operate on a different conceptual model from that of the Americans, a model that structures what and how services are actually delivered. While some Americans, especially those at the local level (where services are actually delivered and utilized) are aware of this different model, their perception is either ignored by or withheld from Americans in policy positions, thus preserving the public version of Mutual Assistance Associations as providers of social services on the American model. Both refugee leaders of MAAs and Americans on all levels preserve the myth that all actors are participating in utilizing a common (i.e., American) model of social service provision.

In order to better understand the development of two social service models operating under the mutually-developed definition of one quasi-mythical model, I will review the history of MAAs in the United States, looking particularly at MAA development among Southeast Asian refugees since 1975.

HISTORY OF MAAs IN THE UNITED STATES

1975-1979: Early MAAs: Prior to 1975 there were no known, formally organized Southeast Asian self-help groups in the United States. By the late 1980s there were over 1,000 incorporated, non-profit refugee self-help groups in

17

the country, in addition to numerous other informal associations.[5] The first refugee self-help groups begun in 1975 were small and informal. Ha Ton Vinh, describing these early groups, writes that "the formation of an Indochinese association often begins with a small group of two-three people; sometimes with one person who has initiatives and resources to foster a plan of action."[6]

Ha describes five kinds of mutual assistance associations that came into existence in the late 1970s-- religious, political, self-help, professional, and student, categories that continue to be useful today. Religious groups focus on establishing temples (or congregations within churches). Political groups hope, in Ha's words, to "counteract Communist propoganda and biases against the refugee community, to nuture a dream of future triumphant return to the homeland and openly criticize the dictatorship of the Communist governments."[7] Self-help groups engage in activities designed to foster friendship and mutual understanding among refugee groups and the American community, to bolster community spirit, to offer special services such as native language classes, information and referral services for those people with limited resources, senior citizens, and those recently arrived in the area.[8]

Much of their attention focuses on producing cultural and musical performances. These self-help groups, in Ha's description, "usually do not have an official membership list because most of the programs are organized for the general public, and they are not incorporated and do not have non-profit and tax-exemption status."[9] However, Ha notes that already some groups formed between 1975 and 1979 were beginning to apply for official status. Professional and student groups arose as refugees began to find themselves in similar educational and occupational settings, with similar experiences and goals.

He notes that there were approximately 200 mutual assistance associations as of 1979. He saw these MAAs placing their focus on gaining security in sameness, preserving their culture, and creating a kind of bridge for newcomers to American society. These refugees believed "that at any price they have to preserve their heritage and also expose the richness of their culture to the people of the host country." At the same time, they are caught in a dilemma; they have to let go of what they hold dear in order to survive.[10]

Although Ha's discussion of MAAs through 1979 describes some MAAs as self-help groups, he does not include a discussion of them as service providers, an important point for my analysis. He does, however, make a series of recommendations to help MAAs play their roles in more effective ways in the resettlement program. First, these include encouraging refugees to establish MAAs. Secondly, Ha suggests providing information on how to set up such an organization, write by-laws, file incorporation papers, and complete tax forms. In addition, he suggests helping refugee leaders plan events, expand activities, and uncover resources by "getting the attention of agency people."[11] Certainly Ha sees MAAs moving from informal self-help associatons (i.e., informal clusters of members assisting one another) to formally-constituted associations providing service to a range of clients.

In Ha's opinion, money was the greatest need of these fledgling refugee groups, because seed money and office space would allow refugees to develop their own community programs such as "counseling outreach, information and referral, arts and cultural exhibits and performances."[12] He also urged that refugees be included in policy-making sessions, hired by resettlement programs, and included on the advisory boards set up for various service programs.

1979-1981: MAAs as Service Providers: During the next two years Ha's suggestion became reality. Refugees came to be organized into more and increasingly formalized organizations. By early 1981, more than 500 MAAs existed nationwide, including at least 340 Vietnamese, 75 Cambodian, 45 Lao, and 35 Hmong, as well as five Southeast Asian ethnic Chinese associations and an additional number of mixed ethnic group MAAs.[13] Of these, a small number were receiving funds for the fiscal 1981 year from the federal government's Office of Refugee Resettlement.

A survey conducted in 1981 by the newly established Indochina Refugee Action Center, itself a nationwide assistance association, documented the stated purposes, goals, and achievements of the 60 MAAs surveyed. The results (categories of which do not total 100% due to multiple responses) were as follows:

Purpose Founded	Current Achievements
80% social/fraternal	65% social/service delivery
68% educational/cultural	50% preservation of heritage/cultural education
13% professional	23% building the association
12% religious	8% provision of professional and related services

Have Been Unable to Provide	Reason for Inability to Implement Goals
37% social and resettlement services on regular basis	67% lack of funding
18% cultural heritage and educational services	18% lack of staff and staff time
15% professional/training and employment opportunities	13% relative unreadiness of the association
12% association expansion	5% non-acceptance by "the system"

These data clearly demonstrate the desire on the part of the MAAs to provide social services, and to obtain funding for that purpose. Half the associations surveyed stated that in five years time, they planned on providing social services with funding; 12% planned on developing the MAA into a resettlement agency, and 33% wanted to serve as the focus of a refugee community through such activities as forming a community center.

Not only had the goals of MAAs changed in the two years since Ha's article was published, but their structure had also changed. Of the associations surveyed by the Indochina Refugee Action Center in 1981, all but two of the groups had been granted (or had pending) federal tax-exempt status, and 80% either had or were waiting for a Federal Employer Iden-tification Number, required for groups receiving federal grant funds. Most organizations now had a board of direc-tors, necessary for incorporation. Those MAAs surveyed reported a shift from occasional large community meetings to monthly board meetings.[14] Indeed, recently-funded MAAs re-vealed a difference in board composition from older funded and non-funded organizations: 45% of the MAAs reported that their boards included American-born, non-refugee board mem-bers, an indicator of new awareness on the part of refugee leaders of resources available to them and the need for Americans' advice and know-how.

This increase in the number of MAAs being established and the concommitant shift in focus often occurred at the behest of American-born social workers and sponsors, who expressed interest in assisting refugees in organizing them-selves in order to obtain newly available funds. This occurred on both local and national levels. Two Americans have written about their experience in helping refugees es-tablish a local MAA. According to them, in order for the group to function as a "formal organization," it was neces-sary for the group to acquire the symbols and tools of legitimacy, authority, and effectiveness. Selecting a board in becoming incorporated, obtaining the essential tax-exempt status, designing a social service program, and managing an organization--all are crucial activities.[15]

The refugee group being assisted by Granville and Powell, however, soon ran into difficulties. In Granville and Powell's perception, the organization often could not make decisions because it lacked a quorum. When confronted with the responsibility to participate in management, group members did not attend but left the decision-making up to a few leaders. Granville and Powell were then prompted to compel the refugees to operate as they thought they should, by calling the refugees repeatedly to remind them of meet-ings, giving them rides to meetings, and applying repeated pressure to individuals to particiapte in the group.

At about the same time, American sponsors were encouraging the local refugee population of a small east-coast town, herein referred to Freetown, to establish an

20

MAA. Their effort was motivated by the possibility of obtaining government funds. It failed, one American sponsor said, because "it didn't come from them" and "they were not ready for it."[16]

The rhetoric for encouraging MAA development also continued on the national level: MAAs should be formed, consulted, advised, trained, and funded.[17] In 1981 alone, the Indochina Refugee Action Center published seven papers on refugee resettlement. The two most often repeated themes about MAAs were clearly articulated in these publications: 1) "There is increasing recognition by public and private agencies and organizations at all levels of the need to build the capacity of MAAs to assist in the resettlement process;" and 2) "many MAAs need assistance to improve staff skills and service capabilities, especially accounting and record-keeping systems and generally augment their role as service providers . . . ."[18]

Thus, it was thought by Americans at the beginning of the 1980s that refugee leaders must be trained for social service delivery.[19] This training must include not only technical aspects, such as the accounting and record-keeping mentioned by Harmon and Robinson, but education in the very concepts of democratically-conceived social service provision. To prove the need for educating refugees in basic democratic and bureaucratic concepts, Americans cited struggles between local MAAs and their American sponsors and "helpers"--and with other social service agencies--over issues such as representation and client - service provider relationships.[20]

From Americans' viewpoints, major concerns with several aspects of representation in MAA establishment can be distilled from these discussions. There is representation of the larger community, representation by board members once chosen, and representation of clients (to the extent that these differ from community representation). Granville and Powell's 1981 difficulties with establishing a quorum are echoed in Ledgerwood's 1986 depiction of the attempt to establish an MAA in a city on the west coast. The strategy to get members--either from the community or the board--to attend meetings was a constant item on every agenda, particularly at meetings where lack of a quorum prevented discussion of any other matter. The issue of representation and of differing goals can be seen in the following case.

In Gadding, a large west coast city, a "Central Registry Task Force" comprised of American service providers and refugee MAA leaders was set up to decide how to spend funds locally available to refugees.[21] A major--but exceedingly polite--disagreement arose between American agency personnel and MAA leaders over whether to spend the funds on a "central refugee registry" or a "refugee-run service center." The Americans said the central registry would evidence need at the same time it identified clients, who could then be served by existing agencies. Refugee leaders called the proposed registry an infringement of their "freedom and

rights" (a basic reason they gave for having come to
America). They claimed they needed their own service center
controlled by refugees. A series of meetings was held to
decide how funds would be spent in such an effort. The min-
utes of these meetings make clear the struggle between non-
refugees and refugees over agenda: Non-refugees kept trying
to discuss their issue (a registry), while refugees kept
trying to discuss theirs (a refugee service center).

After several months of such meetings, the refugees
came to one session with a specific suggestion; they proposed changing the name of the "Central Registry Task Force"
to the "Hudson County Refugee Service Center." One
Vietnamese MAA leader suggested centering all refugee services and case management in the refugee service center (an
interesting idea to present to a body composed of American
social workers already providing those services). The
Americans finally yielded, saying privately they had done so
because of the national interest in MAAs, the unyielding
stance of local refugee leaders, and a secret conclusion
that the refugee-run center would not last, because "refugees don't know how to do this like we do."[22]

The refugees got their refugee center, but the
Americans' conclusions seemed prophetic. There were constant struggles among participating MAAs over staff hiring,
conflicts with other agencies and bilingual workers, and
ill-attended board meetings. After several years, the
center essentially dissolved in a welter of accusations
among competing MAAs, and between Americans and refugees
over alleged corruption, misrepresentation, and misuse of
funds. However, despite this crisis and declining funding,
the center remained open six years later, primarily through
the efforts of bilingual workers for whom the center's loss
would have resulted in serious blows to their reputation,
and through Americans devoted either to the empowerment of
refugees or the preservation of their refugee friends' jobs
and honor.

This local MAA coalition, like MAAs nationally, had
slowly and rather traumatically come of age. Because MAA
leaders and staff could speak the language and "knew the
hearts" of their fellow refugees, this like others came to
be touted in various publications and in national and local
arenas as the new answer to refugee service provision.
These came to be seen as being able to provide a broad range
of services to refugees, and in so doing, relieving refugees
of many of their anxieties relating to life in a new country. In this way, MAAs also came to be seen as a positive
factor in combating refugees' mental health problems.[23]

<u>1981-Present: Continued Existence as Service Providers:</u>
Today, refugee mutual assistance associations continue to
provide social services to refugee clients but with different variants and approaches. Some MAAs offer a full range
of services, from employment placement to counseling.
Others offer only one service. Some MAAs operate out of

homes on shoestring budgets; others are funded in the hundreds of thousands of dollars, operating with offices and
large staffs.[24]

In addition to MAAs that operate primarily in the
social service field, there are other types of MAAs that
also act to redistribute goods and services, and that affect
refugees economically. There are homeland-oriented MAAs,
whose activities (at least implicitly) include raising money
to support resistance armies in other countries and attempting to affect American foreign policy as it relates to such
areas. For example, leaders of Vietnamese and Cambodian
MAAs have testified before Congress, compiled documentation
from refugees regarding issues in their homelands, and published public letters of support for various American
political leaders and human rights initiatives. The Hmong
author of another chapter in this volume, Vang Pobzeb, has
done the same. In reciprocal support of these activities,
MAAs in the United States receive "legitimacy" from
governments-in-exile, or attention from the American government. This attention can come in the form of United States
senators or representatives making appearances at events
sponsored by MAAs, such as the Scholars Seminar on Khmer
Culture held in Washington, D.C., in 1985. It was sponsored
by Save Cambodia and attended by Senators Robert Dole and
Malcolm Wallop, as well as Congressman Stephen Solarz. The
conference itself took place at the Dirksen Senate Office
Building and the Old Executive Office Building, which
further legitimized its being for both refugees and
Americans.

Many MAAs continue to be concerned with cultural
preservation. Some operate as temples, or on behalf of
temples. As clients, refugees offer financial aid and, to a
lesser degree, services to the temple. In return, the temple not only offers a place to worship and to fulfill
spiritual goals, but various other services--weddings, fore-
casts for planning one's life, English and refugee language
classes, and religious rites important for physical and
mental well-being in this new country. A temple is usually
run by a secular leader, who is also often a leader of an
MAA and sometimes employed as a bilingual worker, either for
his own MAA or for another social service agency in the
area.

MAAs also act as "freelance entrepeneurs" by operating
businesses providing specific social services. MAA offices
serve as consulting firms for fee, providing educational
services to both refugees and Americans; offer various
training programs to refugees, such as job training, and
citizenship classes; and give assistance with the completing
of forms (the bane of many a refugee's life in America).

An intriguing recent development is the creation of
refugee-owned medical clinics. Refugee owners, often operating also as an MAA, offer space, interpretation and
translation, and clients to hired medical personnel. Some
time ago, I received a long-distance telephone call from a

refugee friend who owns such a clinic in a large city on the west coast. He asked about medical doctors who might want to earn up to $7,000 a month working at his clinic. When asked how things were working out, he replied, "Okay, but American doctors take too long with each patient and are lazy." He added that it was too bad that I was an anthropologist, the "wrong kind" of doctor.

A number of MAAs continue to provide federal- and state-funded services to refugee clients. MAAs also may receive training to assist them in providing such services. For example, in 1988 the Refugee/Entrant Assistance Program of the New York State Department of Social Services funded workshops presented by an MAA which provided technical assistance to other MAAs.

In addition, MAAs are increasingly viewed by the government as active participants in public-funded refugee resettlement. The State Department's Bureau for Refugee Programs holds regular consultations in Washington, D.C., with MAAs from across the country on issues relating to specific sub-populations of refugees (e.g., Amerasians, Vietnamese political prisoners, Cubans). Of even greater importance may be the development seen recently of MAAs becoming national resettlement agencies. In 1991, an Ethiopian MAA began operating nationally to resettle refugees in the United States.[25]

MAAs continue their efforts to provide services to an ever-increasing refugee population (which they also attempt to influence legislatively) and, as Van Arsdale notes, to obtain a larger share of refugee-directed funding.[26]

These efforts continue amidst growing evidence that Southeast Asian refugees and American government and social service personnel operate through different models of social service and according to different definitions of mutual assistance associations. For example, Finnan and Copperstein note that refugee organizations providing resettlement services have a "curious" concept of membership; that although "most claim some membership, manifested in governing boards and volunteers, their real measure of size and penetration is the number of clients served."[27] Few so-called members were found to be active in such organizations, even to the extent of attending meetings or paying dues,[28] but many take advantage of whatever services and resources may be available. To support this contention, an alternate model of social service will be presented, first, as its "prototypes" operate in Southeast Asia, and second, as it is subsequently utilized by refugees living in the United States.

SERVICE MODELS

Southeast Asia: In Southeast Asia, resource and service distribution is based on a patronage system, i.e., a reciprocal, asymmetrical, face-to-face exchange relationship

between patron and clients, in which a patron with superior
power and influence assists and protects clients in return
for their loyalty and personal assistance.[29] The patron
role often includes the role of broker, with the patron
assisting his clients in obtaining resources that are not
directly under his control but to which he has access,
usually through someone--his own patron--with whom he himself relates as a client.

Patronage is viewed, by and large, as normal and proper
in Southeast Asia. It is the way things are done. In the
absence of social service bureaucracies and a large portion
of the population not having the resources to access government agencies directly (e.g., through literacy, transportation, knowledge of forms and procedures), patronage assures
that clients obtain these necessities.

Southeast Asian strategies for gaining services and
resources are group-based. These groups consist in the
first instance of the immediate family, the extended family,
and the village.[30] The second type of group is the patron -
client cluster. Hanks' classic work on merit and power in
Thailand notes the composition of such groups: "Groups form
only when a man has gathered resources and can distribute
them as benefits to others."[31] Hanks continues with a description that demonstrates the relationship of individual to
group and patron to client: "Groups themselves are tiny
hierarchies with a superior showering benefits on his
nearest inferior, who in turn relays a portion to someone
standing beneath him."[32] Therefore, groups that form around
such patrons are not united as groups but rather are linked
personally to the individual patron.

United States: This patron - client relationship differs significantly from provider - client relationships in
industrialized, bureaucratic societies, as has been discussed elsewhere.[33] In centralized bureaucracies, individuals
gain access to resources directly and on an individual
basis, according to universal and impersonal criteria.[34]
Most clients attempt to overcome this impersonality, and
patron - client models in American bureaucracies are common-
place, but these stand outside the formal structure.[35]

Therefore, it is not surprising that American scholars
have tended to look at refugee resettlement and adaptation
in the United States as a process involving individuals,[36]
since American social service agencies view clients as individuals and determine eligibility and grant services and
resources on the basis of individual criteria.

However, SEAR resettlement strategies are not based on
individuality; refugees act in their new world on models
that come from their old world, using strategies that are
patronage- and group-based. Thus we see the old model of
patronage being fit into a new environment, with several
authors having described these patron - client clusters as
they pertain to Southeast Asian refugees in the United
States.[37]

While in Southeast Asia groups are defined primarily through kinfolk and geographical proximity, group definitions of SEAR in the United States have changed due to escape and resettlement realities. "Family" is now a reconstituted group of kin, consisting of relatives who were able to escape together or join one another after resettlement. "Village" may now be public housing neighborhoods, or friends from the refugee camps who have been able to gather together after resettlement. Alternatively, "village" may include family and friends who remain geographically distant, but are connected by telephone, mail, and visits. In the U.S. "village" also may now mean Mutual Assistance Associations, to the extent that these fulfill the tasks of resource and service distribution previously provided by family and village leaders.

Refugee MAAs in the United States operate on this Southeast Asian model and, in so doing, are influencing how SEAR enter into and operate in the American environment. The refugee Mutual Assistance Association acts as a patron, with its members as clients. In the distribution of resources and services in the social service economy, these associations-as-patrons are of two general types: First, following what has been presented, MAAs act as direct social service providers; and second, an MAA--through its leader employed as a bilingual worker at an American social service agency--provides services to refugees.

Since the MAA leader/bilingual worker is modeling activity on the patron - client system, we see two different patterns of activity, as we do with all refugee patronage systems operating in the United States. First there is a visible American model of service provision, with refugees applying for services, being processed for services, and then receiving services through a system that emphasizes eligibility, compliance, professionalism, and compartmentalized solutions applied to specific problems. Second, there is an invisible system of patronage, with patrons supplying and brokering resources and services to their own clients. The visible American service system and the invisible patronage service system operate both when an MAA acts as a direct service provider, and when an MAA leader is simultaneously employed as a bilingual worker providing services on behalf of an American social service agency.

MAAs and MAA leaders act as intervening groups between Southeast Asians and Americans in two major ways. First, they assist refugees in entering the economy as workers. They help refugees get jobs, obtain language and work skills necessary for jobs, and assist them through additional services that, in the words of the federal government, "are intended to overcome barriers to refugee economic self-sufficiency."[38] When publicly funded, their primary mandate is to help refugees get jobs, keep jobs, and move on to better jobs.

Second, MAAs and MAA leaders assist refugees in obtaining social services, primarily cash assistance, food stamps, and Medicaid. In effect, they help refugees obtain and maintain welfare services, and move on to a better level of services, such as from general assistance (which is temporary) to social security insurance (which tends to be permanent).

DEFINITIONS OF MUTUAL ASSISTANCE ASSOCIATIONS

The American definition of "mutual assistance association" conceptualizes refugee MAAs as refugee self-help groups whose fundamental purpose and operation can be seen in their public statements, i.e., by-laws and publicly-stated goals. If one MAA leader states the purpose of his MAA as provision of social services to members of his ethnic group, that is what the American assumes the MAA is or will be doing. If another MAA leader says his organization exists to support a Buddhist temple, the American will assume that is the case, and will approach the first MAA for discussions of service provision and the second for information on Buddhism. Most importantly, if refugees say their MAA has been formed to provide social services to refugees, then Americans assume the social services will be provided on an American model of social service, as they expect public funding to be spent in ways acceptable to Americans.

Refugees from Southeast Asia, however, see American-defined MAAs as vehicles through which they can fulfill private agendas while appearing to provide public services to their fellow countrymen. They perceive the groups they have formed, usually for other purposes, as appropriate for Americans' definitions of MAAs; in return for viewing their own MAAs as American-defined, refugees are able to obtain funding to do not only what the Americans see the funds as doing (i.e., provide social services), but also as facilitating their other--occasionally sub-rosa--agendas.

The implicit assumption when Americans are talking about groups providing services and receiving funding to do so is that these groups existed previously (or emerged) as "acceptable entities," and indeed that they originally were formed by communities to meet the needs of communities. Similarly, the American government has seen these self-help groups concurrently serving as community representatives and helpers (whatever their other goals), whose activities can be brought to serve even more needs of the community.

In fact, many refugee self-help groups have been formed in response to governmental interest in community-based organizations.[39] The usual pattern is for an English-speaking refugee to learn of the government's interest and potential funding, and then to create an MAA to receive some of that funding. Alternatively, an American or group of Americans sees the opportunity and encourages one or more refugees to initiate action.

The structure, activities, and evaluation processes of any one of these MAAs are created by a limited number of

27

refugees to conform to governmental views of legitimacy and conceptions of what constitutes a fundable organization.[40] Van Arsdale suggests Americans have a preconceived stereotype of what an MAA's purpose should be and what it should do. In addition, he stresses:

> [T]he perception by agency representatives as to what an MAA's purpose should be often does not match the perception of purpose held by the MAA's own leaders and members. Cultural preservation and intra-ethnic support are common themes underlying the stated purposes of most of the MAAs . . . yet service delivery and community outreach per se--while included among the activities of some--are not.[41]

The notion of refugee MAAs being democratically-organized groups responding to the needs of the community by obtaining funding to meet those needs is a myth. The reality is that Mutual Assistance Associations in the United States (SEAR and otherwise) are created by individuals in response to governmental conceptions of what should be. These individuals then perpetrate the myth of the group that is democratically-based and run in order to obtain funds while incidentally offering services. Although their activities attempt to benefit particular groups, SEAR groups often are not the groups named on MAA charters, but rather the personal clientele and extended family of the patron. In these cases it is this patron - client cluster that is the real MAA.

ISSUES OF EMPOWERMENT: A CASE STUDY

This examination of Mutual Assistance Associations began by analyzing how they are defined by those who act and react in relationship to them. We find that MAAs are differentially defined, depending upon whether the definer is American or refugee, and upon whether the definition is being created publicly or privately.

Yet MAAs also are "mutually defined" in a way that benefits both Americans and refugees, and thus are empowering for those who participate in them. As long as Americans and refugees agree that MAAs are as they appear on paper and are as their leaders present them, then American individuals and organizations (including private and public funding sources) can continue to act towards them as if they do what Americans want to assume that they do: Provide services on the basis of standard eligibility and impartiality to specified groups of clients. Refugee MAAs are then empowered to enact not only those agendas that Americans assume they have, but whatever agendas--sub-rosa and otherwise--the MAAs actually may have.

A number of issues discussed in this chapter are illustrated in the following case of a "composite" refugee leader who arrived in the United States over a decade ago.[42] In the beginning, he placed himself under a powerful patron and volunteered his time for an agency providing a variety of services to refugees. After two years, he broke with this powerful patron, taking with him a large number of clients he had personally assisted in resettling. He then helped in the formation of a Mutual Assistance Association, which combined Vietnamese, Lao, and Cambodians through a refugee service center.

The loyalty and service of this leader reciprocally empowered his first patron by providing services in his patron's name to Cambodian clients, and by bringing him additional clients. At the same time, it provided him both training and knowledge about patrons and American customs which stood him in good stead when he in turn became a primary patron. He then took power himself when he led clients away from his previous patron to begin a new MAA, thus empowering a new refugee organization, a new set of refugee leaders, and--perhaps through future opportunities-- a new set of clients.

The idea for this center came from Americans. The manager of the project was an American. But the center itself was funded by the federal government with funds earmarked for MAAs. In his capacity as a bilingual worker for the MAA, this Cambodian refugee leader was viewed as representing a constituency of Khmer people living in the community. This patron was challenged by other refugee leaders in the community who were similarly based, either as bilingual workers in social service agencies or as presidents of MAAs, or both. Through a series of events, he eventually faced charges of corruption, resigned his position, and thereby supposedly relinquished a particular constituency which he represented.

Americans supposed that this refugee leader gained legitimacy as a leader by his service to his community as a bilingual worker. When his work was challenged by either Americans or other refugee leaders (in fact, competitors) and he lost his position with the MAA, it was thought by Americans that he also had lost his role as a community leader. In fact, his leadership was not empowered by his position in the American-run, American-funded refugee center but by his activity as a patron to his fellow refugees.

While he was employed by the MAA, this leader had sponsored monks from the refugee camps in Thailand, and had established himself as president of a temple committee. In this capacity, he had primary control over the substantial financial resources of the temple. He also simultaneously engaged in providing freelance services to refugees for direct cash payments, some of these payments coming from courts and hospitals and others coming directly from the clients served.

Today, this man is employed in a low-level business position. He no longer is directly connected to an MAA nor employed by a social service agency. Nevertheless, he remains on the temple committee and continues his freelance work, providing services to refugees in the community. His empowerment as a patron now is based on activities over which he has control--his temple and freelance work--rather than as an employee of an agency with short-term funding and thus little job security.

His empowerment as a patron has been possible because of his ability to attract and keep clients, which has been aided by his extensive contact with Americans. He was involved in the creation of an MAA for building and main-taining a temple, in the creation of an MAA for providing social services, entertainment, native language training, and cultural preservation services for his own people, and in the creation of a multi-ethnic MAA which obtained state funding to provide refugee services. He served as a board member of one MAA and president of another, as a bilingual staff member of yet another, and as an advisor to several MAAs across the country.

His contact with refugees and Americans in the planning and execution of MAA activities, both unfunded and publicly funded, has been constant. He has attended hundreds of meetings in the past nine years, consulted with refugee leaders in numerous towns both in person and by telephone, and spent thousands of hours discussing problems and ob-taining advice from both refugee and American advisors and friends.

Yet despite his activity on behalf of the refugee community and his efforts for a time to comprehend and then follow American definitions of MAAs and social service pro-vision, his clientele has remained more or less constant, and substantially different from that defined by Americans. It is this clientele that has allowed this refugee leader to retain power over such a long period of time, and it is the exact nature of this clientele that is important for our understanding of MAA organizational systems and MAA leader empowerment processes.

An examination of his career reveals that at no time did this man ever represent a constituency in any Western sense. This man does, however, represent and serve the interests of two groups. First are his clients, who have remained the same. These are the people he resettled in his first two years after his own arrival while working both as a volunteer and paid bilingual worker. These are the same people one finds at the temple today. No matter where he is employed, or who provides his paycheck, he has provided services to these clients on a regular basis for more than a decade. Second are the members of his large extended family, numbering over fifteen people. During this long period, his family has progressed from a small rented home and one car to a new split-level home and four vehicles, including a $20,000 van.

Empowerment of refugees is a goal both of refugees and many of the Americans working with them. But my data indi-cate that a conflict can arise when Americans see empowered refugees operating publicly-funded MAAs on a Southeast Asian model of service provision, a model that in American terms (if understood at all) can allow abuse in representation, hiring, hierarchical relationships, client favoritism, and corruption. The patron just described was seen by Americans as working variously as a "volunteer" or a "bilingual worker," whatever his particular public role at the time, serving the clients involved in specific, publicly-defined ways (i.e., by the funding source, according to explicit eligibility requirements). The patron, however, continued to serve "his" clients--family, those being sponsored, friends--whatever his position in the community, with whatever resources were available to him. When Americans saw elements of favoritism and misrepresentation, they saw this as evidence of misuse or misunderstanding of the American model of service provision. By sharp contrast, the patron saw himself operating as a good patron in Southeast Asian terms. This patron has been empowered and his clients have benefitted, but undoubtedly in ways not anticipated by Americans.

CONCLUSIONS

Since 1975 Southeast Asian refugees have been creating self-help groups with multiple goals. These goals have touched on all aspects of refugee life: Religious, political, economic, and socio-cultural. Refugees also have created self-help groups to provide social services to other refugees.

I have demonstrated that Southeast Asian models of service provision differ from American models, primarily in the type and degree of utilization of patron - client relationships. In addition, Southeast Asian definitions of self-help groups, in the United States known as Mutual Assistance Associations, differ from American definitions. Americans view MAAs as refugee groups whose primary purposes are those expressed by their leaders on paper, so that religious MAAs serve religious purposes, social service MAAs serve social service needs, and so forth.

However, Southeast Asian refugees see MAAs as being American-defined. In their endeavors to conform to American definitions in order to obtain American benefits (i.e., money, resources, and knowledge), public definitions and agendas emerge which tend to differ from those which are private. SEAR create MAAs to conform to American definitions, then attempt to fulfill both American and refugee agendas. Publicly, they appear to be created and defined as Americans wish; privately, they fulfill refugees' agendas, which are most often patron/individual- or family-oriented rather than group-oriented (in the American sense).

While Southeast Asian refugees and American government personnel and service providers operate on different models of social service and different definitions of "mutual

assistance associations," they share a general definition of
MAAs as social service providers that allow both Americans
and Southeast Asians to benefit.

NOTES

[1]I am grateful to my former colleagues in Ithaca, New York,
to my children for granting me the time to write, and to J.
Ledgerwood for sharing her ideas and data on this topic.

[2]An article by R.E. Hammond ("The Great Refugee Shakedown:
The Hmong are Paying to Free Laos--But What's Happening to
the Money?" The Washington Post, April 16, 1989) discusses
issues surrounding financial contributions solicited for a
Hmong-led "free Laos" campaign.

[3]Invisibility and sub-rosa activities are discussed in C.A.
Mortland and J. Ledgerwood, "Refugee Resource Acquisition:
The Invisible Communication System," in Cross-Cultural
Adaptation: Current Approaches, Y.Y. Kim and W.B. Gudykunst,
eds. (Newbury Park, CA: Sage, 1987).

[4]While definitions of Mutual Assistance Associations vary,
such associations generally are agreed by researchers,
government officials, social service personnel, and refugees
to encompass any refugee-initiated, American-based self-help
group that is incorporated as a not-for-profit organization.
See P.W. Van Arsdale, "Accessing Human Services:
Ethnographic Perspectives on Refugee Communities and Mutual
Assistance Associations," Information and Referral: The
Journal of the Alliance of Information and Referral Systems
9: 1-25, 1987; and Levin and Associates, Assessment of the
MAA Incentive Grant Initiative (Washington, DC: Department
of Health and Human Services/Office of Refugee Resettlement,
1986).

[5]Personal communication from Truong Ngoc Phuong, Executive
Director of the International Service Center, Harrisburg,
PA, October 1988. Additional information was obtained from
panel discussions chaired by L.X. Khoa, "Mutual Assistance
Associations (MAAs)," panel presented at Refugee Resettle-
ment in the Heartland of America: A Multi-State Conference,
St. Louis, MO, June 1986.

[6]Ha Ton Vinh, "The Indochinese Mutual Assistance
Associations as Socio-Cultural Settlement Patterns," in
Proceedings of the First Annual Conference on Indochinese
Refugees, G.H. Stopp, Jr. and M.H. Nguyen, eds. (Fairfax,
VA: George Mason University, 1979, p. 34).

[7]Ibid.

[8]Ibid.

[9]Ibid.

[10]Ibid. See also N.V. Hien, D.D. Bui, and L.X. Khoa, Final Report: Ethnic Self-Help Organizations (Washington, DC: Department of Health and Human Services, 1983).

[11]Ibid., Ha 1979, p. 37.

[12]Ibid., pp. 37-38.

[13]K.K. Le and D.D. Bui, "The Indochinese Mutual Assistance Associations in the 1980s: Roles and Responsibilities," paper presented at the National Governors' Association Refugee Resettlement Conference, Washington, DC, April 1981.

[14]Ibid.

[15]K.H. Granville and T.J. Powell, "Issues Related to Development of Mutual Assistance Programs among Indochinese Refugees," paper presented at the National Conference on Social Welfare, San Francisco, CA, September 1981, p. 7.

[16]J. Ledgerwood, "Portrait of a Conflict: Exploring Cambodian - American Social and Political Relationships," paper presented at the Southeast Asian Studies Summer Study Institute Meetings, Rochester, NY, August 1986.

[17]For another interesting example of groups forming in response to potential federal funding, see M.P. Fisher, "Creating Ethnic Identity: Asian Indians in the New York City Area," Urban Anthropology 7: 271-285, 1978. In this instance, diverse Asian ethnic groups banded together to request the status of a "minority group."

[18]R. Harmon and C. Robinson, Refugee Resettlement: An Outline for Service Planning and Delivery (Washington, DC: Indochina Resource Action Center, 1981).

[19]Ibid. See also the following issues of Refugee Reports: Vol. 2, Nos. 23, 27, and 30, 1981; as well as ORR's Issues in Refugee Resettlement, Vols. 1 and 2 (Washington, DC: Department of Health and Human Services/Office of Refugee Resettlement, 1981).

[20]See notes 15 and 16, above.

[21]See note 16, above.

[22]See note 16, above.

[23]L.X. Khoa and D.D. Bui, "Southeast Asian Mutual Assistance Associations: An Approach for Community Development," in

Southeast Asian Mental Health: Treatment,, Prevention, Services, Training, and Research, T.C. Owan, et al., eds. (Washington, DC: Dept. of Health and Human Services, 1985). Related information is contained in Bridging Cultures: Southeast Asian Refugees in America (Los Angeles, CA: Asian American Community Mental Health Training Center, Special Service for Groups, 1983), with attention being directed to the chapter by D.D. Bui, "The Indochinese Mutual Assistance Associations." A complementary perspective is provided by T. Scudder and E. Colson, "From Welfare to Development: A Conceptual Framework for the Analysis of Dislocated People," in Involuntary Migration and Resettlement: The Problems and Responses of Dislocated Peoples, A. Hansen and A. Oliver-Smith, eds. (Boulder, CO: Westview Press, 1982).

[24]For a discussion of MAA activities in one state, see P.W. Van Arsdale, "Mutual Assistance Associations: Bane or Boon to Refugee Cultural Adjustment?" Paper presented at the Annual Meeting of the Society for Applied Anthropology, Santa Fe, NM, April 1989.

[25]Khoa's letter from the nationally-oriented Indochina Resource Action Center (IRAC) in Washington, D.C., to a local MAA in August, 1989, asked for support for IRAC's efforts to "provide reception and placement (R & P) services to new arrivals, and the possibility of establishing a national Indochinese VOLAG to negotiate and enter a cooperative agreement with the State Department's Bureau for Refugee Programs."

[26]See note 24, above.

[27]C.R. Finnan and R.A. Cooperstein, Southeast Asian Refugee Resettlement at the Local Level: The Role of the Ethnic Community and the Nature of Refugee Impact (Menlo Park, CA: Social Sciences Center, SRI International, 1983, p. 49).

[28]Ibid. Also see the information contained in B. Dunning, A Systematic Survey of the Social, Psychological, and Economic Adaptation of Vietnamese Refugees Representing Five Entry Cohorts, 1975-1979 (Washington, DC: Bureau of Social Science Research, 1982); and Y.Y. Kim and P.M. Nicassio, Survey of Indochinese Refugees: Methods and Procedures, Vol. 2 of the Research Project on Indochinese Refugees in the State of Illinois (Chicago, IL: Travelers Aid Society of Metropolitan Chicago, 1980).

[29]J.C. Scott, "Patron - Client Politics and Political Change in Southeast Asia," in Friends, Followers, and Factions: A Reader in Political Clientism, S.W. Schmidt, et al., eds. (Berkeley, CA: University of California Press, 1977).

[30]See, for example, M.M. Ebihara, Svay: A Khmer Village in Cambodia, Ph.D. dissertation, Dept. of Anthropology,

Columbia University (Ann Arbor, MI: University Microfilms International, 1968); C.F. Keyes, The Golden Peninsula: Culture and Adaptation in Mainland Southeast Asia (New York: Macmillan, 1977); G. Martel, Village des Environs d'Angkor: Aspects Demographiques, Economiques ete Sociologuiques du Monde Rural Cambodgien dans la Province de Siem-Reap (Paris: Ecole Francaise d'Extreme-Orient, 1975); and G.P. Murdock, Social Structure in Southeast Asia (Chicago, IL: Quadrangle, 1964).

[31]L.M. Hanks, Jr., "Merit and Power in the Thai Social Order," American Anthropologist 64: 1247-1261, 1962, p. 1249.

[32]Ibid.

[33]See note 3, above.

[34]Additional information on the ways in which individuals gained access to resources from an historical perspective is covered in R.P. Saller, Personal Patronage under the Early Empire (Cambridge: Cambridge University Press, 1982).

[35]Personal communication from Nancy Donnelly, University of Washington, 1988.

[36]See, for example, P.J. Strand and W. Jones, Jr., Indochinese Refugees in America: Problems of Adaptation and Assimilation (Durham, NC: Duke University Press/Duke Press Policy Studies, 1985); M.H. Nguyen and G.H. Stopp, Jr., eds., Adaptation and Stress of Vietnamese Refugees and Indochinese Refugees in the United States (Boulder, CO: Westview Press, 1981); and D. Montero, Vietnamese Americans: Patterns of Resettlement and Socio-Economic Adaptation in the United States (Boulder, CO: Westview Press, 1979).

[37]See notes 3, 16, and 29, above. See also J.L. Marcucci, Khmer Refugees in Dallas: Medical Decisions in the Context of Pluralism, Ph.D. dissertation, Dept. of Anthropology, Southern Methodist University (Ann Arbor, MI: University Microfilms International, 1986); and P. Van Esterik, "In-Home Sponsorship for Southeast Asian Refugees," Journal of Refugee Resettlement 1: 18-26, 1981.

[38]For example, such phraseology is found in ORR's request for proposals to serve matching refugee clients, 1990, and in the Bureau for Refugee Programs' request for proposals to provide reception and placement (R & P) services, 1990. It also is found in the request for proposals to serve refugees with state funds issued by the New York State Department of Social Services, 1988.

[39]According to Van Arsdale (note 24, above, p. 12), "it is important to stress that the MAA concept in the United

States initially was engendered and promoted primarily by non-refugees working in institutional/agency settings."

[40]The very nature of non-profit organizations (which MAAs must be to receive certain types of government funds) dictates the structure, as with the board of directors and financial accountability procedures. These rules vary somewhat from state to state.

[41]See note 24, above, p. 13.

[42]The characteristics and activities of several different leaders have been condensed and synthesized into this description, for purposes both of illustration and confidentiality.

THE HMONG COUNCIL EDUCATION COMMITTEE: GRASSROOTS ADVOCACY

Vang Pobzeb
Hmong Council Education Committee

The Hmong Council Education Committee is a grassroots advocacy committee representing Hmong American communities in the United States. It is the nation's first committee to promote educational opportunities and scholarship development, as well as special outreach activities and collaborative linkages, for Hmong Americans and recent Hmong refugee arrivals.

The purpose of this chapter is to discuss the history, principles, and practices of the committee. In order to understand what this organization is about, it is important to discuss briefly the formation and purposes of the Hmong Council itself. The committee functions as one of several council units. As former refugees, it is the committee's belief that by sharing information on organizational development and the goals that have been met, we will be providing a useful, emic, grassroots perspective on how empowerment can be achieved.

HISTORICAL ESTABLISHMENT

In December 1982, the Hmong American National Community Development Conference was held in Fresno, California. There were about one thousand participants, including community leaders, community residents, parents, students, and the general public. The key outcome of the event was agreement to form the Hmong Council. On December 26, 1984, former Lao national General Vang Pao, eighteen clan leaders, and Merced County officials signed the articles of incorporation. On June 17, 1985, the California Secretary of State approved and signed the articles of incorporation and endorsed the by-laws. The approval granted the Hmong Council tax-exempt, non-profit status.

While many non-profit groups are chartered daily in the United States, this was a first for the Hmong. The Hmong Council became the first formal council that Hmong people had formed in some four thousand years of traceable cultural existence.

Hmong regard themselves as Laotians (politico-economically, not culturally or ethnically). In 1975, there were about 650,000 Hmong among the 3.3 million people of Laos.[1] After the Communist Pathet Lao, Vietnamese, and Soviets took over Laos by armed force in May of 1975, about 500,000 Laotian people fled. A large proportion were Hmong.

They joined groups of some 2.5 million people who fled Laos, Cambodia, and Vietnam from the late 1970s through the early 1990s. They became "world refugees," a number which has surged to over 17 million as of 1992. As of this date, nearly 150,000 Hmong have settled in the United States. Of this total, about 60,000 are in California, 17,000 in Wisconsin, and 16,500 in Minnesota, with others spread elsewhere throughout many states.[2] The headquarters of the Hmong Council are in California owing to its exceptionally large Hmong population. Fresno continues as a major center.

OBJECTIVES, STRUCTURES, AND FUNCTIONS OF THE HMONG COUNCIL

Objectives: The national objectives of the Hmong Council are geared toward the development of "productive and responsible citizens." A major theme is unification of the Hmong within the context of American society. Article II of the Hmong Council charter states:

This corporation is a non-profit public corporation and is not organized for the private gain of any person. It is organized [for] non-profit charitable purposes. The primary public and charitable purposes of the corporation include the operation of a non-profit organization for the social, economic, and legal education and counseling and cultural activities for Hmong people in the United States and world wide.[3]

Since its inception, the Hmong Council has been attempting to develop effective modes of economic self-sufficiency and adaptation to the American system, with an emphasis upon recognizing America's multicultural heritage and social, economic, educational, and political sub-systems. The challenge has been to do this while maintaining Hmong cultural identity and heritage.

Structures: Administratively, the Hmong Council is composed of six committees:
   1) Administrative Committee
   2) Legal Counseling Committee
   3) Hmong Council Education Committee
   4) Economic Development Committee
   5) Census and Public Relations Committee
   6) Social and Cultural Committee.
Each committee has a chair and vice-chair who serve as its administrators. These 12 individuals report to the officers of the council, who consist of the president, vice-president, secretary, treasurer, and eighteen members of the Board of Directors. Each of the latter represents a clan, and is elected or appointed for a two-year term. Since July of 1988, Fresno County has been able to grant a rent-free facility for the council's offices. There is an executive

director who has run the daily affairs of the Hmong Council since that date.

Functions: The Hmong Council is committed to providing and achieving the following functions:
1) Economic development and job training
2) National educational development and counseling
3) Language translation and bilingual programming
4) Legal counseling
5) Information and community referral
6) Community and refugee-specific advocacy
7) Cultural and recreational activities
8) Collecting national Hmong census and educational statistics
9) Conducting the national Hmong New Year festival and celebration
10) Maintaining a public bureau for concerned Hmong community members to access state, federal, and individual agencies and parties
11) Counseling regarding minor social problems and legal issues which do not need to be brought to the American courts
12) Mechanisms for enabling Hmong to understand American laws, politics, and customs.

For us, an important "functional milestone" was reached on December 12, 1986. The government of California issued a proclamation that recognized the days for celebrating the Lao-Hmong New Year in that state as December 26, 27, and 28. As a result, these three days also became our national New Year holidays, with the focus remaining on California--some 25,000 attend the events there. Additional recognition for the Lunar New Year was officially received from California in 1988. Symbolically, the Hmong New Year in the U.S. indicates a leaving behind of the bad and an attainment of the good. The New Year symbolizes new life in America.

It also should be stressed that, during the days of celebration, economic, social, cultural, educational, and political issues are discussed.

THE HMONG COUNCIL EDUCATION COMMITTEE

On January 9, 1987, the Hmong Council Education Committee was established under the by-laws and articles noted above. Founders and incorporators of the Hmong Council approved my appointment as committee chair at that time.

Objectives: The Hmong Council Education Committee is a national development committee that aims to promote high-quality educational goals, scholarship opportunities, and economic self-sufficiency for Hmong Americans and Hmong refugees in the U.S. Educational programs, achievement recognition programs, and job training initiatives are the primary vehicles used.

The national objectives of the committee stem from the following seven principles (paraphrased):
1) To promote--and link--quality educational opportunities and economic self-sufficiency
2) To search out and provide counseling, advising, and information regarding educational objectives, careers, and training opportunities to Hmong students at the elementary, secondary, and higher educational levels
3) To reduce the school dropout rate
4) To effectively utilize statistical data on Hmong students
5) To plan and develop long-term educational strategies which build upon the concept of excellency in achievement
6) To enhance cooperation in the coordination of educational objectives among students, parents or guardians, school officials, and the general public, while not duplicating nor interfering with academic freedom and school policy
7) To search for new strategies and actions that will enable Hmong to achieve short-term adjustment and long-term adaptation to the American educational system.[4]

The committee encourages young people to attend colleges and universities, or vocational and technical schools for job training. Options are laid out for them to consider. Advice is provided as to possible professional fields. To accomplish this, the committee regularly conducts orientations, workshops, meetings, and conferences in California, Minnesota, Wisconsin, Colorado, and other states. The committee members regard these types of services as important in motivating individuals in their educational development.

The Dynamics of Support: The Hmong Council Education Committee receives support from the Hmong Council and individual donors. However, since 1987 the committee chair, vice-chair, and other members have had to spend a substantial portion of their personal incomes to cover expenses. Other kinds of volunteers also are expected to spend portions of their incomes for community causes. In the United States, as in Laos, many Hmong intellectuals and community activists see this type of giving--and associated types of voluntarism--as essential for community development.[5] We believe in the concept of "common good and common cause." Historically, voluntarism as generally defined has been practiced widely in Hmong society.

Many students, educators, parents or guardians, public schools, technical colleges, universities, and agencies have been contracting with the committee for information on educational problems and development opportunities. Funds are obtained in this way. A number of colleges, universities, and agencies also have been co-sponsoring orien-

40

tations, local meetings, state workshops, and national conferences on educational development for Hmong Americans and Hmong refugees. The fees charged help defray costs.

An important event of this sort occurred on March 22, 1989. The Hmong Council Education Committee, the California State University at Fresno, and several associations co-sponsored the first state-wide Hmong education conference since Hmong refugees first began settling in California in 1976. There were approximately 500 participants. One outcome was creation of a "road map" and model for the California State University at Fresno, as well as other interested colleges and universities in the state, to provide financial assistance and other forms of support in conducting more conferences of this type.

On June 2, 1990, the Hmong Council Education Committee, the Colorado State Department of Education, the Boulder Valley Public Schools, and the Jefferson County Public Schools co-sponsored the first Colorado Hmong American Education Conference. Again, about 500 people attended. Dissemination of information and the raising of funds were the two primary outcomes.

Conference Development: The committee regards conferences, meetings, workshops, and cross-cultural orientations as key to an overall strategy for motivating community members, agencies/corporations, students, and parents regarding refugee educational goals (see Adkins and Sample, this volume). To this end, the committee has been cooperating closely with the Hmong American United Students Association (HAUSA) of Wisconsin, professional educational associations, Mutual Assistance Associations, colleges, universities, and agencies such as those mentioned above. A coherent set of conference objectives has been developed.

In addition to motivation, among the most important objectives are: (a) systematic sharing of general information and references, (b) introduction of prospective students and their families to college life, (c) creation of a support network, (d) creation of systematized community - institutional linkages, (e) creation of formats for problem resolution, and (f) honoring academic achievement.

As an example, HAUSA conducted its first educational conference in November of 1981. Since then their conference model has been shared with others across the country. The Hmong Council Education Committee itself also has learned a great deal from them.

THE CASE OF WISCONSIN: On December 23, 1990, the Hmong Council Education Committee completed the First National Educational Report of Hmong in the United States. Due to the activities of HAUSA, as well as a number of others, the report contends that Hmong educational development in Wisconsin ranks first in the U.S. Among the 17,000 Hmong in the state, there were about 550 students enrolled in colleges and universities. This yields a ratio of 3.2 to 100, one of the highest for Hmong in the nation. Furthermore,

41

school dropout rates in Wisconsin were found to be the lowest among Hmong American communities in the U.S.

The quality of education has attracted Hmong students from other states to colleges and universities in Wisconsin. Educational quality is complemented by the state's excellent educational support system.[6] The needs of Hmong students are met through targeted college admissions, financial assistance, bilingual programs, and in-kind services and supports. This, in turn, has triggered positive feedback from other states.[7]

Statistical and Census Initiatives: As noted above, the first national educational statistics report was completed in December of 1990. Other of the Hmong Council's committees have produced similar documents as well, in the belief that statistics are one means of gaining attention for a cause.

The college-level educational data was classified into seven regions (centered on key states) as follows:

Region	Numbers of College Students in 1990
Region I: California	1023
Region II: Minnesota	494
Region III: Wisconsin	550
Region IV: Michigan	48
Region V: Colorado	80
Region VI: Washington	65
Region VII: Rhode Island	77
	2337

An additional 792 students were registered elsewhere in the country, bringing the total to 3129.[8]

In terms of higher education degrees, from 1972 to 1990 about 15 Hmong received doctoral degrees in France, Australia, and the United States. As of 1990 there were 22 doctoral candidates in the U.S. alone. During the preceding 18 years, there were approximately 50 persons who completed masters degrees. As of 1990, approximately 30 persons were working on M.A. and M.S. degrees. Nearly 600 persons completed Bachelor of Science and Bachelor of Arts degrees during the preceding period, with several hundred in progress as of 1990.[9] The committee predicts that about three thousand Hmong will have graduated from colleges, universities, technical and professional schools by the year 2000.

On September 7, 1990, the committee received a Certificate of Appreciation from the Bureau of the Census, U.S. Department of Commerce. This was an outgrowth of its involvement in assisting in the collection of data for the 1990 census. Representatives of other refugee groups also took part, with applied anthropologists consulting as to appropriate, culturally-sensitive data collection methods.

Based on statistical and census interpretations, plus other qualitative information, it can be said that the years 1976 to 1979 were the period of initial adjustment of Hmong to the U.S. educational system. The period from 1980 to 1989 was a decade of incipient national educational development. The period of 1990 to 2000 is seen as a time for systematic expansion of educational opportunities. The effort will not proceed tentatively.

In the present decade, our committee recommends that about 70 percent of the Hmong college students be directed toward natural science, mathematics, and technology. Given the importance of liberal arts (especially social science), but the relative lack of jobs in this area, it is recommended that about 30 percent be directed toward this area. This 70:30 equation also must be balanced with our recommendation that Hmong men and women begin to prepare early for medical school and professional fields such as law.

THE DEVELOPMENT OF GRASSROOTS ADVOCACY

The First National Educational Report recommends that Hmong Mutual Assistance Associations (MAAs), Lao family communities (some of which are formally organized), and community/human service agencies work closely with the Hmong Council Education Committee and its affiliates (such as HAUSA) to: (a) enhance educational and youth associations, (b) promote financial developments benefitting youth, and (c) link job-skill development to programs promoting long-term economic self-sufficiency. Grassroots advocacy requires collaborative relationships.

Hmong Community Empowerment and ORR: Linkages of the type mentioned above are doubly essential because members of the committee believe that, for the most part, the Office of Refugee Resettlement (ORR) in Washington, D.C., has ignored the requests and needs for assistance that have been communicated to it.

Our hope had been that financial assistance would be forthcoming from state refugee offices as well as ORR. With few exceptions, state offices have not been responsive either. Indeed, through late 1992 much of their funding had been derived from ORR, and thus was subject to similar constraints.

The concept of empowerment means self-help, as noted in the concluding section, but includes enablement by those in power to facilitate the means, opportunities, abilities, facilities, and other resources needed. In particular, the means to access information must be facilitated. Such facilitated self-help also leads to self-assessment, a process essential to evaluating--and adjusting--the strate-

43

gies being used to adapt. ORR could play a vital role in enabling this to take place.

   Hmong Community Empowerment and Adult Education: Some critics, relying upon their observations and personal experiences, believe that the English as a Second Language (ESL) programs, as well as certain other areas of adult education, have deteriorated in recent years. By way of contrast, others stress these programs' achievements in the face of scarce resources (see Adkins and Sample, this volume). The federal government, state governments, and local agencies have been spending literally millions of dollars to educate Hmong and other refugees in this manner.
   In the U.S. empowerment and English literacy clearly are linked. The critics recognize this, but are concerned that (e.g.) newspaper reading skills are being taught before basic English skills have been mastered. Adult education teachers that our committee members have observed are "teaching" out of the Fresno Bee, St. Paul Pioneer, or Milwaukee Journal in ways which do not promote broad-based literacy. Adult students we have talked to believe many of these teachers are not interested (or motivated) in helping Hmong obtain a real education. Others complain that they have been studying from the same basic books for up to ten years. This is not what we might call "uphill teaching," but rather "downhill teaching." A related complaint is that many of the best teachers move on, choosing not to remain in these essential jobs.
   Administrative inadequacies account for some of these problems as well. The Hmong Council Education Committee believes that the oversight provided by the departments of education in several of the states, plus that of the U.S. Department of Education, is not as stringent as it needs to be. In some situations, adult education programs fall out- side the purview of such departments. In other situations, administrators wink at problems--and continue to promote enrollments--so that funding can continue and jobs can be retained.[10]

   Other Constraints: Members of the committee, as well as other Hmong leaders, believe that some state refugee offices do not really want Hmong to gain full empowerment. Whether based in fact or not, a pervasive feeling has been created that some officials want Hmong to retain a depen- dency relationship. This is exemplified in the relative lack of state support afforded many MAAs in the country as they attempt to establish their operations. The politics of empowerment are significant.
   A lack of coherence in the planning and implementation of community development projects in general also negatively impacts Hmong initiatives. Furthermore, even when good budget proposals are created, these do not always translate into good projects, nor projects which include empowerment options. In those instances where good projects are imple-

44

mented, they more often focus on short-term rather than long-term solutions.

As of December, 1990, we estimated that as many as 70 to 80 percent of Hmong people in larger communities in the United States had not become totally self-sufficient economically. Many thousands of these were still dependent on public assistance and public housing.[11] The problems remain most severe for those living in California.

We believe that much of this problem is due to systems failure. For reforms to be enacted, entire systems must change. Change must occur in concert with Hmong MAAs, Lao family communities, and others. It also must occur with attention being paid to the Civil Rights Act of 1964, affirmative action plans, and other sets of existing laws and regulations. Specific recommendations are found in the final section of this chapter.

ORGANIZATIONAL TENSIONS

While significant achievements have been realized, a number of organizational tensions also have been encountered. General Vang Pao, by the very nature of his status and outspoken suggestions for change, has attracted both admirers and detractors (see Mortland, this volume). To his credit he repeatedly has suggested that problems internal to the council and/or to Hmong communities not be taken to the courtroom, but be resolved internally if possible.

General Vang Pao and current leaders of the Hmong Council recognize that organizational factionalism does exist. For a decade all 18 clan leaders, through the council, have been calling for the factional strife to end. Several believe that the addition of women as elected clan heads would be a positive development, and also would reduce factionalism.[12] Others strongly disagree. I believe that an internal structural analysis is needed.

Beyond the council and committee, one of our greatest difficulties has been encountered as we have attempted to bridge the gap between what U.S. policymakers proclaim, and what they actually do. On a number of visits to congressional offices in Washington, D.C., I have met with staff members who eagerly proclaim their support, yet follow through irratically. However, our recent trip to Southeast Asia to investigate problems of forced repatriation of Hmong to Laos did receive substantial Congressional support.

Our disappointments with ORR and the state refugee offices were covered previously. Tensions continue among some of our committees and some of those offices.

CONCLUSIONS AND RECOMMENDATIONS

Hmong Americans, in concert with newly arriving Hmong refugees, are demonstrating that empowerment processes will work. In this chapter I have outlined the education-related strategies we are employing, some of the successes that have been achieved, and some of the constraints that have been encountered.

The Hmong Council Education Committee is one vehicle being used to empower Hmong. By systematically promoting high-quality educational development, in collaboration with a variety of corporations, human service agencies, colleges, universities, technical and professional schools, and community non-profit organizations (including Mutual Assistance Associations), we have made progress. Progress of a different sort also has been achieved in getting Hmong community leaders and educators to recognize--and in some instances officially sanction--the activities of our committee. The certificates of recognition and achievement we have received are doubly important for this reason.

The committee believes that empowerment and self-help are virtually synonymous. Grassroots advocacy goes hand-in-hand. With Hmong Americans helping Hmong refugees, both short-term adjustment and long-term adaptation can more readily be achieved. The cycle of poverty, which has gripped some Hmong, can be broken in this manner as well. The welfare dependency rate can be reduced. We believe that our educational initiatives will help reduce unemployment among Hmong as well.

The committee recommends that state and federal governments seek a new and more coherent approach to help us address our problems. The focus should be on the youth, rather than on the adults. By more systematically addressing education, as well as social problems of young people, longer-term gains will be realized. If left unresolved, problems of the young become problems of the old.

Recommendations involving the Hmong and refugee-specific state and federal government agencies are as follows:

* Local, state, and national educational and youth associations should be given the opportunity to receive targeted, community-oriented financial assistance from state refugee offices and ORR.

* State refugee offices and ORR must come to recognize more clearly the linkages among job training, job skills, on-the-job experience, and the achievements reflected in post-secondary/higher education. These create foundations that can--and will--contribute to the attainment of economic self-sufficiency by both younger and older generations.

* The Hmong Council Education Committee, and other committees like it, should not only receive cooperation but financial support for its administrative activities from state refugee offices and ORR. Educational associations should receive similar funding. This type

46

of fiscal support does not diminish the process of empowerment.

* State refugee offices and ORR must facilitate more open communications regarding educational needs as perceived by the Hmong. Agency perceptions of needs and Hmong perceptions of needs often are at odds.[13]

Regarding education, coherent teaching techniques should be emphasized. A primary goal of education is to empower people to help themselves in the job market in the long run. State departments of education, as well as the U.S. Department of Education, should closely monitor adult education and ESL programs. The Hmong Council Education Committee believes that the federal and state governments have the responsibility to provide budgetary assistance and human resources to adult education institutions. School administrators and teachers themselves must be strongly supported so they can teach their students properly.

Recommendations for colleges and universities to consider are as follows:

* Each college or university that has more than 50 Hmong students enrolled should hire at least one Hmong American to work in that institution.

* Graduate schools should develop more proactive admissions policies to attract qualified Hmong students.

* Financial assistance packages should be strengthened for Hmong considering entrance to law, medical, and other professional schools.

* Affirmative action policies affecting Hmong student admissions and faculty hirings should be pursued more stringently. Equal opportunity is essential.[14]

Our recommendations extend into the private sector. Corporations and other companies should develop more systematic means of attracting qualified Hmong to the workplace. More systematic procedures for ensuring equitable, cross-culturally sensitive treatment once on the job are essential.[15]

Ultimately, Hmong empowerment rests with Hmong. The MAAs can do more, especially in terms of addressing the most critical problems of Hmong communities. The Hmong Council Education Committee is committed to both lead and assist, as needed. Hmong educators are potential leaders. Hmong intellectuals must contribute substantively to community activities, as well. Information access must continually be facilitated. We must not alienate ourselves from our own people.

NOTES

[1]Vang Pobzeb, Hmong Culture Related to Law and Education
(Boulder, CO: Social Science Education Consortium, 1990, p.
5). See also Vang Pobzeb, Selected Documents on Education
and Economic Development of Hmong in America: 1981-1990
(Denver, CO: Hmong Council Education Committee, 1990).

[2]Ibid., Hmong Culture, p. 5.

[3]The By-Laws of the Hmong Council, Inc.

[4]The By-Laws of the Hmong Council Education Committee.

[5]Voluntarism and its impact on refugee service organizations
is covered in P.W. Van Arsdale, "Secondary Migration and the
Role of Voluntary Agencies in the Resettlement Process," in
Mental Health of Immigrants and Refugees, W.H. Holtzman and
T.H. Bornemann, eds. (Austin, TX: Hogg Foundation for Mental
Health, 1990.)

[6]This support is strongly evidenced in a letter which I received in my role as committee chair, from Gov. Tommy G.
Thompson of Wisconsin, dated May 3, 1988.

[7]On April 18, 1988, Gov. Rudy Perpich of Minnesota sent a
letter of support to the Hmong Council Education Committee.
It expressed the importance of the committee's help for
Hmong educational development nationally. On June 2, 1988,
a similar letter was received from Peter G. Mehas, assistant
for education to the governor of California.

[8]First National Education Report of Hmong in the United
States (Denver, CO: Hmong Council Education Committee,
1991, p. 34).

[9]Ibid., pp. 45-47.

[10]This information is derived from letters sent by Hmong
community members to the Hmong Council Education Committee.
The most recent letters of complaint came from persons in
Fresno, California, and were dated March 21, 1991.

[11]See note 8 above, p. 51.

[12]A Hmong woman was elected to the St. Paul, Minnesota,
Public Schools Board of Education in 1992, a first in the
U.S.   In Colorado, an extremely active Hmong women's
association has been formed. It has succeeded in attracting
significant amounts of funding.

[13]See note 8 above, pp. 51-53.

48

[14]See note 8 above, p. 57.

[15]For example, an evaluative protocol has been developed by P.W. Van Arsdale and D. Ellis, "An Approach to Baseline Employment Assessment" (Denver, CO: Colorado Division of Mental Health, 1991), which builds directly upon the experiences of Hmong in the workplace.

SOUTHEAST ASIAN REFUGEE EMPLOYEES
AND THEIR EMPLOYERS IN THE AMERICAN MID-WEST:
PROPONENTS, PICADORS, OR PAWNS?

Pamela A. DeVoe
Lindenwood College

INTRODUCTION

Much of what is written concerning successful Southeast Asian refugee economic adaptations in the United States centers on the refugee population itself, as employees. This is appropriate in many instances. However, the refugees form only one part of the equation for economic success. An essential missing element is the employer: His or her needs as an employer and perceptions of the Southeast Asian refugees as workers must be considered. In this chapter I examine the employer - refugee employee relationship as these two meet in the economic crucible of the American Mid-West. My basic premise is that the relationship is a product not only of individual determination, but perhaps more importantly, a product of a catalyst outside their immediate control. This catalyst, to which each reacts and which impinges upon their interrelationship, is a function of the broader economic system.

To assist in understanding the employer - refugee employee relationship and systems environment, I use a variant of the world systems theoretical perspective developed by Wallerstein. While this approach necessarily addresses macro-level issues,[1] it also reflects micro-level activities, for example, the complex hierarchy of economic layers due to unequal development in core areas[2] and the paradox found in the negative correlation between the degree of strength among workers and the degree of industrial advantage of a core area.[3] Therefore, through application of the world systems approach, the total economic arena in which the employers and their refugee employees interact is evaluated.

The fissure forming in the United States economy today is an example of change taking place in old core areas.[4] Many American manufacturers choose to invest their capital in industries placed in developing countries. Concomitantly, there have been large numbers of plant closings and job cuts in U.S.-based industries.[5] Significantly, not only do American laborers lose jobs, but also small- to medium-sized domestic industries suffer as global competitive markets are realigned.

Although Wallerstein conceives of the world as belonging to one economic network focused on capitalism, he does not claim that changes and variations in each part of that system can be predetermined. He notes that change results from many individual and disparate factors which are not themselves easily predictable.[6] The flow of refugees from Southeast Asia into the United States since the late 1970s is an example of an unanticipated factor impacting the disintegrating core-area economy.

My research centers on the relationship between American employers in metropolitan St. Louis, one of the largest mid-western cities, and Southeast Asian refugees (SEAR) who have been settled there through the federal government's refugee resettlement program. Whereas much of the extant case study material emphasizes the workers' point of view, in my research the fulcrum for analysis is the employers' viewpoint. Thus, the material presented in this chapter offers a foil for other case studies based upon the employees' perspective.

The presentation is divided into three parts: a) delineation of the employers' perspectives concerning the SEAR as employees, b) analysis of the environment in which both of these groups are immersed, and c) examination of the resultant cultural discourse[7] which molds the specific characteristics of their continuing relationship.

EMPLOYERS' PERCEPTIONS OF THEIR SOUTHEAST ASIAN REFUGEE EMPLOYEES

The main thrust of this study was to gain an insight into the perceptions of American employers of Southeast Asian refugees (SEAR). I conducted open-ended interviews with 40 employers in the metropolitan St. Louis area concerning their SEAR employees. The businesses represented in this sample ranged from various types of factories (e.g., those producing bed frames, shoes, mops, and packaged handicrafts) to a few service industries and restaurants.[8] Twenty-five percent hired part-time SEAR and 95% hired full-time SEAR.

The employers recognized three overriding factors in hiring SEAR. First, almost 50% mentioned that they were contacted initially by the major sponsoring agencies, in particular the International Institute of Metropolitan St. Louis. The International Institute has an aggressive job placement program for refugees, as do several other institutes elsewhere in the country (see Adkins and Sample, this volume). The Institute actively seeks out potential employers, and therefore succeeds in placing a large number of its newly arrived refugees, as well as finding alternative positions for those who are dissatisfied with their posts.[9]

Second, many employers considered the decision to hire SEAR to be in keeping with the general orientations of their businesses. That is, a little over one-fifth (22.5%) mentioned "humanitarian policies" of their businesses as contributing to their acceptance of SEAR. Among this group, employers frequently mentioned hiring of the handicapped and

51

foreigners (i.e., refugees) in the same breath. Extending the parallel a little further, one employer likened a new refugee employee to his deaf employees, thereby underlining the initial problem a lack of English language skills can present. Frequently, I found that these employers responded to their new SEAR with patience and understanding through the job training programs, but also had low work expectations for them (which affected job advancement, as is discussed later). Other employers (15%), who mentioned the general orientations of their businesses, referred to their affirmative action programs as being a factor in their initially considering SEAR for employment.

Positive stereotyping was the third reason given for hiring SEAR. That is, without consideration of the particular individuals involved, the employers mentioned that the SEAR as a group had admirable employee characteristics. Thirty-five percent thought the SEAR were good workers, and that perception influenced them in their decision to hire SEAR for the first time. Thirty percent of the employers had had previous experience with hiring SEAR or other Asian employees. Comments such as "the first Vietnamese man paved the way for the second" and "the first one was exceptional, therefore the line supervisor was impressed and started recruiting them" were common. The employers' positive experiences with their first refugee employees led them to steretype all SEAR as particularly satisfactory workers and therefore, to hire more SEAR employees. Finally, 10% had heard about the quality of their work from other employers, and thus generalizing from this information the new employer was willing to try SEAR workers.

Generally, the employers' stereotyping of these refugees included such employee attributes as positive work attitudes. In fact, this positive work attitude was verbally contrasted by several employers with the poor work attitude exhibited by American workers. Dependability and reliability also were mentioned. As one employer commented, "They haven't become Americanized; they want to work." A few employers even mentioned that one of the original reasons for considering SEAR employees was because they "had trouble keeping a full, reliable crew." Employers repeatedly mentioned how quick and intelligent their SEAR employees were in picking up the task requirements, as well as how they seemed to have "innate qualifications" for certain work (e.g., small hands for detail work, patience for monotonous or difficult tasks, a sense of perfection in achieving quality in their finished product).

The SEAR were put forth as good examples for other American workers to follow. An extreme case was found in a factory where the typical American worker would be employed for at least six months before the employer allowed him or her to perform a job a SEAR employee would be started on the first day of employment. Therefore, according to this employer, the "other workers were awed by it . . . [and] respected them more." Frequently, employers commented to the effect that "as long as you can communicate with them, tell them to do something, they'll do it." One noted that they were "not obstinate" in the way he considered his American employees to be. The examples of satisfied employers are innumerable. In comparing the SEAR to other American workers, one retail merchant complained that "Americans think that work interferes with their social life," whereas his SEAR employee was seen to have applied himself to his work and to be satisfied with his position.

While the Southeast Asian refugee employee might be perceived to be the answer to the American employer's dream, hiring a SEAR is not without problems. Many employers thought of this as a risk-taking venture. In spite of the seemingly humanitarian and economic motives noted above, these employers found themselves actually hiring an unknown quantity. They did not have adequate information on the person's educational or work background, or even on their new employee's level of English proficiency.

Such lack of knowledge can be a significant deterrent for many potential employers. For those young, newly developed businesses (i.e., less than two years old) interested primarily in cheap labor, the prognosis for a successful employer - employee relationship involving SEAR appears to be poor. The reason for this failure is understandable. Most of the SEAR are non-English speakers, and as such, require more support and tolerance during the initial on-the-job training period. The newly developed businesses prime objective is, as quickly as possibly, to carve out a niche and survive in an uncertain economic climate. As a result, placing a non-English speaker in this particular job environment is often a fruitless endeavor. There have been instances where such placements have led to intolerable situations for all concerned; it becomes demoralizing for the SEAR and unproductive for the employer. The SEAR lose face with other refugees as well as their sponsors (who helped them find the jobs), while the employers cannot produce at full capacity because they do not have able workers.

In general, employers frequently commented on the fact that their knowledge of their SEAR employees' abilities was based on what can be called the "discovery method." The employers had no idea what their SEAR employees knew about the machines/tools they were using. As one employer noted, it was "hard to know what they were capable of at first." Through observation the employers came to discover which kinds of equipment were familiar to their new employees.

Further, some employers said that they would like more information concerning their Southeast Asian employees' family situations and ethnic customs. For example, if they knew more about the families of reticent employees, they could help relieve the pressure on such employees by "popping for a telephone call" to a brother in another city, or by "not scream[ing] at him at work" (as one self-described "emotional employer" said). The employers wanted

53

information on customs involving holidays the SEAR celebrated, as well as their ideas on medical care. This information was considered potentially valuable to the employers in that it would enable them to react properly to potentially important scheduling and health situations, and would minimize the loss of workers (e.g., through intra-national migration to rejoin relatives). The initial hiring of SEAR was considered an innovative step which would garner uncertain results.

Employers also were asked open-ended questions concerning the SEAR employees' abilities to advance within their company or business. Of the 40 employers 75% said that it was either "definitely" or "theoretically" possible for them to advance.[10] English was named as the major stumbling block among those who said that "theoretically" their SEAR employees could advance. Another 7.5% (three employers) said that advancement was impossible because of language problems. The remaining 17.5% candidly noted that advancement was impossible in their particular business. These were family enterprises and the management positions already were filled by family members.

In spite of the number of employers who thought refugees could advance, many responded with comments such as: "I don't think they really want that." One employer reflected the same opinion when she said the refugee she employed was "satisfied with his position." Thus, some employers believe their SEAR employees are not ambitious and are happy with their stable/secure positions. Still others commented to the effect that "they are their own worst enemy." This refers to the employers' perception that while SEAR are capable of advancing, the embarrassment or self-consciousness exhibited when they are the lead persons interferes with their being successful in such positions as floor managers and supervisors. Certainly, holding this perception of Southeast Asians as non-leaders allows the employers "in good conscience" to continue to use them in low-paying, dead-end jobs.

Still other employers indicated concern that their SEAR employees may not be able to advance economically. These concerns were reflected in comments involving the need for them to learn English more proficiently, and/or for them to wait longer before entering the work force so that more English study could be completed. "Make sure they learn English" (i.e., learn to read and write) was the single most common response received during the course of this research project. Some employers suggested that the refugees are "turned out in the job market too soon." Therefore, in the short run they might appear to be successful in gaining employment, but in the long run their work history will be marked by lost opportunity. This position was summed up by one employer who said, "to come [into the work place] too soon is bad for their work. They're starting off behind the eight-ball."

Overall, it appears that the employers perceive their relationship with their SEAR employees to be a "win - win" situation. That is, as far as many of the employers know, most of the Lao, Hmong, Vietnamese, and Cambodian refugees come to the United States with little or no English skills, little or no formal education (although there are exceptions), and little or no prior experience in dealing with industrial technology. As a result, the SEAR are perceived to be unprepared to work in an industrial economy and fortunate to be able to move into any job, even at minimal pay.

On the other hand, employers perceive that they also have a problem. That is, they must find dedicated, intelligent, hardworking, and reliable people who can consistently produce a quality product, while limiting production costs. This is often accomplished by keeping wages depressed. Finding such capable employees at or near minimum wage has been a challenge, one being met by hiring untested SEAR.[11]

FACTORS AFFECTING THE EMPLOYER - EMPLOYEE RELATIONSHIP

As Wallerstein points out, a critical element in the modern capitalist system is that profits are made by selling more items at a smaller margin of profit per item.[12] One way this is accomplished is through wage-lag. The profitability of a business rests in part on the underpayment of wages to its employees. It is here that the importance of the SEAR is especially salient, in that it is they who provide a resource for cheap labor.

Wallerstein also noted that it is possible for the most advanced socio-economic areas or polities, where unionized laborers are a powerful entity, to eventually be put at an industrial disadvantage relative to less developed areas.[13] This paradox, where the strength of the workers actually endangers the industries in their area, is due to the advantages gained by an industry becoming involved in cheaper and more efficient international trade.[14] This is what is happening in the United States today.[15] While strong unions have been able to protect their members' benefits and wages in their home areas, at the same time, many large businesses have been moving overseas in order to avoid unions and take advantage of the cheap labor available in what (until very recently) have been termed Third World countries.[16] This removes jobs from the United States. The remaining businesses are faced with labor costs which put them at a distinct disadvantage in the economic market place.

In this economic environment refugees may offer small- and medium-sized U.S.-based businesses a chance to survive. The uncertain environment for American businesses is demonstrated by their high attrition rate nationally. The number of business failures climbed dramatically during the 1980s.[17] In the state of Missouri business failures also

have been high. For example, during the years 1985 and 1986
failures of newly incorporated businesses were 12.2% and
14.5%, respectively; business failures for the same years
nationally were 8.6% and 8.7%, respectively. Further, among
the original 40 metropolitan St. Louis businesses included
in this study in 1982, 25% no longer existed as of 1988.[18]
Clearly, the economic climate for locally-based businesses
is uncertain. There is no doubt that the ability of employers to hold down wages is a critical part of their ability
to keep their businesses alive.

The refugee flow into the United States could not have
been predicted by Wallerstein's theory or derivatives thereof. Yet, in line with his theory, these new workers are
functional in that they help maintain a local economic
system, a system which is losing the competitive battle with
emerging (formerly peripheral) areas not in the United
States.[19]

Two major, intersecting factors have emerged which
allow this maintenance pattern to occur. First, the state
and federal governments pressure refugees to get jobs as
soon as possible. As noted by Mortland (this volume), self-
sufficiency is a heavily promoted theme. Monetary aid (primarily CMA, i.e., cash/medical assistance) is short-lived,
often causing sponsors to place newly-arrived refugees
immediately in jobs for which they are ill-suited (see also
McSpadden, this volume). Often adult SEAR are placed in
jobs within a week to a month's time regardless of English
level or previous experience. In this way, the government
(through the voluntary agencies and sponsors) attempts to
"force" economic independence.[20]

Second, the SEAR enter the United States with "money
illusions."[21] Coming from Less Developed Countries they
have no real conception of the amount of money needed to attain even a minimal standard of living in the U.S.

Initially wages in the United States look good to them,
especially when compared to those in their homeland. As of
1987, when much of this data was being analyzed, a typical
beginning wage of $3.50 per hour meant that a person could
earn $140 per week or a maximum of $7280 per year (if there
were no time lost through layoffs).[22] By 1992 the typical
beginning wage had risen to only about $4.50 per hour. I
found that refugees often do not understand that in the
United States this income, if used to support a family of
four, is below the government-defined poverty level. A job
paying minimum wage virtually guarantees that the refugee
family will struggle.[23]

Therefore, the SEARs' own economic disadvantage theoretically can increase the chance of profitability for the
employer. For a firm in an economically-drained local
market such as St. Louis whose labor force consists of a
large proportion of refugees, the chance of profitability
can translate into the chance for survival.

EMPOWERMENT THROUGH CULTURAL DISCOURSE

Although there is an unequal power relationship between metropolitan St. Louis employers and SEAR employees, the character of the relationship is not necessarily defined and controlled by the employers.[24]   In fact, I believe that refugee self-empowerment is discernible, having developed from the cultural discourse carried out between these two sets of actors. Wolf says:

> [M]en make their own history but not under conditions of their own choosing. They do so under the con- straints of relationships and forces that direct their will, and their desires.[25]

The process of cultural discourse rests on the actors' complementary survival strategies.   On the one hand, employers--particularly those with small- to medium-sized businesses with up to 30 employees--are battling for sur- vival in an economy which is becoming increasingly global. This global orientation is proving to be highly productive and efficient for many large companies, but is restricting the profits and survival chances of the others.   Smaller businesses must deal with this unsettling economic climate by searching out new ways of maximizing profits while keep- ing costs down.   As noted earlier, finding a capable, co- operative, yet cheap labor pool is one such strategy. Although it cannot be proven at this point, the purposeful use of this as a survival strategy can be inferred from my data.[26]

On the other hand, Southeast Asian refugees are bat- tling for survival as well. They come to the United States from war-torn, politically ravaged countries. Many of those entering the St. Louis area (as elsewhere) have little or no English ability, little formal education, and little or no relevant work experience, as previously noted.   Those who were agriculturalists had been used to the vagaries of the weather, interlinked with seasonal fluctuations, such that periods of concentrated and light work were interspersed. During periods of light work they had had leisure time, often used for increasing their sense of solidarity through social, religious, and recreational activities.

Upon their arrival here, the SEAR are faced with the immediate problem of obtaining a steady income. For former agriculturalists the seasonal work cycles which also had allowed sizable periods of leisure time are replaced by con- tinuous periods of repetitive, paid labor. They have little leisure time for socializing, parenting, or personal devel- opment.   The refugees find that they have to spend long hours away from home, with a workload that increases as competency is demonstrated.

One analytic perspective would make it appear that the employers control patterns of choice (as exemplified through refugee labor opportunities and work situations), while the

SEAR have little choice--and thus are unable to empower themselves--due to their lack of preparation for this socio-economic system.

Alternatively, I would contend that the refugees have developed techniques which actually empower them in their participation within the larger U.S. market economy. They have maximized their opportunities through two major strategies: a) geographic mobility, by which they can--and do--move when they feel unhappy with their employment situation, and b) extension of the kin-oriented mode of production, by which they take a family approach to working and the pooling of family income. In concert, these better their chances for economic survival. It should be added that, by transferring their kin-oriented mode of production[27] to the industrialized U.S., they also are able to secure the material amenities brought about by advanced technology (e.g., computerized television sets, video cameras and equipment, SLR cameras), as well as automobiles.[28] Some SEAR also have been able to establish small businesses and buy homes.

Through their ability to maximize a potentially weak economic position, it can be suggested that many of the Southeast Asian refugees are avoiding the role of helpless victims at the mercy of the larger capitalist system.[29] Through a form of cultural discourse, refugees and locally-based businesses are helping one another survive.

PROPONENTS, PICADORS, OR PAWNS?

From the outset, the chapter's subtitle has led me to ask whether employers and Southeast Asian refugee employees, as interacting groups, are proponents, picadors, or pawns.

First, are the employers refugee advocates, i.e., proponents? Are the refugees supporters of their American employers? As indicated earlier, there is quite a bit of variability among the employers concerning their responses to their refugee employees. However, the employers who were most successful in finding and maintaining SEAR employees made certain management changes to accommodate the abilities and needs of their new workers. These included efforts to be initially more patient and understanding in training them, to make allowances for cultural differences, and even to be more personally involved in their lives, especially in comparison with their other, American employees. These individuals reasonably could be considered proponents of refugees as workers, and even in some cases, of refugees as participants in the larger U.S. socio-economic system. As for the refugee employees, their attitude, reliability and performance levels (building upon the work of Wallerstein) may increase the survival chances of their employers' businesses in a difficult economic environment.

Second, could either group be a picador? Could either purposefully be weakening the other, or the larger economic climate, through its involvement in this element of the U.S.

economic system? Probably not. On the one hand, as noted above, many of the employers actually encouraged their refugee employees to succeed (e.g., through learning more English). On the other hand, due to the relatively small number of refugee employees in St. Louis, my research suggests that they could not hurt their employers' businesses in a substantive manner even if they wanted to. Neither side weakens the other, nor by extension, the larger economic community. Parts of the United States were characterized as declining core areas before the Southeast Asian refugees appeared on these shores in large numbers. It is the large-scale exodus of American industry and capital to developing nations that threatens the U.S. economy, not the influx of refugee families working at low-paying jobs.

Third, is either group a pawn? From my analysis of the material, I would say that neither side is a pawn in the hands of the other. Both are parts of a larger economic system outside of their immediate control. Yet, both employers and employees have devised alternative solutions to their short-term employment problems.

What are we left with? Does this interpretation of the employer - employee relationship mean that each group is a proponent of the other? Yes and no. Yes, in that through their economic interactions each either purposefully or inadvertantly supports the other's survival. No, in that both sides necessarily put their own survival first.

CONCLUSIONS

In this study I examined the relationship between employers and Southeast Asian refugee employees in an economically declining core area, metropolitan St. Louis. The primary data were obtained from the employers, rather than the employees, an often-neglected yet vitally important group in anthropological research. While the 40 employers interviewed were candid in their primary concern for the success of their businesses, many also expressed concern for the present and future well-being of their SEAR employees.

Although such employers and employees each come to the system with varying degrees of personal and economic power, both groups are caught in a larger socio-economic web neither can control. Yet, they can--and do--make decisions which increase their respective leverage in the battle for economic survival. By increasing their own chances of survival, members of each group also increase the chances of survival of members of the other. The economic decisions they each make represent the end results of the cultural discourse in which they both are engaged.

[1]Macro-level issues are covered by I. Wallerstein, The Modern World-System (New York: Academic Press, 1974). Of particular interest to anthropologists are the macro-level issues addressed in the chapter by J. Nash, "Ethnographic Aspects of the World Capitalist System," Annual Review of Anthropology, Vol. 10 (Palo Alto, CA: Annual Reviews, Inc., 1981).

[2]Ibid., Wallerstein 1974, p. 86.

[3]Ibid., p. 107.

[4]See J. Nash, "Introduction" and S. Sassen-Koob, "Labor Migrations and the New International Division of Labor," both in Women, Men and the International Division of Labor, J. Nash and M.P. Fernandez-Kelly, eds. (New York: University of New York Press, 1983). Also see L.J. Limage, "Economic Recession and Migrant/Minority Youth in Western Europe and the United States," International Migration (Dec. 1987): 405.

[5]See, for example, an article by the St. Louis Post Dispatch staff, "Spending May Not Raise Productivity," St. Louis Post-Dispatch (August 7, 1988): A1.

[6]See Wallerstein, note 1 above, p. 106.

[7]Note T. Asad's review of E. Wolf's Europe and the People Without History, in Comparative Studies in Society and History 29: 594-607, 1987. The essay is entitled "Are There Histories of Peoples Without Europe? A Review Article."

[8]The data are limited in that the employers were chosen solely from the files of the primary refugee job placement agencies in the area (i.e., International Institute of Metropolitan St. Louis and Lutheran Family Services). Their files were used to locate SEAR employers. The interviews were carried out in 1982 (see P.A. DeVoe, "Employers' Perceptions of Southeast Asian Refugee Employees in Metropolitan St. Louis: A Report," St. Louis, MO: Missouri Institute of Psychiatry, 1982). Follow-up material on these same 40 employers in 1988 was garnered from various sources, including an interview with a job counselor at the International Institute; newspaper reports; SEAR job placement reports over the previous one to one-and-a-half years; and informal interviews.

[9]This and other information in this chapter was obtained from conversations with job placement officers.

[10]While there are (e.g.) several SEAR who have become supervisors at beef plants in Southwest Kansas (Ken Erickson, Kansas Department of Education, personal communication), I know of only one case in St. Louis where a refugee has become the head of a department--and in this instance, it was a department created just for him. Due to the need for floor managers and supervisors, I have no reason to question the forthright intent expressed in the employers' responses concerning SEAR advancement. Nevertheless, through 1988 I had obtained no solid evidence to substantiate the local employers' views that it actually is possible for the SEAR to substantively advance.

[11]P.E. Gauen, "Economic Gap Is Racial Wedge," St. Louis Post-Dispatch (October 30, 1988): A1.

[12]See Wallerstein, note 1 above, p. 125.

[13]Ibid., pp. 81, 107.

[14]Ibid., pp. 121-122, 127.

[15]See Nash, note 4 above, p. ix. Also see Sassen-Koob, note 4 above, p. 176.

[16]See Wallerstein, note 1 above, p. 127. Presenting a complementary perspective is M. Nash, "Work Incentives in Rural Society and Culture in Developing Nations," in Employment in Developing Nations, E.O. Edwards, ed. (New York: Columbia University Press, 1974).

[17]There was a three-fold increase in business failures between 1980 and 1988. Note Statistical Abstract of the United States 1988, Table 834 (Washington, DC: Department of Commerce, Bureau of Census, 1988, p. 500); "Rumblings in the Dust Belt," Christian Science Monitor (September 17, 1988): 19; "Business Failures," The Wall Street Journal (March 3, 1988): 19; and "Business Failures Fell 10% in First Quarter Survey," The Wall Street Journal (May 26, 1988): 4.

[18]The existence of the original 40 metropolitan St. Louis businesses was determined by examining the local telephone book and checking the active job placement files with the current central job placement office for refugees in the St. Louis area. Unfortunately, this method did not provide information concerning the specific reasons for business failures. As a result, it is not possible to ascertain the exact role wages played in the demise of these firms.

[19]See Wallerstein, note 1 above, p. 106.

[20]Job counselors at the International Institute were helpful in discussing this and related government funding issues.

[21]Wallerstein (see note 1, p. 80) originally used this term to mean the inability to accurately perceive the rise in inflation. However, in this chapter its meaning is expanded.

[22]During the period from November, 1987, through August, 1988, the median beginning wage for female SEAR was $3.35 per hour; the median beginning wage for male SEAR was $4.00 per hour.

[23]That the SEAR eventually recognize the need for a higher income is demonstrated by their complaints to job counselors at the International Institute. They indicated that they want jobs with higher wages. Notably, however, staff of the International Institute indicated to me that, as of September, 1988, there were very few alternatives for them. For SEAR in the United States generally, also note G.P. Kelly, "Coping with America: Refugees from Vietnam, Cambodia, and Laos in the 1970s and 1980s," Annals of the American Academy of Political and Social Sciences 487: 138-149, 1986.

[24]See note 7, above.

[25]See note 7 above, p. 604.

[26]Wallerstein (note 1, above) makes numerous references to the impact of this kind of change on the old capitalist centers. It creates what he terms a "multilayered format" (p. 86).

[27]This is suggested in G. Barraclough, "Return of the Natives," The New York Review (June 2, 1983); and by E. Wolf as referenced in T. Asad (note 7, above).

[28]See DeVoe, note 8 above, p. 5.

[29]M.Bloomstrom and J. Hettne discuss how developing countries could avoid colonial exploitation and establish an indigenous capitalist system, in their book Development Theory in Transition: The Dependency Debate and Beyond-- Third World Responses (London: Zed Books, 1984, p. 122).

RESETTLEMENT FOR STATUS QUO OR STATUS MOBILITY: ETHIOPIAN AND ERITREAN REFUGEES IN THE WESTERN UNITED STATES

Lucia Ann McSpadden
United Methodist Church Committee on Relief

INTRODUCTION[1]

This chapter addresses the issue of the self-sufficiency and empowerment of Ethiopian and Eritrean refugees in the United States. It examines contrasting paths to self-sufficiency as these are shaped by common policies and practices of the federal government, specific states, agencies, and community volunteers. I believe that the most significant institutional force dominating refugee resettlement in the U.S. is the concern with self-sufficiency. At all levels--national, state, county, and local community--there is distress about high welfare usage as indicated both in numbers of refugees and in the length of time many are on public assistance. This concern merges the American cultural value of personal independence with the governmental concern to minimize the costs of resettlement. Labels such as "refugee" are central to the formation of social and economic policy and to the accessibility of services for minorities. Refugees are perceived as problems rather than people with problems. "Refugees as problems" becomes reconstructed into "refugees as burdens."[2]

The experience with the resettlement of Southeast Asian refugees (SEAR) since 1975 informs the policies and procedures of resettlement in general, and sets the tone of the debate. As a group the Southeast Asian refugees are the largest refugee population and have been high users of public assistance, especially in highly impacted states such as California.[3] The particular characteristics--job skills, cultural traits, leadership potentials--of Ethiopians and Eritreans, relatively small groups of African refugees, often go unnoticed as policies and procedures are formulated.

THE INSTITUTIONAL CONTEXT OF U.S. RESETTLEMENT

Prior to 1975 the role of the U.S. federal and state governments in actual refugee resettlement was virtually nil. Once a refugee was accepted by the U.S. government, he or she became the responsibility of one of several voluntary agencies (VOLAGs). All VOLAGs were (and continue to be) private, non-profit agencies, most church-related with a few being secular. At that time, all used private funds to support the resettlement of refugees for whom they were responsible. American families, churches, and community groups were involved in the direct activities of resettlement; money was raised by the VOLAGs. The federal government did not provide funds directly nor regulate the resettlement process. The refugees themselves received no public funds.

After 1975 the availability of federal funds on a "per capita of refugees resettled" basis changed the approach of some VOLAGs. They hired caseworkers, developed sophisticated and experienced resettlement offices, and diminished or eliminated their reliance upon volunteers. Today, these agencies depend almost totally upon federal funds and upon the availability of publicly-funded refugee service programs for their resettlement efforts. Their operational procedures, therefore, are directly shaped by the federal government (particularly the Department of State and its InterAction arm). The majority of refugees today are resettled by these VOLAGs using the agency/casework approach.[4]

However, approximately half of the VOLAGs continue to depend primarily upon their volunteer networks to structure resettlement. In this approach, a church congregation is typically the "sponsor of record." The congregation helps to resettle a specific refugee family or individual, e.g., providing housing, helping to access medical care, and helping to find employment. Such VOLAGs resettle fewer than half of the refugees arriving in the country due to the volunteer-oriented nature of their efforts.

Since 1980 the refugee resettlement process has become increasingly complex and institutionalized. The nation, in the form of federal, state and county governments, sets policies and procedures. The policies are aimed at producing economic self-sufficiency quickly, in what until recently was delimited as a three-month period. The procedures rely upon the voluntary agencies to provide specific services designed to facilitate rapid self-sufficiency, e.g., English as a Second Language and job development programs (see Adkins and Sample, this volume). The VOLAGs have contractual obligations with the Department of State and are federally funded to implement the resettlement. Beginning in 1993 a government move toward privatization of certain services will give even more responsibility to those VOLAGs which are successful bidders.

The results of these policies have been an emphasis upon the following:
1) Quick employment at an easily obtained job
2) Training programs most suited for unskilled, uneducated persons with low levels of English proficiency
3) Rapid resettlement rather than agency interaction with refugees over an extended period of time
4) Quick turnover of refugee clients, i.e., "one-step" employment
5) Understanding "refugees" as a unitary category,

i.e., all refugees being the same for resettlement
purposes ("same" being defined by referencing the
largest group, SEAR).

THE PROBLEM OF RESOURCE ACCESS

The research upon which this chapter is based compares
the psychological well-being of Ethiopian and Eritrean
refugees resettled by agency-based VOLAGs with the
psychological well-being of Ethiopian and Eritrean refugees
resettled by volunteer-oriented VOLAGs. I was motivated to
undertake this by the apparent difficulty which these
refugees were having in their resettlement experience.
Depression, resistance to participating in employment training or to the taking of certain jobs, surprising complaints
about the difficulty of low-level tasks, anger, and even
suicide were consistent topics of discussion among agency
staff and volunteers.[5] The Ethiopians and Eritreans seemingly were experiencing more difficulties than the Southeast
Asian refugees with whom the resettlement personnel were
familiar.

In discussions with UNHCR staff, they reported that
Ethiopian refugees were one of the two largest groups of
refugees to request UNHCR's assistance in repatriating even
though at that time (1987) repatriation would have been
especially dangerous (see Campbell, Kreisberg-Voss, and
Sobrepena, this volume). In addition the staff noted that
the refugees often appeared to be mentally ill.

Interestingly, my discussions with agency staff and
volunteers (as well as my own observations) revealed significant differences in the perceptions--and actualities--of
behaviors of these refugees. At times they were reported as
being angry, hostile, volatile, threatening, stubborn, and
difficult. By way of contrast they also were reported as
being shy, soft-spoken, diffident, hesitant to be assertive
on their own behalf, and dependent upon Americans for help.

In this chapter I argue that these differences are
related to very real differences in resettlement experiences, differences related to contrasting access to
resources for economic self-sufficiency and to their perceived and real potential for status mobility. I further
argue, as does Vang Pobzeb (this volume), that such differential access to societal resources is shaped by the ideological premises of the state which inform policy and
practice concerning self-sufficiency. DeVoe (this volume)
couches her analysis of SEAR in much the same terms.

Methods: Agreeing with Bach that an essential theoretical premise is that the sponsoring situation, the mode
of resettlement, is a major factor in the refugees' experience socially and economically,[6] I wanted to understand
whether there was a significant difference in the psychological well-being of Ethiopian and Eritrean refugees

65

resettled by agencies utilizing caseworkers and those resettled by agencies depending upon volunteer networks.

I limited my analysis to single men because they constitute the largest percentage of Ethiopian and Eritrean refugees admitted to the U.S. and because they do not have families to assist them in resettlement. Investigating their experiences allowed me to focus more clearly upon the differentials related to the mode of resettlement uninfluenced by variations in family support. In my research I utilized several complementary methodologies:

* Life histories of 59 single Ethiopian and Eritrean men who had been in the Western United States between 6 and 24 months.[7] They were divided approximately equally between those resettled by volunteers and those resettled through agency-based methods.

* The short form of the Goldberg self-administered questionnaire (12 items) for the detection of non-psychotic mental illness translated into Amharic and Tigrinya (as well as being available in English).[8] The items deal with issues of life stress which easily connect to the refugee experience, e.g., "Have you recently felt capable of making decisions about things?" I judged the Goldberg questionnaire's short form to be more acceptable to a person unaccustomed to survey instruments.

* Cantril's Self-Anchoring Scale ("The Ladder of Hope"), an open-ended scale which explores the refugees' perceptions of their current life situation and their hope for the future as they are located between the two "anchors" of a Good Life and a Bad Life. This scale honors the refugee's own categories and allows a view into the discrepancy between the refugee's aspirations and perceived achievements, exploring hopes and fears based in the present real situation.[9]

* Participant observation within resettlement agencies, and of Ethiopian and Eritrean organizations/events.

WHO ARE THESE MEN?
ETHIOPIAN AND ERITREAN REFUGEES IN THE U.S.

African refugees in the U.S. are a relatively unknown, "invisible" entity. Most African refugees in the country are Ethiopian or Eritrean. Although approximately one out of every 200 Ethiopians and Eritreans was a refugee as of 1991--a total of over 1.25 million persons--only some 23,500 had been granted resettlement in the U.S. since 1980.[10] Even this small number is historic, for the U.S. had not before admitted Africans as a refugee group. The lack of previous experience, the small numbers of mainly single young men, and the scatteredness of the Ethiopian and Eritrean refugee populations all contribute to the public's lack of awareness of both the presence and the needs of these refugees (although events in Somalia in 1992 altered this somewhat). The majority of Ethiopian and Eritrean refugees in the world are poor and illiterate, reflecting the reality of their country. However, most who have reached the U.S. are well-educated by the standards of their nation. Many come from a small urban or semi-urban elite segment of society. Typically they left for political reasons, fearing arrest, imprisonment, torture, and death. Some were caught up in the civil war involving Ethiopia and Eritrea either as combatants or suspect combatants. Because of their relatively high levels of education (often through 12th grade, some through college), most have a functional knowledge of English. Had they remained in their country under normal circumstances, they would likely have assumed positions of social, economic, and/or political importance.

The refugees are single and without close families. Their ethnic communities are geographically scattered across the U.S. as well as being fragmented by political, ethnic, and linguistic differences brought from their homelands. In Ethiopia and Eritrea they would depend upon close friendship ties with agemates, yet, even though single and alone in the U.S., their suspicions of strangers from their homelands are rampant. Additionally, they often face discrimination due to being black. Being young and having been students they have little work experience. What skills they do have usually were obtained during the refugee flight and are not easily transferable to the U.S. work environment.[11]

A Typical Case: A typical young refugee is Berhane Habte,[12] a recent arrival to Northern California. Berhane's father was a member of Haile Selassie's government and was killed soon after the change in government. Berhane was imprisoned briefly and then released. Later he, his brother, and his sister were jailed. His brother died after one week in prison. After Berhane was released, he went to live in the village of his mother for six months. From there hiring guides, he and other refugees walked into Sudan at night. Living in Khartoum, working as a waiter at times, he supported himself until he was sponsored by a church in Northern California. When I met him he was 24 years old, single, and proficient in English, having completed two years at Addis Ababa University. His mother and sister were still in Ethiopia.

After he arrived in California, housing was found for him with two other Ethiopians. However, this arrangement lasted only a week. He asked to move to another situation since his Ethiopian roommates purposefully spoke their own language (not intelligible to Berhane) even though all three had another language, Amharic, in common. He says he felt uncomfortable and left out. Berhane typifies the characteristics which, combined, put the single male Ethiopian refugee under significant psychological stress during the resettlement experience.

   Socio-Demographic Characteristics: In the population studied[13] the refugee men average 26 years of age, are single, urban and well-educated by Ethiopian standards (ninth to twelfth grade is typical), with a large proportion being university students.   In total slightly more that 71% have education ranging from 9 to 17+ years.   Their status in Ethiopia and Eritrea as evidenced by their fathers' occupations was comparatively high.   In countries such as this, with sharp distinctions between economic and professional groups, and with access to secondary and higher education related to these status differentials, the occupation of the father is an excellent predictor of the education likely to be achieved by the son.   Such occupations as government official, member of parliament, judge, professor, teacher, lawyer, large landowner, and military officer were the most common (64%), although the range included illiterate farmers and small shopkeepers.
   The majority (53%) of the young men had been students: 83.8% had completed at least 7th grade.   Of those who were not students, many reported having had their education disrupted by the political and military conflicts.   This disruption of education is significant in that, had the men been able to continue their education, many would have continued on to college--a notable achievement in Ethiopia and Eritrea.[14]   An additional 6.8% were professionals such as teachers or accountants.   Following Bach, one could assume that there are important implications for their perceptions of themselves, their social status, their sense of loss, and their expectations for themselves in the experience of resettlement.
   Their levels of education are reflected in the flunctional to fluent English exhibited.   Almost two-thirds were functional in English with 44.0% being relatively advanced.   Since English is taught in Ethiopian and Eritrean schools from the 7th grade on, proficiency in English logically reflects the level of schooling achieved.[15]
   With self-sufficiency the focus, employment is important.   On average, these men demonstrated a high level of employment for the short time they had been in the U.S., with 77.9% being employed at least part-time.   However, their employment was found to be financially marginal. Fifty percent were employed in entry-level, semi-skilled, or unskilled jobs.   Only 8.5% lived alone; the majority lived with other Ethiopians or Eritreans.   A large proportion (18.6%) lived with Americans.

                STRESS, STATUS, AND ASPIRATIONS

   Analyzing the responses to Goldberg's questionnaire for the detection of non-psychotic mental illness, i.e., the felt presence of stress and psychological distress, it is apparent that most of these Ethiopian and Eritrean refugees operate daily under high stress. Although the individual responses varied from zero items out of 12 (a "normal, non-stressed" response pattern) to a high of 10 items out of 12 (indicating persons at great risk for mental distress), the data show significant differences in the mean responses by group. The agency/caseworker resettled men averaged 3.98 items out of 12 and the volunteer resettled men averaged 1.75 out of 12.[16] The differences were especially significant during the second year of resettlement, and in the group of men with 9-12th grade educations where English proficiency was held constant.

The responses to Cantril's Self-Anchoring Scale reveal that these young men are focused clearly at getting educations which then will produce good jobs in terms of status and money, and which will bring them the respect perceived as being intrinsically connected to their societal status. In using Cantril's scale one is looking at the aspirations of these young men, the difference between such aspirations and current reality, and the relative discontent experienced. With this scale no categories are offered to the respondent; he determines what is important. Given the openness of the scale, the consistency of the responses was striking. Having a good job, supporting oneself, and going to school were identified by nearly all of the men as characteristics of a good life whereas having no job or a "bad job," living on welfare, and not being able to support oneself were perceived as characteristics of a bad life. The responses to what is a bad life consistently included "to be a beggar."

In Ethiopian and Eritrean cultures "refugee" can imply a "beggar," a handicapped person who cannot be independent, who is not healthy and whole. A person in either the Ethiopian or Eritrean context who is physically whole but who begs is ridiculed. It is seen to be shameful behavior. The men frequently agonized over this construct.[17] The emphasis upon being independent and helping themselves was a constant theme intertwined with needing help from a sponsor--"someone to guide me."

In examining the responses to Cantril's Self-Anchoring Scale it appeared that the difference in psychological well-being between the two groups of men might relate to the differential ability of the two approaches to help them obtain jobs, especially jobs of higher status with good salaries, or jobs which related to some future goal. In analyzing the employment situations and stress levels of these young men, the contrasts are striking--unemployed men had a mean response rate of 4.82 items whereas the employed men had a mean response rate of 1.86. Thirty-one percent (31.0%) of the agency-resettled men were unemployed compared with 13.3% of the volunteer-resettled men. There also were important differences in the type of employment typical for each group. The agency-resettled men more often were in entry-

69

level positions with no training opportunities or schooling to prepare them for future possibilities (65.0%), compared to only 38.4% of the volunteer-resettled men. Volunteer-resettled Ethiopians and Eritreans more often were employed in professional or "acceptable status" (by emic categorization) jobs or were in regular schooling (61.6%), compared to 35.0% of the agency-resettled men. Importantly, 50.0% of the volunteer-resettled men combined going to school--usually college--with some type of employment, compared with 5.0% of the agency-resettled men.

These differences in employment and schooling related to differences in stress levels. For the entire sample the difference between the mean responses of employed refugees with entry-level jobs and those with good-paying or higher-status jobs and/or enrolled in school is significant. The mean response rate of employed refugees resettled through agency/caseworkers was 3.28 items whereas the mean response rate of employed refugees resettled by volunteers was 1.44. Using their own categories/perceptions of a good life, the opportunity to combine schooling with employment or to have a job with more pay or higher status would likely decrease psychological stress and be perceived as enabling a more hopeful future.

INCENTIVES AND CONSTRAINTS TO SELF-SUFFICIENCY

These data suggest that there are indeed two paths to self sufficiency for these Ethiopian and Eritrean refugees, paths which are presented to them by the VOLAGs which happen to sponsor them and which are shaped by the at-times idiosyncratic procedures used (even though the national and regional offices of all VOLAGs maintain the same structural connection with the Department of State and other government entities). One path is shaped strongly by governmental policies which emphasize immediate self-sufficiency. VOLAGs which depend upon state-funded service providers and upon government funding for their resettlement expenses naturally are vulnerable to governmental pressures. A constant theme in conversations with staff is the concern with employment; how many have jobs--any kind of jobs--and how quickly can employment be found. As of the time of the research, the agency was required to report employment statistics as a percent of the case load which was employed within three months. The type of employment is essentially unimportant; funding and recontracting depend upon a satisfactory level of employment, i.e., what percentage are not utilizing public welfare and are employed at least part-time.[18] These VOLAGs resettle the majority of refugees with the staff handling comparatively large case loads. Their connection with any particular refugee is time-limited. My interviews with agency staff indicate that they did not normally stay in contact with refugees who were employed, and hence these refugees were not perceived to need the agency's services any longer. In fact, given the pressures to move many refugees through the system, the staff could not allow themselves the time to stay in touch even if they personally wished to, as many said they did.

Single men on welfare are usually mandated to be in regular contact with the VOLAG office, at least with a job developer, until employed. Any refugee who after a specified time turns down an offered "appropriate" job while on welfare losses his cash assistance in the state of California. So the system as presented in this path forces the refugee into virtually any job and then leaves him alone to fend unassisted.

The second path, shaped "on the ground" by volunteers, is basically removed from the governmental pressures described above. In this path the volunteers are rarely aware of the state policies or expectations for resettlement. They, like agency caseworkers, are committed to the Ethiopians and Eritreans quickly becoming financially independent, partly for the refugees' sake and partly because they, as Americans, espouse the value of personal independence. The difference is in the personalization, made possible by the small number of refugees any one congregation or community group resettles at one time and the volunteers' sense of personal responsibility for particular refugees.

This mode of resettlement encourages strong, direct links between the volunteers and the refugees. The volunteers have many more contacts in the "normal" job arenas, are able to put more time into job searching, and more often become personally "connected" with the refugees. Their responses often become individualized. Because there is more than one volunteer per refugee, there are more skills and insights to draw upon. The volunteers rarely utilize the track of public refugee services.

This personal relationship, which can cause its own problems,[19] appears to encourage the Ethiopians and Eritreans to move on to other jobs, and to explore alternatives such as juggling a part-time job and going to school. The volunteer has time for this. There is no governmental pressure to move on to the next refugee.

The results of this personal, long-term involvement can be seen in the quantitative data cited earlier. From a qualitative perspective, one Ethiopian summarized his experience as follows:

> I could not have had all this happen without so much help--so many people helped me. The woman at the college helped me get my registration changed to a resident: I had to fight alot to get that to happen. They kept telling me "no." A man showed me how to get a Pell Grant. One woman gave me $750 of her own money as a gift so I could go to school. A man at the church got my transcript translated from Russian to English-- an official transcript with a seal. The college

71

accepted it then and transferred my 61 units. I am a
junior now. [Everything in my apartment] is from the
church. I haven't had to buy anything. I have had so
much help. I couldn't do it by myself. By myself I
would give up; it is too much to do alone.

PROCESSES OF CULTURAL AND SOCIO-ECONOMIC ADAPTATION

These two different paths likely account for much of
the difference in psychological well-being as well as the
different descriptions of Ethiopians and Eritreans given by
the Americans working with them. The "typical refugee
journey" is, in fact, markedly different for these two
groups, and the difference is in social structure (not culture or ideology). They have been connected to different
resources and different rewards of the socio-economic system
and have had access to different vehicles for upward social
mobility.

The agency-resettled group, for the most part,
continues to remain in the lower socio-economic class, not
much different than during their early months in the U.S.
The volunteer-resettled group, although for the most part
still not well off financially, is nonetheless in jobs with
some recognizably hopeful future, is receiving regular
schooling, and/or has jobs that pay reasonably well. These
men are working very hard, and are still discouraged at
times and often exhausted. As an example, a man named
Yohanes Hailu came to dinner at my house one afternoon and
fell asleep at the table. He was attending a community college in the day and working the graveyard shift at a warehouse at night. He said he had never been so tired and
worked so hard in his life.

However, as their psychological well-being scores and
responses to the self-anchoring scale show, these men are
hopeful and understand themselves to be moving, albeit
slowly and with some confusion, toward a good future.
Interestingly, a recent training seminar emphasized that in
the workplace an individual can work 16 hours per day for
three weeks without any damage, and will only suffer
fatigue.[20] The crucial dynamic for this to occur, without
burnout, is that the individual have a "challenge with a
chance." A challenge with minimum or no chance leads to
collapse. The volunteer-resettled men appear to perceive
that their culturally confusing, extremely fatiguing,
situationally-specific new behaviors will finally pay off in
ways recognizable to and accepted by them. Some of the jobs
would have been considered unthinkable and even shameful
before. One young Ethiopian man said:

I never tell my parents what I am doing! My mother
would be so shamed. We are all the same. We don't
tell our mothers what we are doing. These jobs we
have--never in Ethiopia--never! It is a shame. Only

if you are poor do you do what we do here. To work in a restaurant--oh! But here it is what we have to do so we can live, so we can go to school. But we never tell our mothers.

They are adapting in remarkable ways. This appears to be fueled by their awareness that success is possible, success in their terms if not in their ideal setting or along their ideal timeline. They are increasingly able to take control of their lives in ways important to them.

The feedback process is negative with the Ethiopian and Eritrean refugees resettled by the agency/caseworker approach. As they find themselves stagnating in minimum-wage jobs with no access to better jobs nor to college educations, they begin to despair. Their lack of success in accessing the meaningful and workable resources of U.S. society generates anger and (in some) depression. They become less able to take on culturally-stressful behavior, to make culturally strange but effective short- and long-term plans. They experience an increasing sense of hopelessness, a lack of ability to control their life course, to control the important variables in their social situation. A man named Fissaha Giorgis agonized with me:

They are all dumb, dumb, dumb. When they suggest a dishwasher's job, they look at me as if I were an animal. They see a dishwasher. I am not a dishwasher. I am a good man. I must have a good job.

The ability of the sponsor to utilize some aspects of the traditional cultural values of the Ethiopian or Eritrean refugee in resettlement is crucial, especially during the early stages of the process. Enabling personal interaction, and developing short-term plans that are realistic in the U.S. context but which also take the goals and tactics of these young men seriously, are essential in order to reduce stress and promote appropriate and successful activities. The young refugee, "away from his mother" as he frequently says, without a cohesive ethnic community, without a realistic way to build or rebuild a family, without the financial resources to act out his own "cultural track" of moving into independent adulthood, depends often unrealistically upon his sponsor for clear guidance and concrete help.[21]

How these cultural differences affect the resettlement experiences of the young men I studied is shaped by the different methods of resettlement. Both agency personnel and congregational volunteers are socialized by the American values of individual initiative, individual responsibility, and economic self-sufficiency. However, such cultural values are given a systematic "procedural rules" approach with the agency/caseworker method. "We are required . . ." is often heard. The available options are framed by local refugee service programs and government regulations. The expectations and procedures are made as uniform as possible.

73

There is little if any flexibility allowed in the system, which ironically is important to the agency personnel since they are dealing with large numbers of refugees and are dependent upon a complex network of refugee programs to provide the core services. The responsibility is put upon the refugee to conform to the regulations and procedures, and to take the initiative to come into the agency for further advice or information.

Although there were certainly some congregational volunteers who were culturally and procedurally inflexible, the typical interaction took the interests and felt needs of the refugee men into consideration. This interactive concern was especially evident over the long term. In the short term, new volunteers were extremely anxious about finding jobs (usually any jobs) for the men. However, as the volunteers continued to interact with them, they became better acquainted personally and learned more about their needs. The more flexible volunteers took seriously the Ethiopians' and Eritreans' interests in specific jobs, training, or schooling. For some men who had specific employment interests the volunteers attempted to match those interests with actual employment openings (although not always successfully). Typically the volunteers accepted the wishes of the men to get back into school, at least part-time, and would work with them to make that possible.

Over time relationships of increasing trust and familial-like interactions frequently developed. Those refugees who were closely involved with their sponsors were often housed with Americans. They had Americans to turn to for advice and referred to their sponsors as "their family." It is probable that they experienced lower levels of stress. Facilitating this were sponsors who tolerated an initial "un-American level" of dependency, emotionally if not financially. These sponsors encouraged high levels of personal interaction, gave advice directly and openly, and took the concerns of the refugees seriously--even if they could not meet all of them to the refugees' satisfaction. They worked tirelessly to open doors of opportunity for the refugees, while attempting to be clear in communicating the steps needed to reach their goals. These sponsors fit, in some important ways, the Ethiopian and Eritrean cultural models of the family, the parent, and the patron (see also Mortland, this volume). Personal connections perceived as caring connections were developed. One man said of his sponsor, "I owe her my life. She sacrificed so much for me, got me in school, found me a place to live."

A Systems Perspective: For refugees of all ethnicities, the common assumption in refugee resettlement, made by agents of the state, VOLAG staff, and sponsors, is that refugees are "outside" the American socio-economic system in which they need to be incorporated. Few if any service providers expect incorporation to happen easily or quickly; however, it is accepted that for the process to happen at

all, the refugee must be acculturated into certain appropriate "American behaviors." This is seen as especially
urgent when "they," the refugees, are perceived to be
markedly different from "us."

However, I would argue that the assumption of the
refugee being outside the socio-economic system of the
United States--and needing to change in order to "get in"--
is erroneous. A systems-analytic perspective makes it clear
that, as soon as the refugee physically enters the United
States, he or she becomes an actor within the U.S. socio-
economic system. He or she immediately begins to affect it,
and to be affected by it. One key element of the system is
its status-by-achievement class sub-system, tied to the
capitalistic economy and undergirded by a belief in individual initiative and achievement (see DeVoe, this volume). In
such an environment, class position is determined by a
person's access to the appropriate and effective resources
for social mobility--educational certification, personal
connections, training, information, money, and work experience. When these are coupled with job advancement, one can
ascend the "status ladder."

The challenge for the resettlement entities is to
present a realistic version of this system to the refugees,
along with the options available to access these resources.
Sponsors and others must lay out anticipated interactions,
and the probable consequences of the actions the refugees
may be taking.

Initially most refugees are incorporated into the
American socio-economic system at the bottom of the class
structure. While immediately interactive with the system,
he or she likely will have few (if any) economic or political resources to draw upon. The refugee is lacking connections, as well as the knowledge of how to act on his or her
own behalf to gain information about resource access. This
socio-economic status correlates with dependency--upon the
particular VOLAG initiating the resettlement, upon the
regulations which guide VOLAG actions, upon the cultural
values that frame and fuel the actions of the significant
resettlement actors.

With specific reference to the Ethiopians and Eritreans
I studied, all of the above applies. In addition, a highly
individualistic process of incorporation also is taking
place. The refugee is not strongly connected to a family or
cohesive ethnic community that could envelope him in a more
understandable or more supportive environment, that could
provide him with a subculture to ease and define the way.

Ethiopian and Eritrean refugees' goals of self-
reliance, accumulation of economic resources, a "good job,"
and enhanced education are congruent with general American
cultural values, i.e., independent action and success as
defined by job, money, and education. The discongruity--and
associated stress--emerges as the means to attain these
goals are pursued in conjunction with the resettlement
agency and/or sponsor. Americans push these men to take any

75

sort of initial job, understanding that such jobs serve a functional rather that a structural (i.e. status) role, the function being to become economically self-sufficient as quickly as possible. The refugee resists, because for him such a job does not connect to his long-term structural goal (i.e., status and a good job), linked to a respected "social place." The initial job is perceived as demeaning, humiliating, and frightening. It is perceived to be an indicator of his future social situation, a "social place" lacking respect. The more he resists the functional approach, the more he is pushed by the Americans who are increasingly anxious that he become independent.[22]

For the Ethiopians and Eritreans I studied, their hostility, anger, and lack of cooperation typically produce strong negative reactions from staff and volunteers. A negative feedback process is created, wherein each comes to push against the other in more and more counter-productive fashion. The refugee's resistive behavior is countered with actions intended to "get him going" in the "right direction."

However, as Merton in his work on social structure and anomie has shown,[23] a socio-economic system has within it both cultural goals and institutionalized norms that theoretically can be accessed by all the actors. He states:

> The sacrifices occasionally entailed by conformity to institutional norms must be compensated by socialized rewards. The distribution of statuses through competition must be so organized that positive incentives for adherence to status obligations are provided for every position within the distributive order. Otherwise . . . aberrant behavior ensues. It is, indeed, a central hypothesis that aberrant behavior may be regarded sociologically as a symptom of dissociation between culturally prescribed aspirations and socially structured avenues for realizing these aspirations.

From this theoretical perspective, when subgroups within a socio-economic system have incorporated the goals of the society but are systematically and structurally cut off from actualizing them, deviant or maladjustive behavior may result. This behavior can be anti-social (even gang- or criminal-oriented), or directed against oneself. Alternatively, the person can overly accommodate, or remove him- or herself from the system through subcultural behaviors or mental illness (especially adjustive disorders). Ethiopian and Eritrean refugees, socialized for membership in the more elite segments of their societies, rarely engage in overt anti-social or gang behavior. In fact, they state explicitly their need to avoid groups associated with such behavior--"I will lose my future," one said. The psychological stress shown in anger, depression, and for some, mental illness and even suicide, appears to be the response when negative reactions do occur.

RECOMMENDATIONS FOR EMPOWERMENT

When the Horatio Alger myth of pulling oneself up by the bootstraps is used to justify the "quick fix" of resettlement, we ignore the reality that for a refugee to work him- or herself effectively "up the socio-economic system," he or she must have the tools to do so. These tools are information, connections, and the active, ongoing facilitation of Americans or others who know the system intimately. Also needed is work experience to use as a base upon which to reflect, plan, and act. All this takes time, much more than three months.

The irony in this is that many well-meaning Americans do not question this quick fix. If the refugee has a job, "how can a stranger in our country be expected to be doing much better than that?" The access to status-mobility tools, if considered at all, is judged to be the responsibility of the refugee--in most circumstances an unrealistic expectation. This process produces resettlement for status quo, usually in a lower socio-economic class.

By way of contrast, I would argue for an approach which focuses upon changing the normal refugee resettlement process along with expected changes in the refugees themselves. These changes would incorporate aspects of resettlement which were typical in the U.S. prior to 1980 and, today, are more commonly found in volunteer-guided initiatives. These changes would emphasize empowerment. They would include development of systems to assist refugees in moving from dependence to independence which pay greater attention to the cultural values of the refugees themselves. As this occurs, the refugees' psychological well-being likely would be enhanced as well, to the extent that stressors are reduced. Refugees would have to be active partners in this process. Specific recommendations (both concept- and action-oriented) include the following:

* Extend the time period that a VOLAG is expected to work with a refugee.

* Utilize a core of volunteers to extend staff capabilities and resources.

* Develop with the refugee a long-term plan with short-term steps, and work with him or her to monitor progress.

* Set aside the notion that moving to a better job and/or getting a college education, is a luxury for a refugee.

* Develop a tracking system which more readily identifies--and allows resettlement workers to more easily

adjust--to the differing skills and backgrounds of individual refugees.

Taken together, these would enhance the possibility of resettlement for status mobility rather than status quo. When integrated into the resettlement system, these become a strategy for empowerment.

Since the policies and procedures for refugee resettlement in the U.S. are instituted and monitored by the federal government, and since the funds to support refugee resettlement are appropriated by Congress, changes must occur in concert with governmental inputs. Refugee service providers then will be more likely to respond. Without such changes Ethiopians, Eritreans, and other refugees will continue to experience heightened tensions between processes promoting self-sufficiency and those promoting dependency. Their psychological well-being and their potential for making concrete contributions to U.S. society will be unnecessarily diminished.

NOTES

[1]The research reported here was partially funded by two graduate research fellowships from the University of Utah, and was initially reported in the International Migration Review 21: 796-819, 1987. The larger body of research material is found in L.A. McSpadden, Ethiopian Refugee Resettlement in the Western United States: Social Context and Psychological Well-Being, Ph.D. dissertation, Dept. of Anthropology, University of Utah, Salt Lake City, UT, 1989.

[2]S. Waldron, in "Blaming the Refugee," Refugee Issues 3: 1-18, 1987; R. Zetter, in "Editorial Introduction," Journal of Refugee Studies 2: 327-328, 1989; and H. Moussa, in The Social Construction of Women Refugees: A Journey of Discontinuities and Continuities (Ed.D. dissertation, Grad. Dept. of Education, University of Toronto, Canada) each discuss the relationship of governments and service agencies to the delivery of refugee services as well as the differential position of women refugees.

[3]The difficulties in obtaining employment for newly arrived Southeast Asian refugees is discussed in R.L. Bach and R. Carroll-Seguin, "Labor Force Participation, Household Composition and Sponsorship Among Southeast Asian Refugees," International Migration Review 20: 381-404, 1986. Even more recently, the public assistance debate became a significant focus of the 1992 California budget crisis as well as the California senatorial campaigns.

[4]For a more extensive description of the relationship of voluntary agencies to the U.S. government in the task of resettling refugees, see R.G. Wright, "Voluntary Agencies and the Resettlement of Refugees," International Migration Review 15: 157-174, 1981.

[5]Information related to this was reported by S. West, "Bay Area Ethiopian Refugees Pushed to Suicide," Oakland Post (June 3, 1987); S. West, "Helplessness and Hopelessness Behind Refugee Suicide," Oakland Post (June 10, 1987); N. Van Prang, "From Ethiopia to the USA: A Difficult Transition," Refugees (Jan. 1986), No. 25, pp. 15-16; and two papers presented by T.W. Giorgis at the Ethiopian Community Development Council Workshop on Refugee Mental Health, San Francisco, CA, July 1984. They are entitled "Cross-Cultural Counseling of Ethiopian Refugees" and "Psychosocial Adjustment of Ethiopian Refugees."

[6]See note 3, above.

[7]Over 100 Ethiopian and Eritrean refugees, predominantly men, were interviewed. From these, a comparison was made of the data for 59 single men regarding resettlement experiences and their relationship to psychological well-being, as well as the development of "social place." This sample reflects the same characteristics as the Ethiopian and Eritrean refugee populations admitted to the U.S. during the same period. See D.J. Cichon, et al., The Economic and Social Adjustment of Non-Southeast Asian Refugee, 2 volumes (Falls Church, VA: Research Management Corporation, 1986); and P. Koehn, "Resettled Refugees from Ethiopia: Who Gets Into the United States?, Refuge 10: 15-20, 1991. Related information is contained in B. Stein, "The Refugee Experience: Defining the Parameters of a Field of Study," International Migration Review 15: 320-393, 1981, where it is noted that it is during the early resettlement period of 6 to 24 months after arrival that the greatest stress can be anticipated in the struggle to acquire a job, a home, and a supportive social network.

[8]D.P Goldberg, The Detection of Psychiatric Illness by Questionnaire (London: Oxford University Press, 1972).

[9]A.H. Cantril and C.W. Roll, Jr., The Hopes and Fears of the American People (New York: Universe Books, 1971). A. Hansen (this volume) also used this research tool with non-literate Angolan refugees in Zambia.

[10]Refugee statistical updates are presented regularly in Refugee Reports, published by the U.S. Committee for Refugees, Washington, DC. These statistics on Ethiopians and Eritreans appeared in the December, 1991, issue, pp. 10-11.

[11]For more extensive descriptions of Ethiopians and Eritreans, see the Center for Applied Linguistics' "Refugee Fact Sheet," Ethiopians, Series No. 1 (Washington, DC: CAL, 1981); Y. Ford, "Ethiopian Cultures: Diversities and Similarities," prepared for the Ethiopian Community Development Council Workshop on Refugee Mental Health, San Francisco, CA, July 1984; D.N. Levine, Wax and Gold: Traditions and Innovations in Ethiopian Culture (Chicago: University of Chicago Press, 1965); and L.A. McSpadden, Ethiopian Refugees in the United States: A Guide for Sponsorship (New York: Church World Service, 1989). Informative updates can be obtained from the newsletter African Refugee Network, published by the Ethiopian Community Development Council, Arlington, VA.

[12]While pseudonyms are used for those refugees named in this chapter, all personal accounts and quotations are accurate.

[13]See note 6, above.

[14]At the time the majority of these young adults were children, Ethiopia was one of the most underdeveloped countries in Africa. The literacy rate was about 10%; during the early 1960s, less than 1% of the elementary-aged children completed school. Life expectancy was only 39 years. See C. Legum, Ethiopia: The Fall of Haile Selassie's Empire (New York: Africana Publishing Co., 1976, p. 63); and D.N. Levine (see note 11 above, p. 193).

[15]Overall, English proficiency ranged from poor to excellent in both groups of men. However, there was a large difference in the number of men rated excellent: 29% of the agency-resettled men and 57% of the volunteer-resettled men. When correlated to education in Ethiopia, men with the same level of education in Ethiopia or Eritrea exhibited significant differences in English ability in the U.S. as related to their mode of resettlement. Those who were volunteer-resettled had achieved a large increase in their English ability since arrival in this country.

[16]See note 8, above.

[17]This concept is discussed more fully in L.A. McSpadden and H. Moussa, "I Have a Name: The Gender Dynamics in Asylum and in Resettlement of Ethiopian and Eritrean Refugees in North America," presented at the Third International Refugee Advisory Panel, Refugee Studies Programme, University of Oxford, England, January 1992.

[18]Federal changes being enacted in FFY1993 as part of a trend toward privatization may cause changes in certain of these procedures.

[19]Paternalism, reinforced by personal sacrifices of the volunteer, led some volunteers to expect the refugees to follow their advice, to "do as they are told" because they "should be grateful." Under such circumstances, the refugees typically extricated themselves from the relationship. Although it might be expected that church volunteers would put pressure upon refugees to attend church, such sectarian, proselytizing behavior was not evident in the resettlement situations that I researched, covering mainline Protestant congregations (rather than more evangelical ones).

[20]The training was conducted by Dun and Bradstreet, a Wall Street firm, and was held in San Francisco, California, during July 1989.

[21]The concept that mental health and psychological well-being require the prior fulfillment of certain physical and relational needs is well-known through A.H. Maslow's work. S. Adler's discussion of this in relation to immigrants can be extended to refugees, following the article "Maslow's Need Hierarchy and the Adjustment of Immigrants," International Migration Review 11: 444-451, 1977.

[22]The tensions and confusions regarding understandings of timelines and ways of achieving independence and self-sufficiency are discussed more completely in L.A. McSpadden, "Cross-cultural Understandings of Independence and Dependence: Conflict in the Resettlement of Single Ethiopian Males," Refuge 10: 21-25, 1991.

[23]R.K. Merton, "Social Structure and Anomie," in Social Theory and Social Structure, revised edition, R.K. Merton, ed. (New York: The Free Press, 1957).

THE SPRING INSTITUTE FOR INTERNATIONAL STUDIES: COMMUNITY EMPOWERMENT THROUGH REFUGEE TRAINING

Myrna Ann Adkins
Barbara J. Sample
Spring Institute

INTRODUCTION

In the early days of refugee resettlement the focus of training seemed to be on teaching refugees about the "American way," whether this was in terms of short-term adjustment to the work place or long-term adaptation to a new community. Refugees and other immigrants have taught service providers and other educators that this focus is not sufficient. Individuals usually function in a familiar environment without a conscious awareness of the cultural contexts in which they are operating. Comparing cultural contexts (not "right" and "wrong" values) can assist individuals and communities alike to become proficient at cross-cultural communication, to function comfortably in both "old" and "new" environments, and to devise conflict resolution strategies that work in a multicultural setting. This requires an understanding of the traditional communities as well as the new communities, and of the processes of individual and community change. The acquisition of knowledge and skills needed to network, communicate, and thrive can then proceed effectively.

Refugees, whether they are from Southeast Asia, the former Soviet Union, Eastern Europe, the Middle East, Africa, or the Caribbean, have experienced massive change, including disruption of their familiar work patterns, family norms, and community structures. They have experienced the trauma of war and flight and often many years in refugee camps where they despaired over the past and were uncertain about the future.[1] Immigration brings feelings of uprootedness and vulnerability. Stressors are exacerbated.[2] The barriers refugees encounter to understanding communication, learning new skills, and adapting to new communities and patterns of employment contribute to their loss of self-esteem, and increase their needs for cross-cultural awareness. They often depend on ESL and VESL (special English as a Second Language programs), as well as pre-employment programs, to aid in their cultural adjustment.

Once helped to function competently in English, to find and maintain appropriate employment, and to operate effectively in the larger community, refugees can gain renewed control over their lives. Many "world of work" and ESL programs exist, particularly those funded through the Office of Refugee Resettlement, the Job Training Partnership Act, and Adult Education sources, to help move refugees toward self-sufficiency. In addition, empowering bilingual/ bicultural workers who are employed by health, mental health, social service, and educational agencies to assist their own community members with cultural adjustment and adaptation builds resource strength for both the "minority" communities and the "mainstream."[3]

Working to empower refugees through training is key to the mission of the Spring Institute for International Studies. The Institute is an independent, non-profit corporation chartered in the State of Colorado; its programs span the Mid-West. The staff works with individuals, groups, and organizations to facilitate communication and the acquisition of new skills and technologies. The content of programs designed by the Spring Institute to empower individual refugees and their communities includes promoting intercultural sharing and communication (which also enables individuals to develop skills related to employment), under-standing the impact of cross-cultural change, and developing related personal and professional language skills. While Spring Institute encourages refugees to take advantage of other opportunities for formal education and credentialling through academic degree programs, the training the Institute offers usually is different. While training and education are not mutually exclusive, intensive training programs and focused workshops and seminars can meet specific needs for rapid transfer of skills and information, particularly through hands-on and experiential approaches. The Institute's training programs are all designed to empower through skill building, the disseminating of information, and the raising of cultural awareness.

Spring Institute programs designed to empower refugees and their communities are as follows:
1) WorkStyles
2) Mental Health/Cross-Cultural Communication Intensive Training
3) Vocational English as a Second Language Training
4) Case Management Intensive Training.
The first two are covered herein. Each section includes information on the refugee experience, as well as what we know about the needs and barriers resulting from it. Each analysis then moves to program development and consideration of training outcomes.

WORKSTYLES

The Refugee Experience: All refugees have experienced loss. The inability to earn a living, doing what they are able to do well, is a major problem for most. Not only does this usually mean that refugees lack a means of economic support, but also that they suffer loss of status.[4] This loss is felt by all those who can no longer practice their profession, whether fishermen and farmers from Southeast

Asia without formal education, or technical engineers from the former Soviet Union with strong academic backgrounds.[5] The loss, of course, is not only that of the refugees; the host country misses the richness of talents and strengths these people bring.

Why are refugees unable to utilize their skills effectively and productively? This is the result of a number of factors. First, many of the technical and professional skills people bring are simply not directly transferable to jobs in this country. For example, fishing in Vietnam or Cambodia has traditionally been an individual or family enterprise utilizing the ability to handle small boats and hand nets; the fishing industry in the United States depends on very different technical skills. Russian engineers in government factories have very different responsibilities from engineers in American high tech companies.[6] Second, while many professionals have credentials from their homelands, their degrees and licenses are rarely recognized in this country. Vietnamese physicians, Polish physical therapists, Ethiopian teachers, Romanian truck drivers, Afghan pilots, Russian psychiatrists, and Iranian accountants all must pursue further education, pass examinations, and qualify for American credentials in order to practice their professions. Third, limited English language skills prevent many not only from functioning effectively on the job but also from performing successfully in courses and on credentialling examinations. And fourth, refugees lack the cultural knowledge to unlock the system for gaining and retaining employment in this country, as well as the cross-cultural communication skills for getting along in the work environment.

Barriers and Needs: The challenge is substantial. Faced with the discrepancy between their experience and training and the expectations of the American employment situation, discouraged by the lack of recognition of their expertise in the face of licensing requirements, and overwhelmed by the need for improved English language and cultural skills, many refugees understandably have lost confidence in their ability to handle the challenge. Many have become so discouraged and fearful that they have given up trying to cope. For some, this manifests as lack of motivation; others are immobilized by depression.[7] Cultural adjustment and mental health issues are major barriers not only to functioning successfully in an American work environment, but paradoxically also to accessing services that are available to help them with these very adjustment problems.

Other barriers impact refugees' abilities to deal effectively with the challenge of economic self-sufficiency. Child care becomes a much more important issue when an extended family support system is no longer available. Aunts, grandparents, and cousins are no longer part of the community that provides a natural safety net for children.

Many families are reluctant to leave their children with strangers in day care facilities; others allow their children freedom to roam, once appropriate in homelands where everyone was responsible for the children, but a practice which is deemed irresponsible and even illegal in an American city.[8] Transportation also is a substantial barrier for people who are used to convenient public buses or other easy access to their work, but who now must consider buying a car if they are to get to work reliably.

However, perhaps the most critical barrier is decreased confidence and self-esteem born of discouragement and fear of failure. This can be most destructive at times when such attributes may be key ingredients for successful employment.

Programs: Spring Institute offers a program designed specifically to address the barriers arising through lack of confidence and self-esteem. WorkStyles is a two-week intensive course focusing on pre-employability and personal effectiveness skills, utilizing a competency-based approach. The content includes developing resumes, completing application forms, practicing interviews, and making phone calls about jobs. Training strategies include videotaped role-plays, brainstorming, skits to demonstrate cross-cultural situations, small-group problem solving, as well as didactic presentations and individual exercises. The skills to obtain and keep employment are the focus, with emphasis on identifying those valuable personal qualities that each person needs to bring to an American employment situation.

The course is taught by a team of trainers who have ESL backgrounds and who provide a positive, encouraging, yet challenging classroom atmosphere. The rationale for this approach is that people are able to meet and overcome major obstacles--and therefore are empowered--if they become proficient at dealing with other more manageable barriers. Confidence is gained as they do so. Participants are encouraged to "push their edges," to do all that they can in each of the course content areas, in an environment of trust and support. The trainers teach skills needed in the American "employment culture."

An example of the WorkStyles training approach which combines encouragement and challenge can be seen in the practice interviews. Each person is required to participate in at least two videotaped interviews during the course. Participants have an opportunity to interview with a guest interviewer and then debrief as they view their videotape with the entire class. Many of the participants initially are resistant to the idea of doing an interview on video. As much as possible, an environment of support and safety is created in order for them to be willing to overcome their reluctance, and to be able to "hear" and benefit from the feedback. At the same time, the type of "everyday English" the guest interviewer uses, in concert with the video camera, creates a significant challenge for each refugee participant. When the challenge is met, they discover that they indeed may have broken through a very real barrier of fear. The result is more self-confidence, a more positive attitude, and greater willingness to see the opportunity for growth in other challenging situations. After the first interview, we have found that some of the participants even ask to interview with the toughest "practice employer," believing that they will be better prepared when encountering a real boss.

Several training strategies used in WorkStyles are ultimately empowering for the participants. First, much of the content is generated by the participants themselves in short brainstorming sessions and recorded on flipcharts. The flipchart sheets are then hung around the room for the duration of the training. When students see their own words on the walls, not only does it become clear to them that they already knew much of the information at some level, but they also gain a larger measure of control over the learning of related, new information.

Second, the intensive nature of the training, both in terms of time (60 hours in two weeks) and content ("a year's worth of learning in two weeks," as one participant said) is instrumental in creating a strong group spirit that transcends cultural boundaries. Participants discover how learning can become more efficient when people work together. We believe that such cooperation is ultimately empowering.[9]

Third, most of the learning activities are designed to intensively involve participants. As people work through the interviews, the applications, the development of resumes, and the employment case studies, it becomes more apparent to them that observation and participation are two strategies that are effective not only in getting through the WorkStyles content, but also in coping with new cross-cultural situations. They discover they can choose to have control in any new learning situation by first observing and then participating. Having strategies to cope with new situations is empowering.

And fourth, active listening is a core element of the training.[10] It is a simple communication feedback technique.[11] Not only is it modeled by the trainers in eliciting information from the participants, it also is consciously taught as a strategy that people can use to positively affect any verbal exchange. Active listening involves the listener repeating what he or she understood the speaker to say. It gives the speaker a chance to clarify anything that may have been misunderstood, and gives the listener a chance to check his or her understanding.[12] For people who do not speak English as their first language and who frequently feel powerless to affect the "communication loop," active listening is a powerful tool. Participants come to see how it can help them on the job: By repeating each step in a series of instructions, one is less likely to make mistakes. By using active listening in telephone conversations, one is more likely to get all of the pertinent information. Repeating during a coffee break what a co-worker has said in an earlier conversation lets that person know the refugee worker is listening and cares about what was said. It may lead to closer friendships and a more cooperative atmosphere. It may even defuse a potential argument triggered by misunderstanding. Active listening is an empowering skill.[13]

While the WorkStyles curriculum provides a consistent base for the training activities, the modularized format allows for flexibility. For example, case managers and job developers from the Colorado Refugee and Immigrant Services Program have been instrumental in suggesting issues that need to be addressed and which effectively can be dealt with in a training environment. Different customs related to personal hygiene and principles of the traditional English system of measurement were two areas suggested. Participants' own suggestions led to our incorporating additional information about culture shock in the curriculum.

The underlying philosophy is that "people are capable." The trainers come from the position that, although interviewing in English is very difficult, the refugee participants will be able to complete the task successfully. By the end of the two weeks the participants come to know that they will complete actual interviews in the "real world," with the probability that they will find appropriate employment. Empowerment is engendered, as they themselves must take the steps to gain employment.

Outcomes: Most WorkStyles participants have utilized the skills they learned in the program to obtain employment. Appropriately, they also have taken advantage of services available to them, particularly those which are refugee-specific. However, it has been their willingness basically "to do it on their own," to take responsibility for building their own self-confidence--and ultimately their own self-esteem--that has been the inspiration to those who work with them.

A Hmong woman who came to the United States as a widow with four young children had been living on AFDC and had absolutely no interest in getting a job. The case manager for Joua Yang (a pseudonym) insisted that she attend WorkStyles. Even after she got to the class, she gave reasons as to why she could not participate: She had no transportation, she could not speak English, she lacked written literacy skills. Each barrier was acknowledged and dealt with, but the trainers had little hope for a breakthrough. It appeared that her face would crack if she attempted a smile. During the second week of the program Joua's case manager visited the class during her mock interview. The case manager watched in amazement as Joua showed the "boss" examples of her sewing skills, smiling and answering questions (or asking for a repeat when she did not understand). The grim, stoic, terrified Joua was gone and a self-confident person the case manager did not recognize was in her place. Joua was the first person in the class to get

employment as a seamstress. A year later she was still on
the same job, and shortly thereafter changed jobs on her own
initiative for better pay and benefits.

As a young Soviet computer programmer attended
WorkStyles, he constantly asked questions, challenged the
trainers, practiced the skills, and asked for more. One of
the activities, designed to deal with realistic expectations, asks participants to set a three- to five-year goal
and chart the steps required to get there. Alex Ghurziev (a
pseudonym) stated that he would skip the steps and go
straight to his goal. After WorkStyles ended he frequently
contacted the trainers to rewrite his resume and ask for
suggestions. Getting a job was a full-time task for him; he
made numerous calls, sent dozens of letters, and went to
every interview he was invited to. He was successful. It
took longer, but Alex got the job he wanted as a computer
programmer. It has not been easy; English has been a major
barrier for him in this position. However, by combining
initiative with the skills he learned in WorkStyles, he
built the confidence and gained the skills to successfully
maneuver within the American employment system.

Over 450 clients have been served since the WorkStyles
training first was made available to "hard-to-serve"
refugees in 1986. Two-thirds of the participants have
either found their own employment or accessed services which
helped place them in appropriate jobs. Jewish Family
Service, a Denver-based VOLAG (voluntary agency), compared
the placement and retention rates for clients who had attended WorkStyles and those who had not, and found that the
program's graduates had a higher rate of job placement.[14]

MENTAL HEALTH/CROSS-CULTURAL COMMUNICATION INTENSIVE TRAINING

Experience: By definition, refugees are people who
have left their homelands out of fear--fear of persecution
or fear of loss of life (see also Campbell, Kreisberg-Voss,
and Sobrepeña, this volume). The choice of the United
States, when such choice is possible, usually can be traced
to government or military connections, involvement in U.S.-
linked war efforts, family ties, perceived religious opportunities, or sponsorship offers (see McSpadden, this
volume). Not only have many of the refugees' pre-flight
experiences been incredibly stressful, but the subsequent
flight and resettlement experiences often have been accompanied by inordinate stress.[15]

Studies suggest that approximately fifty percent of the
refugees from Southeast Asia at some time experience
depression severe enough to interfere with their ability to
adjust to their new surroundings, learn English, and obtain
(and function to capacity on) a job.[16] Refugees from Eastern
Europe and the former Soviet Union (e.g.) experience significant cultural adjustment stresses stemming from pre-

arrival psychological pressure and barriers to finding appropriate employment and compatible living arrangements.[17] Responding to the mental health needs of refugees, then, is necessary if new ethnic communities are going to be empowered to contribute within the broader U.S. environment.

Other studies have shown that refugees are not likely to access the mainstream mental health systems when problems present themselves.[18] Prevalent concerns when refugees go to a doctor or hospital are reflected in physical and psychosomatic ailments such as backaches, headaches, stomach aches, and lack of appetite.[19] A common experience is that refugees will not initially access the mental health system, and do not know where to go or how to obtain medical help. Most health care systems that the refugees are financially able to access are already beleaguered by more patients than can be handled efficiently. These facilities do not have the staff to provide language or cultural translation for refugee patients. If a presenting problem is diagnosed to be a mental health concern, referral mechanisms and services often are less than adequate.

The elderly are particularly at risk in these situations. The traditional roles fulfilled by the elderly in their native countries generally no longer exist in the United States. While the elderly often were esteemed and had clearly defined roles related to their perceived wisdom and childcare capabilities, the mainstream U.S. culture makes it difficult to enact them. This is particularly the case where there are two wage earners, and children are busy coping with their own intergenerational issues as they adapt to school life and a new set of familial/cultural norms.[20]

Barriers and Needs: The inability of many refugees to speak English fluently, the lack of medical and mental health personnel who are trained to provide cross-cultural care, and life experiences which do not include the utilization of systems outside the family structure for dealing with emotional needs, all present significant barriers to the access of mental health services.[21] Some no longer have access to indigenous natural helpers such as shaman, soul callers, monks, and herbalists.[22] In U.S. communities where such healers are present, opportunities to build bridges between them and established medical and mental health providers need to be identified. When refugee communities are not systematically aware of their own cultural expectations and do not have adequate information about mainstream health and mental health systems, their members are at a considerable disadvantage in terms of access to the services needed.

Refugee communities, mainstream systems, and specialty service systems all need bilingual workers who can help lift the barriers and provide culturally-appropriate services.[23] While interpreters trained specifically to work in health care settings are desperately required, the need for bilingual workers goes far beyond interpretation. Paraprofessionals from ethnic communities who understand the larger systems and can speak both English and their native languages also are important keys to building bridges for access.[24] There is a need for professionally-trained refugees in the mental health care field in particular. Presently there clearly are not enough.[25]

Bilingual workers are employed in a wide range of organizational settings and exhibit an even wider range of training and experience for their positions.[26] Some have academic degrees in fields related to their work. Others have attended seminars or workshops of varying lengths and levels of sophistication. The range of program models available is extremely broad.[27]

Programs: Spring Institute offers intensive training for bilingual workers in the area of mental health and cross-cultural communication. Although most of the trainees who attend this program are employed by social service agencies, health care institutions, or organizations which deal primarily with refugee resettlement issues, some of the participants already serve as mental health professionals. The Institute also provides on-site workshops focusing on refugee mental health issues to mainstream providers. These are intended to help make the mainstream service delivery system more responsive to a culturally diverse clientele.

The intensive training in mental health/cross-cultural communication is held in two sessions. Each session is five days in length, and participants and trainers reside at the training site together so that training can take place in formal as well as informal settings. Participants return to their jobs for approximately four months after the first session and then come back for another intensive week of training. This enables them to build on experiences and questions generated during the intervening period. This program has been conducted in a number of different locations in the Mid-West since 1983. Many of the trainees receive university credit through the Department of Psychology and the Continuing Education Division of the University of Colorado at Denver.[28]

The curriculum targets both information dissemination and skills development. Bilingual workers and others need to understand the Western service delivery system, gain a background in mental health concepts, and understand the primary adjustment issues facing refugees. Such information is provided both through interactive workshops and written material. Ample time always is provided for discussion and case studies. A significant part of the course revolves around role plays in which participants are given the opportunity to practice counseling techniques and intervention strategies that have been presented. Much of the content of the course is modified as feedback develops from the role plays. These are videotaped so that participants can generate much of their own feedback. Curriculum for this program is continually revised to incorporate emerging issues and augment the knowledge base concerning refugee mental health.

The program, which began as a demonstration program funded by the Region VIII Office of Refugee Resettlement, is now supported by tuition which usually is paid by the agencies and institutions sending participants.[29] The Institute continues to receive positive comments about the effectiveness and impact of this program.

Outcomes: The intensive training in mental health/cross-cultural communication has served over 350 participants from 1984 to the present. This number includes the regular intensive trainings, where participants gather from different states, and the state-specific programs such as those run in Wisconsin and Minnesota. As a result of the program, several participants have entered university-based academic degree programs and become credentialled as mental health providers. Several have become directors of major programs serving refugees, while others have advanced in their careers within agencies focusing either on refugee or mainstream services. For example, members from the very first group of trainees are directors of agencies serving refugees in California and Montana. A substance abuse center in Texas is headed by a former participant, while another works with the elderly for the Denver Regional Council of Governments. Several participants are supervisors and/or have other leadership roles in Kansas social service agencies. Others are performing significant roles in specialty agencies, social service and educational organizations, and mental health-related programs in several other states.

Besides the key roles which graduates play at their work sites, each person trained to understand mental health and cultural adjustment issues of refugees has the opportunity to serve as a bridge between the needs of the communities and the services available. Such community members therefore also serve as information brokers and cross-cultural gatekeepers.

EMPOWERMENT

Every time a refugee is able to access a job through the WorkStyles training he or she has received, the American "employment culture" benefits. Every time a refugee is able to utilize the training he or she has received to assist another in accessing health and mental health services, the community at large benefits. Every time a refugee is enabled to become more fully bicultural so that the benefits of the new society are made available while retaining the richness of the native culture, the community benefits.

Refugee communities are empowered as they come to more realistically understand the challenges they face and the "training and people resources" they have available to help meet these needs. The mental health/cross-cultural communication training gives participants an information

91

base and new skills to be proactive members--and possibly leaders--not only in areas affecting their own ethnic communities, but in the larger communities in which they live. Empowerment ultimately is built upon effective information access and exchange, and on the ability to move from helping one's own community to helping other communities.

CONCLUSIONS

The amazing fact of refugee resettlement in the United States is that so many refugees adjust successfully, become self-sufficient, and thrive in their new land. Their resilience is remarkable. However, the resettlement process is never accomplished without massive upheaval and trauma. To be a refugee means to suffer great loss and the need to grieve.[30] Service providers in the United States need to remember that adults are forced back into roles of dependency until they can gain the self-esteem and confidence to regain control over their lives. Providing educational and training programs which assist individuals in gaining knowledge and skills enabling them to adjust to their new environments (including job and social contexts) is one of the most effective means of helping them regain control. Refugee communities, and thus the larger society, are empowered to the extent that these immigrants come to adjust and deal effectively with the cross-cultural issues they encounter. Those facilitating the empowerment process must understand not only refugees' new cultural contexts and codes, but also the means by which they retain and value "old" cultural traditions and norms. Multiculturalism depends on this systemic interplay of forces.

Programs for refugees, whether they cover ESL, VESL, case management, pre-employment, or mental health/ communications training, must have clear mission statements and specific goals related to refugees' felt needs. When refugees can enter the community and the work place, in whatever capacities, with knowledge to understand cross-cultural issues and skills to help their fellow community members, cultural gaps will be bridged and the empowerment process will succeed.

NOTES

[1]S. Siv, "Coming to America," in Mental Health of Immigrants and Refugees, W.H. Holtzman and T.H. Bornemann, eds. (Austin, TX: Hogg Foundation for Mental Health, 1990, p. 4).

[2]Y. S. Ben-Porath, "Issues in the Psycho-social Adjustment of Refugees," manuscript prepared for the NIMH/Refugee Assistance Program - Mental Health, Technical Assistance Center, University of Minnesota, Minneapolis, MN, 1987.

[3]For more on mental health, see J. M. Jaranson and P. Bamford, "Program Models For Mental Health Treatment of Refugees," manuscript prepared for the NIMH/Refugee Assistance Program - Mental Health, Technical Assistance Center, University of Minnesota, Minneapolis, MN, 1987.

[4]S. Siv discusses loss of status, but the gain of a new status as well, as he rose to become the first Southeast Asian refugee to work directly for a president of the United States (see note 1 above, pp. 3-4).

[5]I. Belozersky, "Psychocultural Frame of Reference of Refugee Groups," transcript, p. 3, Jewish Family and Children's Service, Boston, MA, presented at the conference "Making It In America," New York, NY, September 14, 1989.

[6]Compare this with the comments of I. Porotova-Adler, Illusion and Business: Preparing for Trade and Investment with the Soviet Union, Spring Institute for International Studies Special Publication, Denver, CO, 1990.

[7]P. De Lay and S. Faust, "Depression in Southeast Asian Refugees," AFP (Vol. 36, No. 4, Oct. 1987, pp. 179-184), a publication of the San Francisco General Hospital Medical Center, San Francisco, CA.

[8]"A World of Difference," videotape produced by the Fresno Police Department, California. Production was funded by the State of California, Office of Criminal Justice Planning.

[9]S.A. Brod, "Motivating the Hard-to-Place," in Program Development Guide for Employment Services for Hard-to-Place Refugees, Office of Refugee Resettlement, Region V, Dover, NH, 1987.

[10]B.J. Sample and C. Shoemaker, "Active Listening in the ESL Classroom," paper presented at the TESOL Conference, Honolulu, HA, April 1982.

[11]S.A. Brod, Ideas That Work, Spring Institute for International Studies Special Publication, Denver, CO, 1987, pp 5-6.

[12]T. Gordon, Teacher Effectiveness Training (New York, NY: David A. McKay, 1974, p. 66).

[13]H. D. Brown, "The Optimal Distance Model of Second Language Acquisition," TESOL Quarterly (June 1980), Vol. 14, No. 2, p. 163.

[14]Quarterly Reports and MIS data were obtained from the Mayor's Office of Employment and Training, Denver, CO, 1985 to 1991. Additional information was obtained through per-

sonal communications with staff of Jewish Family Service, Denver, Colorado. (Information about VOLAGs such as Jewish Family Service is presented by McSpadden, this volume.)

[15]See note 2, above.

[16]R.G. Rumbaut, "Mental Health Care System Works to Meet Needs of Southeast Asian Refugees," _Refugee Reports_ (June 1985), Vol. 6, No. 6, pp 1-5.

[17]See note 5, above.

[18]E. Gong-Guy, "California Southeast Asian Mental Health Needs Assessment," Asian Community Mental Health Services, Oakland, CA, September, 1987. Factors needed for successful mainstreaming are covered by P.W. Van Arsdale, "Mainstreaming Mental Services to Refugees," _New England Journal of Human Services_ 8: 36-38, 1988.

[19]Ibid., Gong-Guy 1987.

[20]G. Weinstein-Shr, "Breaking the Linguistic and Social Isolation of Refugee Elders: An Intergeneration Model," manuscript prepared for the Temple University Institute on Aging, Philadelphia, PA, 1987.

[21]"House of the Spirit: Perspectives on Cambodian Health Care," videotape produced by the American Friends Service Committee, New York, NY, 1985.

[22]D. Conquergood, P. Thao, and X. Thao (translator), "I am a Shaman: A Hmong Life Story with Ethnographic Commentary," _Occasional Paper_ No. 8, University of Minnesota, Minneapolis, MN, 1989.

[23]The complexities of this need are exemplified in "House of the Spirit: Perspectives on Cambodian Health Care" (see note 21, above).

[24]E. Egli, "The Role of Bilingual Workers without Professional Mental Health Training in Mental Health Services for Refugees," manuscript prepared for the NIMH/Refugee Assistance Program - Mental Health, Technical Assistance Center, University of Minnesota, Minneapolis, MN, 1987.¡¥
[25]M.A. Adkins, "Role of Bilingual/Bicultural Service Providers in the Delivery of Mental Health Services," in _Mental Health of Immigrants and Refugees_, W.H. Holtzman and T.H. Bornemann, eds. (Austin, TX: Hogg Foundation for Mental Health, 1990, pp. 216-217).

[26]Ibid., pp. 218-219.

[27]J.M. Jaranson and P. Bamford, "Program Models for Mental Health Treatment of Refugees," manuscript prepared for the NIMH/Refugee Assistance Program - Mental Health, Technical Assistance Center, University of Minnesota, Minneapolis, MN, 1987.

[28]M.A. Adkins and C.G. Ray, Intensive Training of Bilingual Workers in Mental Health and Cross-Cultural Communication: A Resource for Trainers, Spring Institute for International Studies Special Publication, Denver, CO, 1987.

[29]Ibid.

[30]Ibid.

PART III

ORGANIZATIONAL CHANGE: THE EXTERNAL DYNAMIC

TOO MUCH OR TOO LITTLE: URBAN EMPLOYMENT PROJECTS FOR SALVADOREAN REFUGEES IN COSTA RICA

Tanya Basok
University of Windsor

INTRODUCTION

Once refugees abandon their country of origin they become dependent on various governmental and non-governmental agencies (NGOs) for subsistence. These agencies distribute emergency aid and, in some cases, provide financing for projects which aim at making refugees self-sufficient. However, distributed assistance does not always bring the desired results and, at times, creates unexpected negative consequences. The delicate balance that must be achieved in delivering assistance is described by Ray Bromley: "Too little support may be useless, too much may be patronizing and may create permanent dependence, and poorly designed and badly delivered support may be counter-productive."[1]

From the perspective of systems analysis as expressed through institutional analysis, this chapter addresses the question of how the nature of the delivery of institutional aid (and its amount) have affected the survival and relative success of refugee projects for Salvadoreans in Costa Rica. Three relevant issues are examined: First, administration of projects by agencies responsible for them; second, paternalistic treatment of program beneficiaries; and third, amount of assistance offered to refugees. The role of the Caritas agency comes under especially tough scrutiny, as do the so-called "durable solution" and "local settlement" programs. The chapter is based upon data which I collected in 1986 on 89 urban employment projects, 67 of which were still functioning and 22 of which had failed. In addition, interview material gathered from members of eight Salvadorean small enterprises which were set up without institutional assistance is presented. Some rural and non-productive projects for Salvadorean refugees in Costa Rica are briefly discussed as well.

THE "DURABLE SOLUTION" APPROACH TO REFUGEE SETTLEMENT

Costa Rica is often cited as a model for refugee settlement because it pursues the "durable solution" approach. This approach to settlement has been analyzed elsewhere (see, for example, Hansen this volume). It has been practiced in Costa Rica since 1981, although NGOs started offering emergency aid to Salvadoreans since they first started arriving in 1980. A number of governmental and voluntary agencies have participated in refugee settlement. They include such domestically located international organizations as Caritas, the Episcopalian Church, the Red Cross, and the YMCA. In addition, refugees themselves formed a number of voluntary organizations, such as OARS (Office of Orientation and Assistance to Refugees) and Productor, aimed at assisting their compatriots. Apart from providing emergency aid to refugees, UNHCR also has financed most of the Salvadoreans' urban projects. Financial assistance has been provided by and through other international NGOs as well. They include Project Counselling for Latin American Refugees, Catholic Relief Services, Swedish Ecumenical Action, and others. To complement and coordinate the work of international organizations and national voluntary agencies, the Costa Rican government set up CONAPARE (the National Committee for Refugees) and PRIMAS (Refugee Program of the Mixed Institute for Social Assistance).

As noted above, in the early 1980s Salvadorean refugees started arriving in Costa Rica and by 1983 they numbered about 15,000. From the very beginning the host government and NGOs concentrated their efforts on settling them. Considerable energy and funds were invested. However, the results were less than satisfactory. In 1985 it became evident to UNHCR that less than half of the 152 projects registered with a government agency were still active. Most of the others had failed.

Consequently a new formula for urban projects was introduced by an ILO worker in 1985 and it was accepted by UNHCR. Prior to 1985, most urban projects were of a collective nature with an average investment of US$1,700 per project member. The new program, called "local settlement," offered small donations of about US$250 to individuals to establish small businesses at home.

The new program could hardly be termed a success either. Of the 49 individual Salvadorean recipients of this program interviewed as part of the present research, only 11 (22%) were working full-time in the occupation for which they had received the donation. Seventeen of these refugees (35%) dedicated part of their time to work in this occupation, and 21 people (43%) were not using machinery or tools they had received through the program at all.[2]

Not all projects for refugees which were still active in 1986 performed equally well. In fact, incomes earned by the beneficiaries ranged widely. Members of some projects earned more than 12,000 colones ($216) per month. Yet others earned less than 3,000 colones ($54) per month. Why did so may projects fail and what explains differences in incomes earned by their members?

PROBLEMS WITH PROJECT ADMINISTRATION
AND TECHNICAL ASSISTANCE

When voluntary agencies started opening projects for refugees most lacked any experience in the field. Therefore, many mistakes were committed in the first two years. Funds were assigned almost at random, market conditions were not investigated, soil and climatic conditions were not examined, and no systematic selection criteria were used to determine which refugees to involve. Anyone could apply for a project regardless of actual job-related skills.

In 1983, voluntary agencies began to analyze the reasons for the high failure rate of the projects. At the same time, CONAPARE conducted an analysis of the projects registered with them. They concluded that out of 145 projects, only 71 were still active, making the failure rate 51.4%. The following causes were identified as leading to failure:

1) Poor structure, organization and planning by implementing agencies
2) Migration of beneficiaries to third countries or return to El Salvador
3) Inter-personal conflicts
4) Irresponsibility of participants
5) Health problems
6) Lack of technical and administrative skills of the beneficiaries.[3]

It was found that urban projects had a somewhat higher failure rate. Caritas, which specialized in urban projects, reported that 89 of its 129 implemented projects (69%) had failed before June 1983.[4]

In response to self-scrutiny and evaluations by CONAPARE, implementing agencies hired new members trained as agronomists, economists or administrators to form technical advisory committees in charge of evaluating project proposals. They also started offering short vocational training and business administration courses to refugees. Technical supervision and control of the projects was strengthened as well.

However, the new approach did not lead to better results. In 1985, when new evaluations were conducted, it was found that 63 out of 152 projects registered with CONAPARE (41.4%) were still active. Thus, 58.6% of the projects had failed. One needs to take into consideration that between 1980 and 1983 Costa Rica was going through an economic crisis which could have affected the economic behavior of the implemented projects. However, in 1983 the Costa Rican economy began to recover, thus creating more favorable conditions, yet Salvadorean projects continued going out of business at a high rate. Those enterprises which did not close down lost many of their members. Caritas, for instance, reported that by 1985 membership in still-functioning projects had been reduced by half.

101

My analysis indicates that one reason the failure and withdrawal rates were high was the nature of technical advice offered by the agencies. According to some informants, advice given to them (especially by representatives of Caritas) was not always useful and, at times, harmful to their businesses. For example, to cope with the lack of administrative skills of the refugees running many of the projects, in 1983 Caritas had started offering three-day business administration courses. Most informants believed these courses were too short for them to learn anything substantive. Another example covers baking skills. Caritas sent refugees to a baking course at the National Institute for Training. They were taught to bake home-made cookies. However, this skill did not prove useful in the overall running of a bakery. Some complaints were more serious. For instance, two shoe-makers expressed their concern about the Caritas team of "experts" who had come to lend them advice. The "experts" knew nothing about making shoes and could not offer any useful advice to the shoe-makers, who themselves had been in this business for many years. (One refugee had owned a shoe workshop employing ten people in El Salvador).

Some advice given by the technical team went against the economic interests of project members. For instance, Caritas advisors insisted that seamstresses and tailors sell their products to stores, arguing that this arrangement guaranteed a stable market for producers. While this recommendation was valid for group projects, individual seamstresses and tailors did much better when catering to private customers. Generally, stores paid considerably less than do private customers, first, because they need to leave room for their own profit margin, and second, because they can purchase industrially-produced textiles for relatively low prices. In the words of one tailor, when he sold to stores he was "working too much for too little." A related problem was found in the TV and radio field. A two-man TV and radio repair project had a poor location, and the men had to work in a centrally-located workshop using their own tools yet sharing profits with the Costa Rican workshop owner. Although that seemed to be the only viable solution to them, Caritas consistently opposed it. Creative interaction with clients and consideration of alternatives were not part of the Caritas formula.[5]

A policy which gave priority to larger, collective projects also led to the high failure and withdrawal rates. I would point to two problem areas linked to this policy. First, while business management skills were less important in individual projects, they were essential in collective ones. Yet, very few Salvadorean refugees had such skills. Most of the implemented projects were of a collective nature, some including as many as 20 members and one including 40. This policy had been implemented for three reasons. The first had to do with economic rationality, i.e., centralizing administrative and technical assistance, increasing competitiveness, and purchasing large quantities of raw materials. The second reason was linked to a policy of international funding agencies which promoted collective projects. And third, Salvadorean implementing agencies believed that by promoting group projects they would be able to unite the community. They believed that once trained to work in cooperatives, Salvadoreans would be able to do the same upon return to their homeland. It was expected that work in a group project would serve as a kind of therapy for refugees with psychological problems.

This policy also was supported by independent researchers evaluating projects for refugees in Costa Rica. An ILO researcher, for instance, contended "the very concept of promoting primarily small projects is the cause of their failure." These projects, argued the analyst, had problems in marketing their products, since they could not generate an "economy of scale." By creating small projects, it was further argued (erroneously so) that implementing agencies were increasing activities of the urban informal sector to the point of saturation. Refugee projects were seen as creating inappropriate competition with the local labor force.[6]

Second, inter-personal conflicts often arose and led to either withdrawal of some members or closure of entire projects. Prior to September, 1982, refugees themselves had formed work groups and chosen the types of project in which they wished to participate. Some of these people had a desire to work in a chosen field but no specific experience. However, in September of that year, agencies began directing refugees to particular projects. One result was that those who had been strangers now had to work side by side. They were all told that they had equal rights and, as a consequence, no one wanted to take orders. This created virtual anarchy in the projects. Conflicts also were provoked because some refugees who had more skills than others demanded higher pay. Equally problematic, people with different political views often were forced to work side by side; their political disputes often interfered with their working relationships.

PATERNALISM AND THE PSYCHOLOGY OF DEVELOPMENT

Agencies administering the "durable solution" program differed in their attitude towards project members. There were some agencies (like Caritas, PRIMAS, and the YMCA) which practiced a paternalistic approach. Other agencies (such as the Episcopalian Church, OARS, and Productor) allowed refugees to develop independently, although still controlling some of their decisions and at times offering more help to them than was required.

In 1985, when an evaluation of projects was conducted by the Caritas technical team, it was observed that one of the reasons for project failure was a "limited sense of belonging to a project" among its members. According to this report, project members maintained interest exclusively in earning a salary and when the slightest opportunity arose, they left a project without even "minimal resistance." It was also observed that there existed a "certain lack of trust" (disconfianza) by refugees towards the Caritas technical assistance team which was regarded as an "external agent" operating in its own interest.[7]

However, my analysis indicates that refugees' failure to identify themselves with the projects stemmed from the attitude assumed by Caritas towards them. Relations between Caritas and project members were defined in the Caritas Constitution (Reglamento) as a set of rights and obligations. The obligations incumbent upon a project's members included presenting monthly financial statements to the technical team, informing it of any change having to do with the employment of new members or withdrawal of the original ones, and updating the socio-economic situation of the members and their economic activities. Members were not allowed to give loans to fellow members with the money belonging to the enterprise. Refugees were under an obligation to provide information to Caritas if the latter was involved in project evaluation activities or research. They were to stay away from any political or religious activities which could interfere with the economic life of their project. Caritas had the right to expel any member who did not comply with the rules it had unilaterally set up. Machinery given to the projects was always the property of the agency and without warning could be taken away from the refugees.

It was the policy of Caritas that all the projects be under its control even five years after implementation. When a project moved to another location, its members were obliged to call the office and provide new addresses. If they failed to do so, Caritas officials called the Office of Migration advising it to discontinue all types of assistance for which the refugees in question were eligible.

Project members were initially placed in the position of wage-laborers under the control of one employer--Caritas. Some of the project members interviewed reported having been told by Caritas that they were "just wage-laborers" (operarios). When asked about the ownership of machinery, most of the informants did not know to whom it belonged. They believed that Caritas was still in control of it, and were fearful that one day it would be taken back.

Most of the informants viewed Caritas as promoting its own interests and not being genuinely concerned about refugees. In fact, there existed wide-spread opinion that Caritas wanted projects to fail so that it would be able to take away the machinery. Some refugees reported that Caritas had closed their projects because the members were having interpersonal conflicts. Rather than solving the problems or re-assigning the projects, it was reported that Caritas would simply close them down and confiscate the machinery. In some cases, Caritas even was accused of instigating the conflicts between project members. Stories about a warehouse full of machinery confiscated from projects which had failed, or from projects where members had left, were often mentioned in the interviews. Whether such a warehouse existed or not is less important than the negative attitudes such stories engendered.

Caritas also was often accused of embezzling funds provided it by UNHCR. Others not accusing Caritas of theft nonetheless believed that the only reason it promoted projects for refugees was so that UNHCR would pay its administrative costs. In fact, Caritas may have retained a large percentage of such refugee funds for overhead. According to one key informant, the agency's administrative costs constituted one-third of the $1,217,759 donated by UNHCR between 1981 and 1985. Even in comparison with other refugee-project implementing agencies, this percentage would be very high.

Many informants had still other stories to tell about Caritas. One woman who was the only participant-survivor of a 10-person project claimed that all her machinery had been confiscated by Caritas. Members of another workshop said they had been forced to buy raw materials left over from a project which had failed. As they discovered later, they had paid three times the amount they could have paid elsewhere. Other people said they were asked to sign blank checks by Caritas employees. When they refused, their project was closed. It was believed by some refugees that while international agencies were interested in aiding them, Costa Ricans working at Caritas were trying to harm them in order to protect the national labor force.

In 1986 Caritas divided the existing projects into three categories: Those which had reached self-sufficiency, those "on the road to recovery," and "deficient" ones. Caritas was planning to "liberate" the self-sufficient projects, transfer the ones on the road to recovery to CASP/ Re (Refugee Unit of the Centre of Socio-Political Analysis, another NGO which joined refugee work in 1985), and close down the deficient ones. By December, Caritas had still not closed down any projects. People from some projects in all three categories had received letters in which Caritas urged them to return machinery to the agency. These were, possibly, some of the "liberating" techniques being used by Caritas.

Examples of the paternalistic treatment of refugees can also be drawn from the experience of other agencies such as the YMCA, PRIMAS, and the Red Cross. The YMCA administered a residence for young Salvadorean refugees who were initially encouraged to form committees for self-government. However, almost all the decisions adopted by the committees were overturned by YMCA representatives. Eventually, these committees disbanded as their members felt powerless.

Many of the boys who lived in this residence acquired a feeling of mistrust towards the Costa Rican agencies that were implementing projects. After the residence was closed in December, 1985, they preferred to work illegally rather than apply for projects implemented by agencies.

The story of Los Angeles, the biggest Costa Rican rural project for refugees, is very similar. At first the project was administered by the Red Cross and then was passed on to PRIMAS. Like the YMCA residence, refugees formed various committees in the Los Angeles project. Similar to their young compatriots, they soon realized that they had no decision-making power. Without decision-making power, there can be no empowerment. Everything was controlled by Costa Rican administrators. In 1981, a UNHCR representative was quoted in a newspaper article as saying: "We want to give refugees participation little by little. But the refugees feel that those who make the decisions, administer funds, and supervise the camp either live in the capital or, like the Red Cross workers, have isolated themselves within the camp."[8] The same article made reference to the misuse of funds and inequitable distribution of goods by the Red Cross. The following incident was reported:

> In December [1980], when the camp was moved from Murcielago to Los Angeles, one of the large gas stoves the refugees had been using was appropriated "temporarily" by the 18 Red Cross workers for their headquarters, even though the post was already equipped with a small stove. [On July 18] five women went up to the Red Cross post to ask for it. Failing to get a positive response, they called their husbands. A bitter exchange followed, and one of the refugees tried to take the stove. The Red Cross called in the Rural Guard, later charging that there had been a "mutiny" in the camp. The arrival of 13 armed guardsmen, who stayed overnight and half the next day, terrified the refugees, many of whom had witnessed massacres of family or village members by uniformed men in their own country.[9]

In 1985, when I visited, the project's farm was run by a Costa Rican agronomist. Refugees were assigned tasks to perform in the field by this agronomist every morning. If the agronomist was not in the field, refugees did not know what to do and, at times, returned back to their barracks. There were no more refugee committees. Most of the project members did not care whether the farm prospered or failed.

By contrast, other implementing agencies such as OARS, Productor, and the Episcopalian Church did not seem to be paternalistic in their relations with refugees. The Episcopalian Church offered more freedom to project members than did Caritas. Its administrative costs constituted only 7% of the total donation per project. Project members were asked to sign a contract which stated that if in two years a project proved to be self-sufficient, all the fixed and fluid capital was to become the property of the project. If

106

self-sufficiency was not reached, the Episcopalian Church had the right to claim back the machinery to be used in other projects. The terms of these contracts were observed and two years after implementation, successful projects were completely "liberated." Episcopalian Church workers often were unaware of the new location of these "liberated" projects. Even when they visited, it was out of personal interest and not in order to interfere with the projects' affairs.

Although relations between the Episcopalian Church and refugees were considerably better in comparison with Caritas, some complaints also were voiced by project beneficiaries. Agency administrators wanted to close down one project which was doing rather poorly. Although this would have been in agreement with the terms of the contract between the project and the agency, the beneficiaries believed that they deserved a chance to keep on struggling for their survival, even though it meant earning a very low income. It is the nature of most implementing agencies to be "rational." Although this particular project was not economically feasible, its members believed that they were fulfilling a political and cultural role, since they were promoting a Salvadorean traditional craft (hand-woven fabrics). In this type of situation, economic rationality in fact plays little role.

It is often important in business to take a risk. It may result in the downfall of the business or it may allow it to prosper. Agencies promoting projects tend to be cautious in their decisions and, by doing so, may slow down development. Members of one project implemented by the Episcopalian Church complained that their entrepreneurial freedom was blocked by the agency and that it was only after their "liberation" that their business began to develop rapidly.

The psychology of development must be addressed. A systems perspective necessitates it. I believe that these complaints do not have to do with special policies of the Episcopalian Church as much as with problems involved in the relations between institutions in general and individuals depending upon them. In such instances, the sooner the relationship is severed, the better it may be for a project.

Since most staff members in OARS and Productor were themselves Salvadorean refugees, there tended to be good rapport between project members and these agencies. However, these two agencies viewed projects as solutions to all refugee problems. They paid more attention to the refugees' social and psychological needs than to the economic aspects of the projects. This may have enhanced refugee - agency relations, but consumed resources and energy that might otherwise have been used to strengthen the economic components.

The Episcopalian Church also was concerned with the psychological well-being of refugees. Its representatives tried to address this problem by organizing retreat-like workshops at which refugees were asked to share their experiences of life and persecution in El Salvador, difficulties of flight and emigration, and impressions of life in Costa Rica. All local employees of the Episcopalian Church participated in these seminars along with several Costa Rican priests. They ate and prayed together as well. At the same time, it is my opinion that the Episcopalian Church workers diligently tried not to ignore the economic performance of projects administered by them.

WHEN INVESTMENT IS NOT SUFFICIENT

In order to understand the importance of the amount of help given, two programs--the "durable solution" and "local settlement"--were compared. The "local settlement" program was a response to the high failure rate of the "durable solution" program. It was based on a different notion of urban development. Instead of promoting large refugee projects, this program aimed at establishing businesses which would be much smaller both in terms of initial investment and membership.

I compared the economic performance of thirty-seven "durable solution" (DS) and 30 "local settlement" (LS) projects.[10] The initial investment per capita in DS projects was found to be significantly higher than the investment per LS recipient (63,314 colones and 13,855 colones, respectively). When total investment per capita was calculated as a sum of initial investment and consequent refinancing, the disparity between the two programs became even more pronounced (71,197 colones and 13,855 colones, respectively). The average investment per capita in the LS program was less than one-fifth that in the DS program. Yet, incomes which beneficiaries earned in these two types of projects did not correlate closely to the amounts of investment.

In order to accurately compare incomes of members of various projects, I adjusted for the amount of time worked; some people were engaged part-time and others full-time. Further, while some beneficiaries preferred treating these projects as their secondary source of income or had to work part-time in order to look after children, others worked less than full-time because demand for their product/service was insufficient to warrant otherwise. Thus, incomes were adjusted to a 45-hour week in a manner which took these factors into consideration:

$$\text{Adjusted Income} = \frac{45 * \text{Monthly Income}}{\text{Amount of Hours Worked Per Week}}$$

The incomes of those project members who faced insufficient demand were left as reported. The incomes of those small producers who worked less than 45 hours per week either because they needed to take care of children or because they preferred working elsewhere, but who also would possibly face insufficient demand if they produced more, were calculated as averages between the real and the adjusted incomes.

Thus calculated, the average adjusted income per DS project member was found to be 7,540 colones per month while for those in the LS program it was 6,570 colones per month (the latter being 87% of the former). In terms of cost efficiency the LS program therefore demonstrated much better results and in absolute terms, those in the LS projects earned only slightly less. Moreover, if refugees--instead of receiving a grant from an agency--had to borrow money from a bank at the commercial rate, their adjusted incomes would be 6,400 colones per month in the case of LS recipients and only 5,810 colones per month in the case of DS beneficiaries. Here the DS program demonstrated worse results. It should be pointed out that there were considerably more beneficiaries of the LS than DS program who worked less than 45 hours per week in these businesses.[11] Real average incomes were 8,080 colones and 5,380 colones for the DS and LS programs, respectively. In other words, it can be inferred that while some LS projects had the potential for offering incomes comparible to those earned by DS beneficiaries, their owners preferred avoiding the risks of investing their entire time in these businesses and continued working in other jobs as well.

With respect to generation of employment, the two programs can be compared in the following way. Seventy-four DS project members created employment for 29 wage-laborers, 11 apprentices, and 19 paid family members. LS project members, on the other hand, created employment for only one wage laborer, one apprentice, and six family members. One DS project member with an average investment of 71,197 colones hired 0.80 worker. One LS member with an average investment of 13,855 colones employed 0.27 worker.[12] Employment of one worker cost 20,366 colones in DS projects and only 10,938 colonies in the LS program. When employment was calculated with respect to the number of hours worked per week (e.g., a worker engaged in the business for 30 hours was equated with a 0.7 job), the difference between the cost of jobs for the two programs became considerably less. The LS program created 23.9 jobs or an average of 0.80 per enterprise at a cost of 17,318 colones per job. The DS program, on the other hand, created 122.7 jobs or an average of 3.32 jobs per project at a cost of 21,445 colones per job.

Therefore, while in relative terms employment generation in the DS program was somewhat more costly, in absolute terms the LS program was much less successful. "Local settlement" did not create sufficient employment-- less than one fully employed person per enterprise.

A more general question is: Does higher investment per project translate into higher salary earned per participant?

Statistically, the correlation between total investment per capita and present income is insignificant (N = 62, P = -0.05, p > 0.7). As is demonstrated later in the chapter, high levels of investment into some projects did not enable their members to earn high salaries. On the other hand, smaller levels of investment often provided sufficient income opportunities for program participants. The level of financial investment is only one factor which influences the economic performance of small businesses. While higher levels are particularly important for projects which require machinery, another significant factor is location. But even when investments in machinery are adequate and location is good, an enterprise may still do poorly due to lack of demand or skill.

A significant range of incomes was found within both the "durable solution" and "local settlement" projects. In order to understand the interactions among three variables--machinery, skills, and demand--it proved useful to divide all the enterprises according to the occupational categories to which they belong[13] and compare the two programs within each category.

   <u>Shoe-Making and Repair:</u>   Salvadorean shoes seem to enjoy relatively high demand in Costa Rica. As far as competition from the industrial sector is concerned, there is an interesting division of labor within shoe production. Large factories specialize in men's and children's shoes, while small producers make ladies' shoes. There is competition from imports and other small shoe-makers, but Salvadorean shoe-makers have a better reputation than locals. Reduction of shoe imports from Nicaragua (as a result of the deterioration of political relations between Costa Rica and Nicaragua) also has created an opening for locally produced shoes.

Shoe-makers sell their products to stores and therefore the type of neighborhood they live in is not important to marketing their product. They require a special leather-sewing machine. Shoe-making projects have been equipped with all the necessary machinery. Those who participated in the LS program received only raw materials. All the LS shoe-makers under study, however, had already established their businesses or had been working in shoe workshops as wage-laborers prior to receiving assistance through the LS initiative. Those working in workshops were able to use the workshop machinery to make their own shoes as well. Other people had been able to purchase sewing machines from their own savings or as presents from foreign friends. One DS recipient, on the other hand, claimed that his project was "<u>desgraciado</u>" (unfortunate) as it had received no machinery. Removing from the analysis the case of one family where production was significantly impaired by the mental illness of the family head, the average income of shoe-makers was 10,216 colones per month. There was no significant income difference between those in LS and those in DS projects. In

110

fact, when hours of work were taken into consideration, LS recipients turned out to be doing better than those in the DS program. Adjusted average income was 10,490 colones per month for those in the LS programs and 6,900 colones for DS recipients. The latter average was skewed because of the effect of one DS project with no machinery whose two owners were making only 4,300 colones per month each. Those in the LS program were able to generate similar or better incomes because they themselves had found solutions to the problem of obtaining machinery, not because of the aid received through the LS initiative per se.

One LS recipient who did not have access to a machine devoted himself to shoe repair. The demand was very low in his neighborhood for this type of work. He did not want to move to a more central location, however, because he would have had to pay a higher rent. He was making an average of 2,400 colones per month repairing shoes and had to work full-time elsewhere to survive financially.

Clothing Production and Baking: In clothing production, as well as in baking, there was a significant income difference between those who had entered a DS project and those who were LS beneficiaries. In DS projects, small-scale clothing producers made 8,350 colones per month on average while seamstresses in the LS program, on average, earned 2,540 colones per month (adjusted average monthly incomes being 7,950 and 3,670 colones, respectively). The average monthly income of bakers in DS projects was 10,000 colones, as compared to 3,500 colones for those in the LS program (or 14,730 and 4,220 colones, respectively, when adjusted for hours worked and demand).

This can be explained by the different amounts of investment into the two programs. When the "durable solution" projects were implemented, the average investment in capital equipment was 38,650 colones, while the average investment in machinery per "local settlement" project (where applicable) was 11,300 colones.[14] In the meantime, the DS projects under study were significantly reduced in size. Those who remained in the projects retained some valuable machinery of an industrial and semi-industrial nature.[15] The machinery offered to people in the LS program, on the other hand, was of a domestic nature. Seamstresses got household sewing machines which were very slow and which did not allow them to finish the edgings well. (Finishing is usually done by a special machine called an "overlock," which usually was provided to the "durable solution" projects.) The stoves given to bakers in the LS program were not suitable for profitable baking as they consumed much energy and, because of their small size, made production slow. These factors hampered the LS producers' ability to compete with other small-scale seam-stresses and bakers.

When DS projects were implemented, the first few months of rent were paid for them. That gave their members oppor-

tunities to find locations in relatively good neighborhoods. By the time the assistance was cut off, each project
already had had a chance to establish a clientele and could
then continue paying the rent on its own.

The situation was different with the LS recipients.
When the LS program started at the end of 1985, it was
intended to create employment mainly for the heads of
families (including many single mothers), who had not yet
been integrated into any project. These refugees had sur-
vived on UNHCR emergency aid and occasional illegal jobs.
Their incomes had been low and therefore they had had to
live in inexpensive houses in poor neighborhoods. The LS
programs offered them machines, tools, and in some instances
raw materials--but no chance to move out of their neighborhoods. Although these small-scale producers saw their
locations as impediments to their businesses' survival, they
nevertheless did not want to take the risk of moving out of
such "affordable housing." Their immediate clients,
therefore, also were low-income people. These clients did
not generate sufficient demand for custom-made goods and
paid little for the products purchased--and even much of
that was on credit.

Paradoxically, clothing-producers and bakers who
received LS assistance often had to join the program because
their emergency aid had been discontinued, this in turn due
to the new approach being taken by UNHCR to deal with the
problem of dependency caused by prolonged distribution of
emergency assistance. CASP/Re social workers tried integrating them into the general labor force, at times ignoring
their actual skills. It was assumed that any woman could
sew and bake and therefore many women were given sewing
machines or stoves. Not surprisingly, it turned out that
their domestic skills did not readily translate into the
skills required to make their businesses work well.

Interviews with members of the 22 failed LS projects
indicated that 13 of them involved seamstresses and 3
involved bakers. Eight seamstresses had had no previous
labor experience working with textiles, and had developed
only rudimentary sewing skills. Out of those seamstresses
and bakers who had received an LS donation who were still
working in 1986, two in each job category had had no previous experience in the field and were earning as little as
2,925 colones per month, on average.

There were two LS recipients who, because they could
not produce clothes competitively, devoted themselves to
clothing repair. Demand for these services was low, especially in poor neighborhoods. Consequently, incomes generated
in this occupation were low as well (less than 2,500 colones
per month, on average).

Other Occupations: In other occupations there were no
sharp differences between refugees in DS projects and those
who had received LS assistance. Painters, repairers, elec-
tricians, and sub-contractors working in construction

(masons and carpenters) did not require significant capital investment. Some basic tools and occasional raw materials were sufficient inputs. Neither did their successes depend so directly on the locations of their businesses since, apart from construction sub-contractors and watch repairers, services were provided at the homes of clients. However, these other occupations require technical skills. If workers already possessed them, grants offered by the LS program were quite sufficient. In the sample, all those in the above-mentioned occupations who had received LS assistance were earning good incomes (between 9,000 and 16,000 colones per month.)[16]

In some occupational categories, even well-financed projects failed to do well due to heavy competition. While one construction carpenter was earning 12,000 colones monthly, all carpentry workshops were experiencing problems because competition with industrially-produced furniture makers was considerable. One carpentry workshop, for example, received 1,200,000 colones from the implementing agency. Yet its six members were earning at most only 5,500 colones per month when they had work; occasionally they did not earn anything for weeks. Another carpentry project, with a total investment of 750,000 colones for six people, provided its members with a salary of 2,000 colones per month. If the money provided these two projects had been borrowed from a bank, their members' salaries would have been negligible. A TV and radio repair workshop consisting of two members received 130,000 colones from the implementing agency, but were able to earn only 2,200 colones per month each--by sub-contracting work from a Costa Rican workshop. A body shop, which had received 150,000 colones for four people, had only one original member left, who was earning 5,000 colones per month.

SMALL ENTERPRISES POR CUENTA PROPIA

The analysis of the impacts of institutional assistance on the economic performance of small enterprises cannot be complete if these small enterprises are not compared to the ones established without institutional assistance (por cuenta propia). I found only eight enterprises por cuenta propia. Although the number is small, some conclusions can nevertheless be drawn from their analysis.

Three of these enterprises had low input requirements. They included one crafts workshop, a street jewel vendor, and a soap-maker. The first workshop received a private loan of 10,000 colones from a friend (with easy repayment terms). The second business started with an investment of 5,000 colones received as a donation from the YMCA.[17] No information is available on the initial investment by the soap-maker, but it could not have been high as the soap-maker only had a few tubs and barrels, and no machinery. Members of these three enterprises had relatively high monthly earnings, being 7,500 colones in the case of three craftsmen from the workshop and the jewel vendor, and 20,000 colones for the soap-maker. The latter worked 66 hours per week; with a machine to cut soap, his productivity would have been still higher.

A photographer whom I interviewed would have required a substantial investment to purchase a camera and photographic materials. However, he was given a camera by the political movement to which he belonged since, in addition to serving a regular clientele, he used to take pictures of political events organized by the movement. He earned about 7,500 colones per month.

Two tailors were under-mechanized. One of them managed to buy two second-hand sewing machines for 10,000 colones. The other was using his friend's sewing machine which likely cost no more than 5,000 colones. Both tailors sub-contracted work from other workshops. While the first one only did so during the two months of peak demand (November and December), the second did so throughout the year. The first earned 14,000 colones monthly (working 70 hours per week) during the busy months, and only 2,000 colones per month when no sub-contracting (maquila) was available. The second earned about 5,600 colones per month year round. If these tailors had had better machinery, they also would have been able to sell to stores or private customers.

The case of one bakery owner provides an example of how a business can grow significantly, even when the initial investment in machinery is low. The owner's wife started the business by making pastries at home and selling them in the street, while he worked in a bakery project. He then left the project (because of inter-personal conflicts) and joined his wife's enterprise. Demand for their product was very high and, as a result, their business grew rapidly. In three years they were able to invest about 250,000 colones into their enterprise.

An important conclusion drawn from the analysis of enterprises por cuenta propia is similar to that found in the case of projects administered by various institutions: There were those enterprises which could function well with low initial investments, as well as those which generated low incomes if under-capitalized.

CONCLUSIONS AND OPPORTUNITIES FOR EMPOWERMENT

One approach to the systems analysis of aid involves the assessment of institutions. Three aspects of institutional assistance are crucial in understanding the relative success and failure of refugee projects. These are project administration, the attitude/approach of NGOs (paternalistic or not), and the amount of assistance offered to project beneficiaries.

One factor which explained the high failure rate among the Salvadorean projects in the first few years had to do with poor administration. However, even when administrative processes were improved and more technical assistance was given to project members, the failure rate among the group projects remained high. An additional factor could be found in inter-personal conflicts among project members, resulting in the withdrawal of some members or the closing of entire projects.

The cases reviewed in this chapter also indicate that the paternalistic treatment of refugees in projects by some agencies resulted in a lack of commitment by project members to these very enterprises, and a consequent high turnover rate. Those members who remained in the projects were very restricted in their decision-making opportunities, especially regarding business risks. Creative ideas that might have led to greater profits were constrained.

As far as the amount of aid is concerned, it cannot be argued that more assistance necessarily translates into a higher success rate. My analysis suggests that the amount and type of help given should be tailored to the input requirements of each business. This must be determined on-the-spot, after costs and benefits are estimated.

Those occupations which require modest inputs of tools and raw materials, but not machinery, and which by and large do not depend on the location of the business (e.g., carpentry) were found to function well with small amounts of aid. Those occupations which require inputs of machinery (e.g., shoe-making) usually cannot survive when offered less-than-adequate equipment. Those producers who cater to private customers in their immediate neighborhoods (e.g., seamstresses) depend on appropriate locations for their businesses to succeed. Such individuals often need assistance to locate themselves well. This certainly was found to apply to shoe-makers, especially those not being provided machinery by the projects. However, better location usually is correlated with the requirement of paying higher rent.

My research indicates that people cannot be empowered in small businesses without being afforded the opportunities to make key decisions, take risks--and make mistakes. The Los Angeles project clearly indicates this. "Project liberation," as successfully exemplified by several initiatives sponsored by the Episcopalian Church, is one important indicator of empowerment. My study demonstrates that "economic rationality" and "controlled" donor agency behavior of beneficiaries do not always lead to self-sufficiency (the latter another possible indicator of empowerment). Flexibility, compassion, and the development of trust between donor and recipient also are essential.

NOTES

[1]R. Bromley, "Introduction," in Planning for Small Enterprises in Third World Cities, R. Bromley, ed. (New York: Pergamon Press, 1985).

[2]According to a 1986 evaluation conducted by A. Carrizo, the proponent of the program, the failure rate of the program was only 25.4%. The discrepancy with the results of my study is significant. When I presented her with my results, Carrizo suggested that the difference could be explained by the fact that her evaluation included both Nicaraguans and Salvadoreans while my research dealt with Salvadoreans only.

[3]CONAPARE (Comisión Nacional Para Refugiados), Situación de los Proyectos Para Refugiados en Costa Rica, mimeo. (San José, Costa Rica, 1983).

[4]V. Jimenez, Analisis de Trabajo Realizado en el Programa de Refugiados por Cáritas de Costa Rica: Período Octubre 1981-Julio 1985, mimeo. (San José, Costa Rica, 1985).

[5]Similar problems were encountered in non-productive projects. Some of the advice offered through the YMCA, for example, was as useless--or at times, as harmful--as was the case with Caritas. In one instance, the YMCA hired a psychologist who used to come to its residential facility every day. Despite the fact that many young men living in the residence needed some psychological counselling or at least someone to talk to, they did not go to see him. His inappropriate comments about "subversives" and "witches," among other things, drove them away.

[6]L. Marmora, Migraciones Laborales e Integración del Refugiado en Costa Rica, mimeo. (Buenos Aires: ILO-UNHCR, 1984, pp. 83, 84, 90).

[7]See Jimenez, note 4 above.

[8]As quoted in an article on refugee resettlement in Costa Rica that appeared in the Tico Times, August 14, 1981.

[9]Ibid.

[10]Major differences between local settlement (LS) and durable solution (DS) programs are summarized through the following economic indicators:

Indicator	LS	DS
Average monthly income	5,380	8,080
Average adjusted monthly income	6,570	7,540
Investment per capita	13,855	63,314
Total investment per capita	13,855	71,197

```
Average # of workers per business    1.27         3.73
Average # of jobs per business       0.80         3.32
Total # of workers                     38          138
Number of owners                       30           74
Number of wage-laborers                 1           29
Number of paid family laborers          6           19
Number of unpaid family laborers        0            5
Number of apprentices                   1           11
```

[11]The number of hours worked per week by project
beneficiaries (by percentage) was as follows:

Hours	DS	LS
Less than 20	3	30
20 - 30	0	17
30 - 45	40	30
More than 45	57	23
	100	100

[12]Unpaid family workers were not taken into account.

[13]The following breakdown occurs when the two employment
programs are compared by occupational category:

Occupation	DS	LS
Shoe-making/repair	3	5
Clothes-making/repair	11	8
Baking	4	6
Soda work	5	1
Services	1	3
Carpentry	3	2
Leather work	1	0
Mechanics	3	3
Crafts	3	1
Commerce	2	0
Other	1	1
Total	37	30

[14]Calculations are based on information obtained in
interviews with project members. There were some discre-
pancies between these data and those reported on investment
by Carrizo (see note 2, above).

[15]Those refugees remaining in the projects did not keep all
the machinery donated, as some surplus was confiscated by
the agencies that had implemented the projects.

[16]Two painters proved to be exceptions. Both had just
started their businesses and did not yet have established
clienteles. However, even by working an average of just a
few hours daily, they were able to earn good incomes. At

117

the extreme, one of the painters earned 6,000 colones in just eight hours.

[17]Although the donation came from the YMCA, this enterprise was not considered to be a "project" because there was no subsequent control of it by this agency.

THE RAT, THE LOCUST, AND THE KURD: REFUGEE CREATION AND RESISTANCE IN THE MIDDLE EAST

Pauletta Otis
University of Southern Colorado

INTRODUCTION

The Kurds are a Middle Eastern people of some twenty million with a rich history dating back to the Medes. They were brought to contemporary attention as unfortunate victims of the chemical and genocidal capabilities of Iraq during the Iran-Iraq War and their vulnerability during the Gulf War of early 1991. The media "discovered" them as refugees during that same year, portraying them as strong, simple mountain people victimized by the terror of Saddam Hussein's Iraq. They were shown as handsome, strong and intelligent, but victimized because they did not have technological, educational, or legal means to protect themselves. Pictures of Kurdish refugees produced an outpouring of world sentiment: The Kurds were to be expeditiously cared for in the name of humanity. Future peace and stability in the region thus would be enhanced.

Much information about refugees is produced for the express purpose of mobilizing public sympathy and financial support for specific situations. Refugees often are portrayed as pathetic, helpless victims who must be cared for and resettled in the name of humanity by those more fortunate. Another type of "refugee literature" is produced by social scientists. Refugees are portrayed as representing the quintessential dependent variable, produced by circumstances over which they have no control nor make no effective efforts to resist. This later kind of analysis elicits two responses: An ex post factor search for causes which to me seems to be morally tardy, or a "blaming the victim" mentality which is scarcely helpful politically or theoretically.

Refugees are more than "Live Aid causes" or dependent variables. Current world refugee problems are too pervasive, complex, fractious, and costly to be relegated to the category of either another emotion-laden global issue or the theoretical realm of academia. My review of the contemporary literature indicates that very few long-term studies of particular cases which might inform general theory have been attempted. Information derived from well-researched case studies with reference to social theory (see, e.g., DeVoe this volume) is required before comparative analysis is possible. Only then can appropriate policies aimed at problem prevention and amelioration be suggested.

119

The story of the Kurds in many ways presents an ideal case history. The Kurds, as individuals and in groups, have fled persecution, famine, and sword. Some have had a choice; others have been forcibly evicted. Some have fled to traditional sanctuaries; some to other areas of the region and others to the Western world. They have fled as individuals and in groups, as children and adults, rich and poor. Civilians and militants alike have left traditional territories. They have been variously received in the places of sanctuary--sometimes with compassion, often with oppression and persecution. As of late 1991 more than three million Kurds were believed to be displaced persons or refugees. Kurdish responses, individually and as a group, have ranged from passive to violent resistance.

The purpose of this chapter is to present the Kurds as refugees within a systems framework suitable for comparative analysis with other refugee groups, with the express purpose of enlightening refugee policy. I provide a short discussion of internal cultural factors which influence decisions to become refugees, external factors as found in the physical, cultural and legal environments, and predicted responses to the perception of threat including the types and efficacies of resistance strategies. Resistance is one form of empowerment. I also provide a short discussion of significant changes in the world's responses to refugee crises as exemplified by the Kurdish situation.

A BRIEF HISTORY OF THE KURDS

The Kurds live in one of the most active conflict areas of the world. For 3000 years they have controlled the area known as Kurdistan, a mountainous area technically divided among the states of Iran, Iraq, Turkey, Syria, and the former U.S.S.R. With a population of some 20 million they form the fourth largest ethnic group in the Middle East.

The Kurds are strongly self-identified. In turn, outsiders see them as very distinct. Although anthropologists do not consider the Kurds to be a single ethnic group, but rather a group of groups, their designation as "Kurds" by outsiders has led to the emergence of a quasi-unified Kurdish cultural and political reality. There is no common genetic origin but they seem to be of Aryan descent. This is supported in that the Kurdish languages (Sorani and Kormanji) are of Indo-Aryan derivation.

Historically, the difficult terrain of Kurdistan provided a buffer zone between the Turkish, Persian, and Arab civilizations. The Kurds who lived and worked in the mountains and valleys allowed neither merchant nor soldier to pass through without permission or tribute. Although this contributed to peace in the region by separating the great empires and controlling contact and confrontation, it made the Kurds few friends or allies. Turks, Persians, and

Arabs as well as the Greeks, Romans and Mongols relegated Kurds to the status of uncivilized trouble makers.

The Kurds, originally Zoroastrian, accepted a form of Sunni Islam in the 7th century and made important contributions to Muslim civilization, notably in the fields of music and art. They continued to play an important role in providing a buffer between the Arabs and the Turks--usually siding with the Turks as co-religionists. In the 12th century Salah al Din, a Kurd, led the challenge to the European crusaders for the Holy Land.[1]

Even during the era of the great empires, the Kurds maintained their separate cultural identity with distinctive language, literature, and religion as well as economic and political autonomy. There was a cost: Remaining separate, they could not, or did not, "keep up with the times." The historical antagonisms of the region, their place as "spoilers" with each of their neighbors, and their "backwardness" at the beginning of the 20th century were to ensure them an ill-defined place in the modern state system.

Kurdish isolation and obscurity in the world was changed virtually overnight with the discovery of petroleum on their land. The Kurds became an "economically complicating factor" in the region. Each of the neighboring states vied for control of Kurdistan. Great power confrontations in the region intensified the competition and conflict between historically antagonistic groups.

The progressive disenfranchisement of the Kurds is related to the inauguration and development of the state system in the region. Even a seemingly positive development, the Constitution of Turkey (which reflected secular, egalitarian principles and promised full equality among minorities, including the Kurds) did not deliver as promised. Subsequent policies were not consistent and massive repression followed. Kurdish groups within Turkey recount the broken promises as evidence of Turkish nationalism and government unreliability.

Another early reversal, the 1920 San Remo Conference, gave Britain a mandate over Arab Iraq and the Kurdish Vilayet of Mosul. By 1920 the Kurds, led by Sheikh Mahmoud, had revolted against the British. The Kurds remember the bombings of villages by the Royal Air Corps and give it as evidence of British treachery.

With the signing of the Ankara Agreement in October of 1921, France (the other local colonial power) took the Kurdish province of Jezireh and Kurd-Dagh and annexed under Syrian mandate. Gradually the promise of sovereignty made possible through the breakup of the Ottoman Empire was diminishing. The 1920 Treaty of Sevres, between the Allied Powers and the Sublime Porte, had provided for the creation of an autonomous Kurdish state in eastern Anatolia. Yet this treaty was never ratified, having fallen victim to realpolitik, and was replaced by the 1923 Treaty of Lausanne. This agreement divided the approximately 500,000 square kilometers of Kurdistan (roughly the size of France) among the five states of Iran, Iraq, Syria, Turkey, and the U.S.S.R.

Thus by the early 1920s the partition of Kurdistan was complete. Kurds had pressed for their own state in the international forum on the grounds of sufficient population, territory, and national distinctiveness. They not only were denied, but denied for reasons which to them remained deceptive and unclear.[2]

In each of the five states mentioned above, the Kurds became a minority population with everything that implies: Lack of legal recognition of the Kurdish languages, the demeaning of religious beliefs and practices, occupation of their territory by "foreign" troops, lack of control over economic resources, little access to formal education, less than adequate human services such as health and medicine, and political exclusion. Even recognition of their separate existence, or identity as an ethnic group, was in several instances denied. Sometimes this was an incidental effect of larger state policies; sometimes it was the result of intentional oppression, repression, or exclusion.

I believe it is very important to recognize that in each case, power (particularly coercive power) has been in the hands of a traditional enemy and that this power has the sanction of the international state system. This system supports the sovereignty of the state and has traditionally shown little sympathy for secessionist movements or internal insurgencies. Internal squabbles and domestic problems are to be solved exclusively by the group which controls the prerogatives of the state.

The Kurds have become refugees because of discriminatory policies and practices of the states in which they are citizens, because of being caught between regional state antagonists, and because of genocidal and ethnocidal state practices. The ultimate cause of refugee creation is found in the history and development of the modern state system. The idea of "state," the organization and power of the state system itself, has failed a number of ethnic nationalities. Kurds and others like them have become its victims.

THE CREATION OF KURDISH REFUGEES

Internal/Cultural Factors: While all cultures react in some common ways to external threat, each individual culture also exhibits certain patterns of unique response. As with other cultures, the Kurds have reacted to threats to their survival in ways in which their culture can be maintained. Some of these are generally predictable: Organizing political resistance, movement out of conflict areas, emphasizing language and religion—generally tightening the cultural boundaries between themselves and other groups. Unique behaviors or attributes seem to include specific attitudes toward movement, patterns of decision-making, values toward personal and group egalitarianism, and the idea of sharaf.

122

The culture of the Kurds is complex. They are not only a nomadic tribal society but settled agriculturalists and urban merchants. As noted earlier, they are a group of groups. Important and consistent characteristics include expressed identity, common language, endogamy, identification with the land of Kurdistan, rules of economic production and distribution, and political fragmentation. As viewed from a systems perspective, their boundary-maintaining practices are extraordinarily rigid: Kurds prefer Kurds in all socio-cultural contexts. They will resist both formal and informal pressures in an effort to maintain their distinctiveness. These attributes are observable in both behaviors and symbolic rituals.

The masses of Kurdish refugees generated by the 1991 Gulf War and its aftermath created widespread knowledge of these displaced people. Yet the migration (especially internally) of these people under stressful circumstances is by no means a new phenomenon. During the 20th century there generally has been a pattern of movement from the mountainous areas to the valleys and back, or from rural to urban areas. Historically, the Kurds also have moved in response to invading armies (chased by Assyrian, Greek, Persian and Mogul warriors), been subjected to persecution by historical empires, moved in response to changes in the ecosystem, and chased each other in intertribal warfare. These movements have had both positive and negative consequences but it can generally be stated that movement within traditional lands is not culture-threatening; movement out of those lands may be. The Kurdish cultural attitudes and behaviors towards movement have been flexible and adaptive.

The values held by a group give some indication as to personal behavior and the cost which an individual is willing to incur to earn prestige. The Kurds emphasize male autonomy and equality, self-expression and aggressiveness, "just about the nearest one can get to a value system whose existence is predicated not only on action, but action which is successful."[3]

In decision-making, it is considered essential to keep the options open until a course of action can be decided upon which is compatible with group goals as well as being judged most effective. The Kurds are adept at defining the relative merit of alternatives and many conversations revolve around choices. The leadership in decision-making is dependent upon the person or persons having the most information, insight or experience with the issue at hand. Thus, leadership is contextual, meaning the person holding the position varies from time to time and from issue to issue.

The concept of sharaf is important for the Kurdish peoples. This involves a corporate concept of society with related notions of honor, knowledge, and completeness in relationship to power. It implies a relationship with other clans and is used to indicate "oneness" of soul with other peoples. An action is never discreet, but falls within the boundaries of known <u>sharaf</u>.[4]

There are reciprocal arrangements between and among groups in this area wherein a refugee group can ask for and receive temporary sanctuary. There is an implication that the giving group will at a future time require sanctuary from still another group. Those individuals requiring temporary help are treated with dignity and respect regardless of historical or ideological proclivities.

<u>External Factors:</u> I have divided the external factors which have helped create conditions wherein Kurds become refugees into three categories:

1) Policies of the states of which Kurds are citizens which have negative effects on the group, thereby threatening viability
2) War or conflict situations in the area, whether or not Kurds were participants
3) Specifically identifiable policies of ethnocide or genocide by states.

For comparative purposes these categories can be applied to other refugee situations as well.

The Kurds have become refugees under conditions wherein the policies and practices of the states in which they are minority citizens were deemed detrimental or threatening to the maintenance of their continued identity and viability. In this situation, individuals or small groups of Kurds have chosen to leave traditional homelands. These people assessed the situation as potentially threatening and moved before it became life-threatening. These so-called "political and economic refugees" generally have been those who, by dint of physical and educational attributes, are most useful in the labor force. Often they simply have been those with the financial capability to leave. Many assumed that conditions in their homelands would eventually change thus allowing their return; however, their situation became permanent as they were progressively integrated into the host country. Many Kurds left for England, Sweden, France, the Federal Republic of Germany, and the United States.[5] They have abilities and attributes which generally make them acceptable and valuable to the receiving or host country.

A second condition involves Kurds who have been caught in the middle of a conflict in which they could not side with either of the antagonists, thus becoming victims of both. In this situation those Kurds who were vulnerable chose to leave the conflict area. The Kurds are recidivistic groups in each of the states of which they are citizens. During times of conflict between the major states, they literally are caught in the middle. Seen historically as spoilers, inhabiting territory on the borders of the states and being potential "fifth columns," the Kurds themselves often have not helped in the process: Insurgent groups with motives which run from helping a specific state, to supporting nationalistic movements, to sheer banditry

124

have complicated an already-untenable situation. During the past 60 years various groups of Kurds have been caught between Turkey and Iraq, between Turkey and Syria, between Iraq and Iran, and between the U.S.S.R. and Iran. In each of these cases some died while many others became refugees.

A third condition which has reduced the Kurds to refugee status has been when ethnocidal or genocidal policies and practices of the states in which they are resident have been activated. This is difficult to contemplate by a seemingly modernized, civilized world but is all too familiar as a side effect of war. Minority groups often become the scapegoats for either of the sides which loses a war, or are labeled as the reason the state did not win "well enough." The long-standing genocidal policies of Turkey, Iran, and Iraq are well known but the current post-Gulf War situation in Iraq differs in both type and severity. Recent policy and practice which included the use of chemical weapons left the Kurds without recourse. Virtually all individuals capable of movement fled the inevitable. The Kurds were not passive victims. They responded by sending the women and children to refugee camps and leaving the men in the mountains to continue the battle. Where entire groups fled, they enjoined political, social, and humanitarian efforts to notify the world of their predicament.

Many Kurdish refugees are temporarily housed in Turkey and Iran where they are neither welcome nor well treated. They seek permanent status elsewhere, but prefer to be in a neighboring area where the climate and culture are more familiar and predictable. These people need a durable solution, either with regard to the state of Iraq or in adjoining states which would welcome them on a permanent basis.

(1) Kurds as Minorities in State Systems: Most state apparatus is controlled by a dominant ethnic group which naturally seeks to maintain and augment its position vis-a-vis other groups. Minority groups, or ethnic nations without states, are comparatively powerless in relationship both to the states in which they are resident and with regard to the international political arena.

To be a viable ethnic group, the group must maintain separate identity, language, religious beliefs and practices, patterns of economic production and consumption, and a socio-political organization adapted to decision-making for the group.

Where policies and practices of the state threaten these aspects of cultural viability, the group is in danger of ethnocide. There are a number of choices available to both individuals and the group. There can be political and/or military resistance. This resistance can generally be initially peaceful but if they experience little success, it can turn more violent. If these actions are not successful, individual members of the minority group may opt to

125

join a contiguous ethnic group or leave the area in hopes of finding a better life elsewhere. From a systems perspective leaving is perceived as more of an option if the contiguous groups are "closed," i.e., will not or cannot accept them either by processes of exogamy or acculturation. Those who leave under these conditions are the so-called "political and economic refugees."

I have conducted research on how the Kurds have fared as citizens and/or as minority groups under each of the various states of the region. Only the information on Turkey and Iraq is presented here.

TURKEY: With the establishment of the Republic of Turkey under Mustafa Kemal Ataturk in 1920, the Kurds in a sense no longer existed--only "Turks" lived in Turkey. When a distinction was necessary, the Kurds were called "mountain Turks." A 1950 Turkish textbook referred to the 1925 uprising as a "gang of ignorant villagers in the eastern provinces." An encyclopedic dictionary explained that Kurds are "of Turkish origin" and the contemporary encyclopedia of Islam tells readers that "one may expect . . . a gradual Turkification among the Kurds, who have no cultural tradition of their own."[6]

Specific state policies deny the separate ethnic existence of 8 million Kurds, nearly 24 percent of the total population of Turkey. Occasionally these policies have been codified in law; most often they have been exemplified in administrative practices. The Kurdish language was banned in 1925. The Turkish government tried to control traditional Kurdish territories with the army, various gendarmes, tax agents, and martial law. Ownership increasingly has come to be in the hands of Turks. Islam, as practiced by the Kurds, was declared improper in doctrine. All cultural organizations were banned including Kurdish schools, associations, publications, religious fraternities, and teaching foundations. Kurdish areas came to be heavily taxed with few state resources reinvested in the people or the land.

Eighteen months of military service are required of all male Turkish citizens. Even here the Kurds have special problems. They are never stationed in Kurdistan, are generally found in only the lower ranks, are seldom given weapons, and ". . . whenever there's dirty work to be done, the Kurds have to do it."[7]

The current situation of the Kurds in Turkey is one of vulnerability. They are the most economically depressed, educationally deprived, politically excluded, and socially persecuted group in the country. The state has made life miserable for the Kurds in Turkish Kurdistan and created internal refugees of as many as one million.

IRAQ: The nationalism articulated in the late 1800s by Sati Al Husrt underlies the preferential policies of the Iraqi state. Arab nationalism was institutionalized in Iraq's formal educational system, supported by the clergy and mandated by the state. Supporting Arabism and Islam, it required obedience, discipline, and sacrifice for the goals of the state and pan-Arabism.

Each of the Iraqi regimes, Hashemites, Kassem, Ba'ath, Aref, and Bakr, have resorted to similar policies towards the Kurds, alternating bribery and persecution.

In 1958, a coup d'etat liquidated the royal regime and brought Kassem to power. Kurds were given key roles in the Presidency Council, government, and administration. The constitution gave official recognition to Kurdish national rights and stipulated that "Arabs and Kurds are equal partners in this nation and state and the constitution guarantees the national rights of the Kurds within the Iraqi national entity." It was quickly apparent that the words belied the actuality.

The Kurdish reaction was rebellion. In March of 1961, some ten thousand "Barzani rebels" were organized. Forty thousand well-equipped Iraqi regulars failed to subdue these Kurds. This failure contributed to the fall of Kassem. The new Ba'ath regime stopped the fighting and negotiated. Kurdish leaders demanded full autonomy, a condition not acceptable to Iraqis. Another offensive was tried; it failed and the Ba'ath regime fell in 1963.

The third regime of the sequence, that of Abd al Salam Aref, also began by negotiating with the Kurds. A cease-fire was declared but the antagonists could not agree on a settlement. Another Iraqi offensive was attempted in 1966 with some 65,000 Iraqi regulars involved. It too was effectively repelled by the Kurds.

A new Iraqi premier, Abd al Bahman al Bazaz, declared a cease fire and opened a new round of negotiations. The Kurds won major Iraqi concessions. However, Bazaz was killed in 1966, thus ending the opportunity to implement the concessions. The coup d'etat of Ahmad Hasan al Bakr brought the Ba'ath party back into power and ushered in yet another round of negotiations. Neither side seemed to be negotiating in good faith and a new Iraqi campaign was launched in 1969. It failed.

The decade of the 1960s cost the Iraqi army 40,000 killed and grave losses in materiel and morale. By way of contrast, the Kurds had fewer men or resources and suffered fatigue, severe losses to their fragile economy, and major disruptions to their way of life.

In 1970 another peace treaty was signed by both parties. The goals of the groups continued to be incompatible: The Kurds demanded political autonomy and some of the profits from the oil in their area. To grant autonomy or distribute state profits according to ethnic group membership was unthinkable for the Iraqis.

During these decades repressive policies in Iraq took much the same form as in Turkey and Iran. Kurdish languages were banned, with all schooling and education conducted in Arabic. Newspapers were closed, street names changed, individual Kurds summarily arrested and executed, and labor and political organizations declared illegal.

In summary, from 1958 to 1975 there was a varying state of low- to high-level, devastating and costly conflict between the Kurds and the Iraqi government. In 1975, the Algiers Accord ended Iran's support for the Barzani insurrection against the Iraqi government. The fact that a Barzani - U.S. connection had been developed was considered a treasonous betrayal of Iraq by the Kurds. The actions of the Iraqi government against the Kurdish population during this era resulted in the killing of untold thousands and the displacement of some 500,000 people. Many individuals and families requested permission to leave Iraq legally. Others fled as refugees to neighboring states to request asylum and live anonymously. When discovered, many of these refugees were forcibly repatriated. Many Kurds fled to Iran; Iran concluded a secret deal with Iraq and the refugees there were told to return.[8]

REFUGEES AND INTERNATIONAL RELATIONS: Whether Kurdish refugees from Turkey, Iraq, or any of the other states in this region are welcomed in a receiving country can generally be understood in the context of international relations. The context of their own laws and public awareness or sympathy are often the determining factors. Although the refugees are sometimes political pawns, their status is generally decided on a case-by-case basis.

Refugees in general often are economically marginalized and have the potential for political disruptiveness. Some incubate guilt for leaving their compatriots in sensitive situations, and assuage that guilt by forming political action groups. The activities of these groups range from propaganda and information exercises to terrorism. Referring specifically to Kurdish refugees, those in Europe (particularly France, England, and Sweden) have engaged primarily in the formation of refugee-welcoming committees, propaganda and information exercises, and cultural preservation activities.

(2) Kurds as Refugees from Conflict Situations: The most common descriptions of refugee situations worldwide are those which occur in conjunction with conflict situations. There are generally three patterns: (a) the states in conflict move civilian populations for their own purposes, (b) civilian populations flee invading armies or civil strife, and/or (c) the resource base of a population is so destroyed or depleted as to engender flight. Each of these has occurred with regard to the Kurds.

The earliest conflict situations which created Kurdish refugees were the internal wars of Turkey and World War I. During this period, Kurds were both refugees and the creators of refugees. Rough estimates indicate that one million Armenians and 700,000 Kurds were killed, with a significant but unknown number of refugees created. There is little information currently available, but from accounts I have heard it is evident that the Kurdish refugees considered the problems temporary and planned on returning to their traditional homelands when the battles were over. Both the British and Russians recorded significant numbers of Kurds fleeing the conflicts and taking up temporary residence in their respective areas.

While the information presented in the preceeding section makes it clear that tensions have been ongoing, it was not until the Iraq - Iran conflict in the period from 1980 to 1989 that a full-scale conflict again produced refugees.

During the Iraq - Iran war the Kurds, as a group, did not side with either antagonist. There are three basic reasons. First, the leadership patterns of the Kurds (discussed earlier) indicate that the sub-groups made their own decisions based on their separate assessments of the alternatives. Second, the Kurds are recidivistic, as previously noted; there are large numbers of Kurds in both Iraq and Iran which would have been devastated with victory for either side. Third, the war was fought on traditional Kurdish territory over petroleum resources found on Kurdish land. Many Kurds believed the Iranians and Iraqis to be fighting over something which in actuality belonged to them.

The Iranians and Iraqis took similar measures with regard to the Kurds. The objective was to keep the Kurds from siding with the opposition while not including them in full participation in the conflict. Various attempts to bribe Kurdish tribes were generally unsuccessful. The Kurds took the bribes without any intention of repayment nor oaths of loyalty.

The Iranian government created a "green line" dividing Kurds from the rest of the population. This was to ensure Persian control over Persian territory and also symbolized lack of control over Kurdish lands. Refugees coming into Iran from both Turkey and Iraq generally headed for traditionally-held Kurdish areas. The government tried to control the numbers but was not very successful. Refugee camps generally were the responsibility of the refugees themselves in conjunction with whatever help they could get from the Iranian Kurds.

The Iraqi government continued to perceive the Kurds as a "fifth column." No distinction was made between traditional resistance groups and civilian populations. All were suspect. There was also the notion that had the Kurds united to fight with Iraq, as Iraqi citizens, the war would have been easily and quickly won with little or not loss of Arab life. When subsequent to the war Iraq pursued policies which used the Kurds as scapegoats, there was little public outcry. It was relatively easy for the Arab press and public to blame the Kurds for the war losses.

Between 1980 and 1989 many became refugees. Those living in valleys moved to traditional highlands. Many Iranian Kurds moved to Iraq; many Iraqi Kurds moved to Iran. Some from Iran and Iraq moved to comparatively peaceful Turkey. Most moved with the intention of returning to their homes after the end of the war. Even rough estimates of numbers, to indicate the magnitude of the problem, are unavailable.

REFUGEE CAMPS AND GROUP ADAPTATIONS: Kurdish groups "caught in the middle" formed the population base of the temporary refugee camps that emerged. The demographic profile of these camps indicated a high percentage of vulnerable populations—women, children, the infirm, and the elderly. Men, whenever possible, stayed in traditional territories to protect their properties and/or conduct guerrilla warfare. Because the situation was deemed temporary, if possible a member of the group remained at or near the homelands and pastures to watch over them. Some men joined the fight with one or the other of the antagonists; others became bandits or took up smuggling. Young boys often became runners between the women in the camps and the men, thus ensuring a degree of communications continuity and control.

This pattern has proven adaptive for the Kurds in the post-Gulf War environment, too. They have had less fear of temporarily splitting up family or clan groups than other endangered populations because of the cultural cohesion (as identified in marriage and exchange patterns), as well as the rigidity of cultural boundaries discussed earlier. The mountains have provided places of sanctuary so men have been able to stay under adverse conditions while sending women and children to protected encampments. Weather conditions are a known factor for them, but not their adversaries, thus providing an advantage for small, fast moving groups of Kurds. There has been a continual use of traditional alliances between tribes, whether inside or outside of formal state boundaries, meaning that temporary refuge often has been assured.

Refugee camps also evidence behavioral patterns which are culture-preserving in expectation of eventual return. These include an emphasis on female chastity, demands for the teaching of language and the establishment of educational facilities, an emphasis on meetings (particularly those of a religious or value-maintaining nature), patience with difficult physical conditions, and retention of symbolic rituals. Resistance to cultural change is high so (from a systems perspective) the boundary-maintaining mechanisms of the Kurdish groups remain extremely rigid.

(3) Kurds as Refugees from Genocide: The impacts and ramifications of genocide and ethnocide are extremely complex, as noted elsewhere.[9] There are two primary causes behind the genocide of Kurds, one tied to long-standing policies and practices of the states involved, the other a spin-off of the Iran-Iraq War. Again, space limits my discussion, here to factors involving Iran and Iraq only. Turkish and Syrian impacts also have been significant.

IRAN: Iran has only sporadically pursued policies of genocide or ethnocide and never to the extent of Iraq, Turkey, or Syria.

When the Shah instituted land reform and troops were sent in to enforce the law, he met with firm resistance. Losing patience, Iran proceeded to bomb the Kurdish areas of Hemalon, Saqqiz, and Kermanshah. Casualty figures and information regarding refugees in unavailable. It is known that Kurds fled Iran to Iraq, Iraq to Turkey, and Turkey to Syria, Iraq, and the U.S.S.R, all during 1946. Casualties in Javanrudi in 1950 numbered some 2,000. By 1958, with renewed hostilities between Kurds and the Iraqi government, Iran encouraged the Kurds to think of Iran as their "motherland."[10]

I have heard it reported that the Ayatollah Khomeini asked civilians to "hunt down Kurds" in 1979 but when that action failed, offered them one day's worth of oil, or about $75 million, to cooperate with the government.

Reports of the treatment of Kurds in Iran vary. Government sources state that there is still a Kurdish insurgency which must be controlled and that the refugees from Iraq present an untenable problem. The government denies any specific program aimed at full-scale forced repatriation of Kurds to traditional territories, assimilating them through education and economic integration, or annihilation of the group as whole. I would expect the government to enforce policies of Persian nationalism and Islamic fundamentalism more rigidly during the 1990s.

The reports by Kurdish partisans vary from the official government position. They indicate a policy of repression and annihilation on the part of the Iranian government. As evidence of Iran's basic hostility towards Kurds, they cite the occupation by soldiers of Iranian Kurdistan, the absence of legal protection of cultural distinctiveness, and their exclusion from the political and economic life of the state. This does not necessarily constitute actual genocide. It does represent the fears of the Kurds based on their historical relationship with the Persians and may indicate the possibility of future genocide or ethnocide.

IRAQ: Iraq is a different story. Partially because the Kurds form a significant percentage of the population and partially because they control the economically most valuable parts of the country, the Arabs of Iraq continue to view them as a threat. Iraq has tried two major methods to get rid of the Kurds--removal and physical annihilation.

One form of removal is refugee creation. Another is forced relocation. There has been continual fighting between the Kurds and the government, as stressed earlier. Many instances have created refugees and internally displaced persons, usually Kurds. As the Iraqis tried to exert control over Kurdish provinces, the Kurdish civilians in the region were forced to flee. For example, in 1931 the British bombed the Turkish - Iraqi border in an attempt to control the Kurds. Refugees were created. In 1946 Kurds fled from the fighting near Kirkuk where Zolfaghari troops were fighting against Azerbaijani troops. In the period of 1957-1958, with renewed hostilities between the Iraqi Kurds

and the government, many fled to Iran. Five hundred Iraqi
Kurds were stopped at the Turkish border by Kassim and arrested and returned. In 1959, some 5,000 crossed the border
from Iraq into Turkey, and another 2,000 left for Iran.[11]

The 1974-75 assault on Kurdistan by the Iraqis left
some 500,000 homeless. Over 300,000 Iraqi Kurds fled to
Iran where they were housed in camps which were inadequate.
There were reports of tuberculosis, typhoid, measles, menin-
gitis, anthrax, and chronic lung disease. Food was scarce
and housing insufficient. Subsequent to the Algiers agreement, the refugee flow was two-way.

Where military efforts were successful, the government
tried to diffuse future resistance by removing Kurds from
traditional lands and from the support systems of the larger
cultural group. Large numbers were moved to places within
the country, while others were forcibly evacuated to
locations outside the country.

Removals have probably wreaked more havoc than any
other policies. As early as 1927, the Iraqi government
tried to move Kurds out of Kurdish territory. Fifteen hundred were forcibly transferred to western provinces. These
policies reached an apex during the 1970s. Practices have
included buying Kurdish lands from individuals or families,
forcibly removing entire villages, moving Arabs into Kurdish
territories, and heavily taxing to force eviction.

In 1972 in the Mosul area 300 Kurds fled to the hills
after being attacked by MIG jets. In 1973, some 30,000
Boyan and Omeryan Kurds from the Mosul area were forcibly
expelled to Turkey. The entire city of Kai Sanek fled to
the mountains in 1974. In 1975, approximately 180,000 Kurds
fled to Iran and 5,000 reportedly fled to Turkey. In 1976,
the first 600 Kurdish refugees were accepted into the United
States.

During the period of 1977 to 1979, the state of Iraq
forcibly moved thousands of Kurds from the petroleum-
producing areas into southern Iraqi deserts. The precise
numbers are unknown, but estimates range up to 1.5 million.
The Iraqis proceeded to bulldoze villages and other communities, and repopulate them with "reliable Arabs."

There are other unfortunate aspects to this situation.
Where thousands of Kurds were forcibly transported to
concentration and relocation camps outside Kurdistan, death
rates on the journey and within the camps were unexplainably
high. In one instance alone, 8,000 men apparently disappeared.

Physical annihilation has been systematically attempted. Much of the Kurdish area is not amenable to
conventional weaponry. Getting at the Kurds was difficult
for Iraqis, particularly during harsh weather conditions.
Subsequent to the Iraq - Iran war the Kurds were singled out
by the Iraqi government as the single reason for defeat, and
a different non-conventional technology was used. Chemical
and biological weapons ostensibly maintained for use against
external enemies (i.e., the Iranians) were turned against

these citizens of the state. Only sheer numbers and the inaccessibility of mountain hideouts precluded easy anni-hilation of Kurds by these means. The evidence of this use is incontrovertible.[12] The Iraqi government, while officially denying the actions, continues to assert its legal right to control its domestic populations in any way it sees fit.

Refugees reported that they were able to fight invading armies which used conventional weapons and tactics in the traditional manner: Use of the weather, use of the geo-graphy of the area, and use of standard hit-and-run guer-rilla tactics. They could not, however, withstand the onslaught of chemical and biological weapons. My evidence suggests that many seemed panicked at the possibility of attempting to defend themselves under such circumstances.

In spite of overwhelming evidence of collusion between Iran and Iraq during the war to eliminate Kurdish strongholds and the subsequent use of chemical and bio-logical weapons, widespread public knowledge of the use of such weapons did not lead to international sanctions. Since the Kurds were relatively unknown, the Iran-Iraq War a seemingly hopeless situation, and the Middle East chroni-cally conflict-prone, international attention focused on the internal control of chemical and biological weapons. The devastation of Kurdistan and its people was used as an example of what might happen to others rather than eliciting international help for the Kurds.

RESISTANCE AND EMPOWERMENT

Much of public sympathy to the problem of refugees is contingent on how much they "fight back," or do not allow themselves to be victimized. The Kurds are certainly not a victim group. They have fought back with political astute-ness and military effectiveness. They have mounted significant resistance efforts and through these, empowered many of their number.

Three broad stages in the Kurds' struggle are high-lighted in this section:
1) 1880-1920: Drive for statehood within the modern state system
2) 1920-1980: Drive for autonomy within states
3) 1980-1991: Drive for survival.
Each of these stages is related to actions and policies of regional and international interests, perceptions of threat, stated goals of various Kurdish organizations, and increasing levels of violence and conflict. Their appro-priate understanding is linked to the analyses presented in the preceeding sections.

1880-1920: The reports of the late 19th century, including those in geographic and travel publications such as the National Geographic magazine, described the Kurds as a peaceful, colorful, cheerful, and hospitable mountain folk without the capacity for fighting.[13] While these descriptions may have been somewhat naive, later descriptions of Kurds being raised from childhood to be cruel and bloodthirsty were equally overdrawn. What is certain is that Kurdish leaders were painfully aware of the development of ideas of nationalism among their neighbors, the Turks, Arabs, and Persians, and that to survive they also would have to be accorded a place of equality in the modern state system. The demand for statehood was articulated in journals, newspapers, Kurdish clubs, and formal delegations to England and France. Led by Sheikh Ubeidullah, one of the first Kurdish nationalists, the demands were pressed firmly and articulately. Although failing to achieve their goal, the efforts indicate an ability and willingness to adapt to modern requirements of political organization. They also indicate that leadership empowerment was occurring in highly visible regional--as well as local--contexts.

1920-1980: After the Treaty of Lusanne in 1923 split the Kurdish population among the states of Iran, Iraq, Syria, Turkey, and the U.S.S.R., Kurdish activities also split. As minorities within these states, they showed remarkable capacity for political organization and the pressing of their demands within acceptable political forums. Only when these efforts failed, and their lives and livelihood were threatened, did they resort to violent resistance. The peshmergas ("those who face death") became renown for the strategies and tactics which helped protect Kurdistan during this stage.

In general, Kurds in each of these states cooperated when some degree of autonomy was granted, resisted when autonomy was threatened, and reacted in proportion to the perception of the threat's extent. In each state, the Kurds organized peacefully and politically. They presented their positions in delegations to central administrators and in well-written documents.[14] Their requests were for some measure of cultural autonomy in exchange for allegiance and support of the state in question. For various reasons, the states could not or would not acquiesce but pressed for control over Kurdish territories and resources. Sometimes this was done in the name of development and modernization, more often simply in the name of the "power of the state."

The Kurds were aware of the penalties of violent resistance only too well. The legitimate use of force is the monopoly of the state. Any group attempting to challenge that force faces insurmountable odds with a predictable outcome--loss of life and livelihood. Nor could outside intervention be hoped for. Insurrections and insurgencies threaten the very nature of the international state system.

As the decision to undertake violent resistance was being argued by the Kurds, the perception of fragmentation was furthered. Many Kurdish groups opted for incorporation

134

within the new states; others believed that incorporation
would lead to assimilation, this in turn leading to a lower-
class station and eventual annihilation. Some of the latter
opted for physical resistance. Kurds knew they likely would
lose in direct confrontation with the superior military
forces of Iraq, Iran, and Turkey. Their strategy thus
became one of attrition. This meant employing a panoply of
guerrilla tactics within Kurdish territories, thereby re-
ducing the states' effective control. Over time, however,
this strategy also incurred unsustainable costs to the Kurds
themselves in terms of loss of live and economic viability.

Various conflict resolution schemes were proposed and
some tried. The most notable was that of the Mahabad
Republic of 1946. Iraq and Iran intermittently offered
limited amounts of regional autonomy, generally when a new
leader required their support. Each of these processes
failed because there was never agreement over a basic definition of autonomy. Turkey never permitted any discussion
of regional or cultural differentiation. The question did
not arise in the Alawaite state of Syria.

There were rumors of international support. Some
materialized. The Kurds were variously associated with
Great Britain, the United States, Israel, the U.S.S.R., and
even the P.R.C. The Kurds came to believe that external
alliances have a price and cannot be trusted over the long
haul. To many it seemed better to deal with a known neigh-
bor, even though an enemy.

1980-1991: A view that has come to be held by the
various states of the region is that the armed struggle in
Kurdistan will continue as long as there are Kurds. By the
late 1970s several leaders came to believe that they would
have to practice a comprehensive policy of ethnocide or
genocide either to terrorize the Kurds into submission or
eradicate them altogether. The recent policies and practices of chemical and biological warfare, forced removal,
concentration camp development, and conventional warfare
must be viewed in this light.

While empowered in some ways, and more visible to the
world's humanitarian agencies, the core problem for the
Kurds during the past decade simply has been survival.
Individual and group strategies of resistance suggest an
analysis of the situation as desperate. Key Kurdish leaders
have become discouraged.

Other empowerment strategies have been employed. Pres-
sure has been maintained on humanitarian groups such as the
International Red Cross, the United Nations High
Commissioner for Refugees, Physicians for Human Rights, and
the Minority Rights Group as well as various religious or-
ganizations. Legal advocates have supported the Kurds in
the U.S. Senate Foreign Relations Committee, the European
Parliament, in letter writing campaigns to the embassies of
Turkey, Iraq, and Iran, and in the petitioning of Permanent
Members of the United Nations Security Council.

The communication of political and cultural demands has taken myriad forms. The use of native dress in public demonstrations, coupled with support for art, music, dance, and handicrafts, has proven helpful in both Kurdistan and Europe. Clandestine radio stations have been set up wherever Kurds have organized resistance movements. Advocacy on behalf of the Kurdish languages has occurred through partisans in Europe and the states of the Middle East. Workers associations, relief associations, cultural associations, friendship societies, student and youth associations, community centers, and women's groups also serve as communication channels.

While much of the Western world has been notably tardy in its response, NGOs (mentioned in other contexts by several of the authors in this volume) have been helpful in putting public pressure on governments to cease the most blatant of the human rights abuses. Their efforts also have aided Kurdish refugee integration in Western countries and led to improved documentation of the horrors of chemical warfare.

CONCLUSIONS

The Kurdish refugee situation is extraordinarily grim. Neither specific numbers nor adequate information with regard to current conditions is available. Oral reports indicate that as of 1991 as many as three million Kurds were displaced persons or refugees. Iran accepted refugees during the Iran-Iraq War only to send them back at the war's conclusion. Prior to and through the Gulf War of 1991, Iraq maintained concentration camps or "relocation camps" in the south. Eight thousand men are said to have disappeared. The most notable or perhaps, most influenceable, international situation is that of the camps in Turkey wherein the estimates run from 20,000 to 200,000 persons in conditions described as running from "adequate" to "atrocious." The post-Gulf War intervention of aid workers did not eliminate these problems.

Unique and specific cultural patterns and practices affect how the Kurds react to and adapt to refugee-producing situations. Several factors are notable. Kurdish cultural norms, reciprocal relationships, and diverse survival strategies have enabled a great deal of adaptive flexibility to occur. This is reflected (e.g.) in the fact that Kurdish military groups far from home territory (with or without local historical precedence) are rendered extensive support. Being a traditional "refugee" or "freedom fighter" in this cultural context is recognized as an honorable and necessary option which individuals and groups take to preserve both their own lives and the integrity of their ethnic group and specific tribe. David Edwards states:

". . . if an individual seeks asylum because he has
been involved on the losing side of a feud or in some
other meritorious endeavor, then he will likely be
received as an honored guest who is entitled to
respect. However, in cases where the individual has
fled . . . in a state of disgrace, the individual and
his family may be absorbed as clients of the asylum
giver. Thus, the context in which asylum is granted is
critical in how the whole interaction is perceived and
interpreted."[15]

This implies that if the refugee is a "refugee of
honor" he or she is accorded an honorable place. If not, he
or she must accept a subordinate position in the camp and
the family may be integrated or forcibly assimilated. The
treatment accorded the refugees will indicate whether their
status is considered honorable in the eyes of their hosts.

This may help explain why Kurds are particularly
culturally disoriented by formal refugee processing situations. Officially sanctioned international refugee camps,
relying as they do on elaborate bureaucratic organization,
require refugees to submit to daily indignities, i.e.,
behaviors not required of "honorable" men and women seeking
asylum. Practical illustrations include not being treated
as an autonomous equal in daily decisions and camp administration, being forced to stand in lines without regard to
honor or rank, putting personal information on printed forms
which may be used against one in the future, and receiving
inequitable food stuffs. Even modest levels of empowerment
are difficult to achieve or maintain under such conditions.

Until the spring of 1991, there was little hope that
the future of the Kurds would be much different than the
past. Yet dramatic world events may impact the Kurdish
situation in unpredictable ways. The fragmentation of
Eastern Europe is leading to greater acknowledgement by the
rest of the world that the state system may not be the only
critical unit of action and analysis in international politics. A "new look" may be required in ethnic/nation-state
definitions. For the Kurds, the best possible outcome of
these new definitions and arrangements probably would be
full autonomy, or a significant degree of autonomy within
one of the states of the region.

The spring of 1991 also saw a post-Gulf War "refugee
shuffle" begin in the Middle East. Over three million Kurds
were refugees--and openly portrayed as such on world-wide
television. Whereas the use of refugees as "media events"
was not particularly unusual, the response of the United
States and others was unprecedented. "Normal" refugee assistance organizations were overridden and a humanitarian
effort by military forces on an unprecedented scale was
initiated. A coalition of thirteen countries provided some
500,000 Kurdish refugees with food, clothing, and tents
within weeks. Where there were few pictures of the results

of the bombing of Iraqi cities, there was extensive coverage of the military's relief efforts in Kurdistan.

Apart from important questions about this use of the military (and its own motivations), the immediate problems of food, water, and shelter were assuaged temporarily. It is certain, however, that there will be dire ramifications. The Kurds were seen by many Arabs, Turks, and Persians as inappropriately accepting the help of powers outside the region. This liaison with "the enemy" may again set them up for future targeting once the attention of the world is diverted.

For the world, and those particularly interested in the problems of refugees, the Kurds present a fascinating case. For the Kurds themselves, the future remains enigmatic.[16]

NOTES

[1]No complete volume detailing early Kurdish history is available. The most accessible information can be found in A.R. Ghassemlou, People Without a Country: The Kurds and Kurdistan, G. Chaliand, series ed., revised edition (London: Olive Branch Press/Interlink Publishing Group, 1992).

[2]No volume is currently available which focuses on the Kurds as a single political group. The documents which are avail-able generally are written from the perspective of the "national development" of each of the states in the region. An example for Turkey is H. Basbug, Iki Turk boyu, Zaza ve Kurmaclar (Ankara: Turk Kulturunu Arastirma Enstitusu, 1984); for Iraq, A. el Haff, L'Iraq Nouveau et le Probleme Kurde, Essai Politique (Paris: Les Editions Khayat, 1977).

[3]R. Paine, "The Stamp of Swat: A Brief Ethnography of Some of the Writing of Fredrik Barth," Man 17: 328-329, 1982.

[4]M.E. Meeker, "Meaning and Society in the Near East: Examples from the Black Sea Turks and Levantine Arabs," International Journal of Middle Eastern Studies 7: 253-270, 1976. See also F. Barth, Principles of Social Organization in Southern Kurdistan (Oslo: Brodrene Jorgensen A/S, 1953).

[5]Information on the activities of Kurds in Europe and the United States is available in "Facts on File," the New York Times Index, several Keesings reports, and from various documents published by The Research Center of the Kurdish Institute, Paris.

[6]S.D. Salamone, "The Dialectics of Turkish National Iden-tity: Ethnic Boundary Maintenance and State Ideology," East European Quarterly 23: 237, 1989.

[7]A. Hottinger, "Forbidden Identity: The Kurds in Turkey," Swiss Review of World Affairs 39: 21-23, 1989.

[8]A key source on Iraq is el Haff (see note 2, above).

[9]M.A. Sills, "Ethnocide versus Acculturation: Issues for Fieldworkers," in Applied Field Methods: A Manual of Practice, P.W. Van Arsdale and S.R. Vemuri, eds. (Denver, CO: Center for Cultural Dynamics, 1991).

[10]Information on the era of the Shah is found in R. Cottam, Nationalism in Iran (Pittsburgh, PA: University of Pittsburgh Press, 1979).

[11]Regarding details on Iraq through the 1960s, see note 5, above. Also see S. Jawad, Iraq and the Kurdish Question 1958-1970 (London: Ithica Press, 1980). Much of the information on the 1970s and 1980s is based on personal accounts, unpublished documents, and first-hand field work.

[12]Journalists and other investigators were able to document the use of chemical and biological weapons, as exemplified in Iranian photographers' "A Photo Report on the Chemical Massacre in Halabja," Iran Photo Foundation, 1988 (volume available through the School for Oriental and African Studies, London); and P. Sluglett, "The Kurds in Saddam's Iraq," in Saddam's Iraq: Revolution or Reaction, 2nd edition, CARDRI Staff, eds. (London: Zed Press, 1989).

[13]Examples of these 19th- and early 20th-century publications include Major F. Millingen, Wild Life Among the Kurds (London: Hurst and Blackett, 1870); and W.R. Hay, Two Years in Kurdistan: Experiences of a Political Officer 1918-1920 (London: Sedgwick and Jackson). From the perspective of Middle East studies and political history, see R. Olson, The Emergence of Kurdish Nationalism, 1880-1925 (Austin, TX: University of Texas Press, 1989).

[14]See Ghassemlou, note 1, above.

[15]D.B. Edwards, "Marginality and Migration: Cultural Dimensions of the Afghan Refugee Problem," International Migration Review, 20: 313-325, 1986, p. 318.

[16]Much of the information in this chapter is based upon first-hand oral sources, the accounts of key informants, and unpublished papers. My own research on the Kurdish problem was conducted from 1989 through 1991. Additional publications of importance include S.C. Pelletiere, The Kurds: An Unstable Element in the Middle East (Boulder: Westview, 1984); and G. Chaliand, Les Kurdes et le Kurdistan: le Question National Kurdi au Proche Orient (Paris: Maspero, 1978).

LONG-TERM CONSEQUENCES OF
TWO AFRICAN REFUGEE SETTLEMENT STRATEGIES

Art Hansen
University of Florida

INTRODUCTION[1]

Policy-Oriented Research: The displacement of refugees and their subsequent settlement in receiving societies are important development issues because they disrupt peoples' lives and primarily affect poor countries. About 80 per cent of refugees originate in poor countries and find asylum in other poor countries. A key question is how best to settle refugees to, on the one hand, relieve their distress and speed their rehabilitation and, on the other hand, minimize any deterioration in living and working conditions of the receiving host populations. This is particularly acute in Africa, the world's poorest continent, because most of Africa's 4.6 million refugees remain refugees for many years. The long-term consequences of refugee settlement are important for refugees and their hosts.

There are two apparent settlement strategies for African refugees, most of whom are rural. Many African refugees organize their own settlements and establish new livelihoods themselves in new or already-existing villages, often without any government or international assistance. This strategy is known as spontaneous settlement, or self-settlement. African host governments place many other refugees in agricultural settlement projects (or schemes), where the refugees can farm and, hopefully, attain self-sufficiency. These refugees receive governmental and international assistance, often for many years. This strategy is called scheme-settlement.

What are the consequences of the different settlement strategies for refugee well-being, both in the short and the long term? In the simplest terms, which refugees are better off? The advantages and costs of the two strategies have been debated.[2] My earlier research examined the shorter-term (1966-1972) consequences for Angolan refugees in Zambia. I concluded that, in self-settlement, the refugee "retains more power over other people and, thus, more stability and control over his or her own life."[3] This chapter extends my earlier research to examine the long-term (1966-1989) consequences of these two rural settlement patterns.

My 1989 research highlights another issue: "Durable solutions" for refugees. Durable solutions occur when refugees stop being refugees. There are two logical ways for someone to drop the refugee status: (a) repatriation to their country of origin, and (b) integration in a host country (see also Campbell, Kreisberg-Voss, and Sobrepena, this volume). Integration could be into: (a) the first host country, where the refugee first sought refuge, or (b) a second host country; the latter option requires resettlement from the first host. My research concludes that the Angolan refugees in this study achieve a durable solution (integration into Zambia) through self-settlement. This raises certain other questions. If self-settlement achieves a durable solution, then why is it illegal? Who benefits by denying refugees their human rights and forcing them to remain long-term aliens?[4] Why do African countries refuse to allow refugees to become naturalized citizens?

I must caution the reader about generalizing from this case (Angolans in Zambia) to all of Africa. Africa is large and complex; there is a lot of variation in refugee situations and in refugee-host interactions (see also Daramola and Mozia, this volume). I do not claim that these Angolans represent all African refugees, or that Zambia represents all African hosts, but this research is the first scientific and controlled comparison of these two refugee settlement patterns in Africa.

Methodology: Research was conducted in Zambia from May through November, 1989, on comparable cohorts of men and women refugees in the Meheba scheme and the Chavuma villages, where I have conducted extensive prior fieldwork. All informants (interviewed using the Luvale language) share these key characteristics. They fled Angola from 1965 to 1969 because of the war, entered Zambia through the same frontier district, and were adults (i.e., at least 15 years old) in 1972.

The village sample was selected randomly from a 1972 census that I had collected during previous fieldwork. A random sample of host Zambians who were living in the villages when the refugees arrived was selected from the same 1972 census to serve as a control. Equal samples of men and women were selected. A different sampling strategy was followed in the Meheba scheme. Agencies had carried out a number of censuses over the years, but no baseline census could be located from which to draw a random sample. I had to locate in Meheba a population of scheme-settled refugees that was similar in key features (the three criteria noted above) to the population of self-settled refugees. This was accomplished, and 73 per cent of that population was interviewed.

ANGOLAN REFUGEES IN ZAMBIA: AN OVERVIEW

Angolan refugees began fleeing into Zambia in 1966, when the war for national liberation against Portugal opened its eastern front. Although national independence was achieved in 1975, a civil war was continuing in 1989, with intermittent flows of refugees fleeing or repatriating as the war became more or less intense. Peace talks began in 1989 among the government of Angola, the opposing UNITA movement, and mediating African governments, so the war may

141

be over within the next several years. As of 1988, however, approximately 94,000 Angolans were refugees in Zambia, comprising two-thirds of the 140,000 refugees being hosted by Zambia.

The Zambian government has always required all refugees to live in settlement schemes, and self-settled refugees who were discovered by immigration authorities were relocated to a scheme. Therefore, successful self-settlement required concealment. I conducted field research in the border villages for two years in the early 1970s. I lived in the villages for an entire year before the first refugee made himself known to me. The primary research method that allowed me to discover the extent of refugee self-settlement was long-term participant observation.

Although the government requires that all refugees live in schemes, 86 per cent of the Angolan refugees are self-settled. The self-settled Angolan refugees studied in this research live in the Chavuma border area of Zambezi District. Most (83 per cent, or 11,600 in 1988) of the scheme-settled Angolans live in the Meheba Scheme in Solwezi District. Both districts are in North-Western Province, but the scheme is on an asphalt highway that connects it with nearby cities, while the border villages are nearly 500 kilometers of not-so-good gravel road away. The difference in location (or relative isolation) is an important variable affecting current well-being of refugees. Another important factor is language and ethnicity. The refugees studied are Luvale-speaking, as are their village hosts in the border area, but the villagers around the scheme in Solwezi District are Kaonde-speaking.

THE 1989 STUDY[5]

Accumulated Wealth: The house is used in many studies as the single most reliable indicator of accumulated wealth, but there is little variation among the refugee samples in this indicator. Ownership of a bicycle or radio clearly differentiates the two categories of refugee men. No self-settled refugee man was found to own one of these, while about one-fourth of the scheme-settled men did. Few women in any category owned either item. Many people in the villages were embarrassed when questioned about the number of blankets that they owned. Many self-settled refugees and some hosts did not own even one blanket. Scheme-settled refugees were fortunate because many blankets had been given to them. Even in 1989, new arrivals to Meheba (from border areas of Zambia, where they had been living for several years) were receiving free blankets from the United Nations.

Annual Cash Incomes and Their Sources: People in the study earned money from five major sources: (a) crops, including the sale of food crops, (b) livestock, mainly goats with a few cattle, (c) fishing and trading in dried

fish, (d) brewing and selling beer, and (e) miscellaneous--
owning a grinding mill, peddling drygoods, cutting planks as
a sawyer, carpentry, being a security guard at the scheme,
and collecting honey (especially important at Meheba).
Everyone participated in agriculture and, to varying
degrees, received some cash income through crop sales. The
other four sources of cash income were sex-specific, i.e.,
linked through the customary divisions of labor and responsibility to one gender or the other. Men earned money
through livestock, fishing and fish trading, and other commercial or wage-earning activities. The only money-earning
activity specifically for women was brewing and selling
beer.

Men earned more cash income than women in all categories. Refugee men in both locations had similar average
incomes, approximately ZK 2,200, but there were different
distributions. The incomes of scheme-settled men were distributed evenly across the range, with a small percentage
not earning any cash. Even distribution means that the
average income is not unduly influenced by one or two
unusually high incomes. The incomes of self-settled refugee
men were clumped with many not earning any money, half
earning between ZK 530 and 960, and one earning ZK 16,130.
If this wealthier individual's income were excluded, the
average would fall to ZK 800. The average cash income of
scheme-settled refugee women was extremely high compared
with any village women (host or refugee), and the incomes of
individual refugee women in Meheba were well distributed
with ten women earning more than ZK 1,000. No woman in the
village earned more than ZK 950.

The difference between the incomes of scheme-settled
and self-settled refugees, both men and women, was primarily
due to the importance of cash crop agriculture (soybeans in
1988 and 1989) in Meheba. About three-fourths of the men
and women in Meheba earned cash income from selling food and
cash crops, while half of the village hosts and only one-
fifth of the self-settled refugees earned money from crop
sales.

Other sources of cash income demonstrated Meheba's more
favored access to resources, both natural (such as trees and
honey) and infrastructural (such as urban markets and good
roads). Meheba is located on a tarred road not too far from
several major urban areas with markets for planks, furniture, vegetables, fruits, and honey. The border villages
are about 580 kilometers by gravel road farther away, and
that distance and the quality of the roads prohibited their
sale of anything other than dried fish--and their labor--to
the cities.

Food and Food Self-Sufficiency: Village men, whether
self-settled refugee or Zambian host, were found to be much
more self-sufficient than scheme-settled refugee men. Self-
sufficiency for men and women correlates fairly well with
differences in the average number of cassava fields, sup-

porting the impression that variable control of home-produced cassava is the single most important factor in terms of food self-sufficiency. Approximately one-fourth to one-fifth of the women in each category were found to be totally dependent on others (usually close relatives) for their staple food, but total dependency was not very common for men, especially for refugee men.

There were greater differences between men and women in the refugee populations than in the host populations, but the differences were not always in the same direction. About the same percentage of host men and women claimed to be self-sufficient; they had the same average number of cassava fields. Ten per cent of host men were totally dependent. Self-settled refugee men were more self-sufficient and had more cassava fields than self-settled refugee women, while scheme-settled women were more self-sufficient than scheme-settled men.

Cassava has been the staple food in the Chavuma border area for at least sixty years and was the most important staple food of the Meheba refugees during the 1970s and 1980s, even though sorghum is the most common staple food of the Kaonde-speaking villagers around Meheba. Most of the cassava was killed in 1985-86 in both locations by the appearance of the cassava mealy bug, and cassava production dropped dramatically throughout the region. That infestation transformed many families and both areas from food self-sufficiency to dependency on maize imports. This dependency was still widespread as of 1989.

The other major staple in these locations is maize, which was more important in Meheba than in the Chavuma border villages, where it was grown more for brewing beer or as a snack to eat early in the rainy season. The mealy bug infestation caused people to plant more maize and rely on it more as a regular staple. In both locations maize grows poorly unless fertilized. People in Meheba are able to buy fertilizer (or get it on credit), although many refuse because they think the price is too high. People in the Chavuma area are unable to obtain fertilizer because the government, which maintains a legal monopoly, fails to transport fertilizer to the isolated border area. Much of the maize consumed in both locations during the years since the mealy bug infestation has been imported by truckers and traders from the rest of Zambia.

Maize is usually imported as grain, less commonly as flour. Maize is harder than cassava to pound by hand into flour, and most women prefer to take maize to a grinding mill. In both locations the switch from cassava to maize means that families are dependent on grinding mills to process their staple food. There have always been grinding mills in Meheba because maize grain was the staple in the food rations that the United Nations supplied. The grinding mills wore out over the years, however, and became less important as cassava became more common. With the recent change, the remaining mills have become overworked, and

Meheba refugees report that they sometimes have to wait in line at a mill for three to five days to have their maize ground. This is the reason why scheme-settled refugees sometimes purchase maize flour to eat when they still have maize grain stored in their houses. This is also one of the reasons why some people are not eating the normal two meals a day. A maize grinding mill was installed in the Chavuma area in the late 1980s to grind locally-grown and imported maize. The huge demand for the mill was expressed in the millowner's income (ZK 1,687,700).

The variable of food self-sufficiency appears to show that men in the villages (self-settled refugees and their hosts) were better off than refugee men in the schemes, but self-sufficiency is a concept that needs further examination. In practice, my study established the degree of food self-sufficiency by asking several questions about the informant's behavior during the past year:

1) Has the informant obtained all of his or her staple food from his or her own fields?
2) Which staple foods has the informant eaten?
3) What crops did the informant plant last year?
4) How many cassava fields does the informant have currently?
5) Has the informant purchased any cassava, maize, or flour?
6) Has the informant sold any cassava, maize, or flour?
7) Has the informant received any staple food as gifts?
8) If there were purchases, sales, or gifts, who else was involved, and what were the amounts and prices?

The answers to these questions provided a multidimensional picture of the relationships among the production, local distribution, purchase, and consumption of staple foods. I also was able to verify in several ways whether home production provided enough staple food for the person and household, and whether the informant was partially or totally dependent on relatives or others (perhaps members of the same congregation) for staple food.

The study did not measure the level of consumption, however, which is a problem for analysis. Self-sufficiency in production, i.e., no purchases or gifts, may mean that the informant produced enough to satisfy his or her hunger, or it may mean that the informant restricted consumption ("tightened his or her belt") to the level of food available. Not purchasing staple food may mean that the informant was satisfied with what he or she produced, or it may indicate a lack of money to purchase enough food to satisfy hunger. Self-sufficiency may mean plenty or poverty. I do not know whether the informant needed (or wanted) additional food or meals.

Meals and the Frequency of Eating Meals: A meal for the Luvale people consists of a staple food (e.g., cassava, maize) prepared in the traditional manner (as shima, a thick stiff mass prepared by stirring flour into boiling water)

145

and accompanied by a cooked side dish (ifwo or "relish") of
leafy vegetable, fish, or (infrequently) chicken or meat.
Only the combination of shima and ifwo is a meal; other sub-
stances that we would call foods and other means of
preparing them are categorized by the Luvale as "snacks"
(visakwola). People who have eaten only snacks have not
really eaten a meal. Luvale people think that two meals a
day are normal, usually one around mid-day and another in
late afternoon. Wealthier people may eat something (por-
ridge or a snack) in the early morning as well. The major
reasons for people not eating two meals a day are that:

1) They have no flour to fix shima
2) They have nothing to use as ifwo (relish), or the
   only relish is the same leafy vegetable (usually
   cassava leaves) that they are tired of eating
3) The woman is working in the fields in the morning
   (when most agricultural work is done) and returns
   too late or is too tired to fix more than one meal
   around mid-afternoon or evening. The customary
   sexual division of labor also requires the woman to
   draw water in the afternoon for cooking and bathing.

Some people eat less than twice a day because they have no
appetite, but fewer than two meals a day is usually understood by the Luvale as a sign of lacking critical resources
(flour, relish, or labor). In the Meheba scheme, there is
an added complication that was noted above. Some families
had not eaten because they had no flour, even though they
had maize in the form of grain. In the Chavuma area there
was less delay at the mill, and no one in the study complained of not eating because they had been unable to grind
their grain.

Village men, whether refugees or hosts, were found to
have been more likely to have eaten two meals a day than
scheme-settled men. The differences in meal frequency
between married men and women is influenced by marital
patterns because a polygynously married husband will receive
food from both wives. Women eat less frequently than men,
reflecting the relative poverty of women, particularly those
who are unmarried. Of all categories, self-settled refugee
women were found to eat least often. A few people in the
study had not eaten a meal for two days. For the men, there
was general agreement between the data on meal frequency and
food self-sufficiency. Village men, both self-settled
refugees and hosts, were found to be better off in both
indicators than were scheme-settled men. The data for women
were not as consistent. Self-settled refugee women were
better off in terms of total self-sufficiency and numbers of
cassava fields, but worse off in terms of meal frequency.

Integration into Zambian Society: The survey also
measured the attitudes of refugees and hosts about refugee
integration into Zambia (by both locality and country).
There were significant differences between self-settled and
scheme-settled refugees. In essence, the self-settled

146

refugee men and women were found to be completely integrated. All of them felt settled and at home; their local
Zambian hosts considered the refugees to be part of the
community. Also, all the self-settled refugees had acquired
Zambian registration cards (reserved for citizens) at one
time or another. Many scheme-settled refugees also felt
that they were well-established in Meheba, as might be
expected since they had lived there for up to 18 years. In
contrast, approximately one-fifth of the scheme-settled
refugee men and women still considered themselves to be
"strangers" to Zambia, even after all these years. An
important factor contributing to this feeling of strangeness
was the attitude that nearby villagers around Meheba had
toward the scheme-settled refugees. These villagers had not
accepted the refugees, and many refugees were well aware of
this, as a key informant named Nsolo Mijere explained to me.

I did not investigate attitudes toward integration by
asking the individual informant point-blank whether he or
she felt integrated or not. Attitudes toward integration
were measured in two ways: (a) using a little model ladder
with five rungs, and (b) asking about relations in general
between local refugees and local Zambians, and whether local
refugees were well integrated.[7]

In the Chavuma area, most people placed themselves on
rungs 3, 4, or 5, i.e., towards greater integration. The
most common reasons for self-placement from both refugees
and hosts, both men and women, were as follows:
1) I belong here. I am _mwenyembo_, or a member of the
village
2) I have built my house. I have my fields
3) I have lived here a long time, or I have grown old
here.
Among the four sub-populations in the village area, refugee
women were found to score themselves lowest, while there was
little difference in the average scores of the other three
categories. Only one person in Chavuma scored himself a
stranger (i.e., on the first rung). He was a very ill, 83-
year-old host who had spent three months of 1988 in the
local clinic in a coma. He said that everyone he knew--the
other elders--had already died, and he was now left to die
among people he did not know. This was a unique response to
the question, and a unique way of defining "being a
stranger."

The answers from scheme-settled refugees revealed an
important difference. The majority of the refugees in
Meheba answered in the same way as the self-settled
refugees. In contrast, one-fifth of the men and women
placed themselves still on the first rung because they were
still strangers to Zambia. They thought that they were not
part of the local district, and that they would never
belong. The primary reason that these refugees considered
themselves permanent strangers was because local villagers
(who are, in African custom, referred to as "the owners of
the land") continued to complain about the presence of refu-

gees in the district and to emphasize that the refugees did not belong there. Scheme-settled refugees said that Zambians in Solwezi District often called the refugees names, such as "refugee, refugee" (in English), mukameheba (person from Meheba), or muka-kuchitajita (person who fled the war). This name-calling emphasizes the distinctiveness of the refugees. Scheme-settled refugees, including some who indicated that they were better-integrated, also mentioned how quarrels and fights sometimes broke out between refugees and local villagers when they met in the woods.

The Desire to Repatriate: These differences in attitudes of self-settled and scheme-settled refugees, and differences in their experiences with local hosts, were vividly expressed by different responses to a question about their desires to repatriate to Angola when the war is over. None of the self-settled refugees wanted to repatriate, while approximately half of the scheme-settled refugees desired to go back to their country. The desire to repatriate was always prefaced by the qualification that the war must really be over, since the refugees were well aware that the war has died down in the past, only to begin again, as in 1992.

Statistics on attitudes toward repatriation do not represent all of the refugees since 1966 who have ever self-settled or have ever been scheme-settled. The people interviewed in 1989 were those who still remained in the villages and in Meheba as of that year. Over the intervening years (1966-1989), an unknown number of refugees had already repatriated. The sample of people in the Chavuma village area suggests that nine per cent of the self-settled refugee men and four per cent of the women had already repatriated since 1972, while three per cent of the host men and one per cent of the women had moved (not repatriated) to Angola during the same years. It is unknown how many refugees repatriated to Angola from Meheba since there is no early census for comparison, but informants in Meheba mentioned that many people had left over the years, especially in 1975 (the year that Angola became independent, and the war seemed to be over). Official Meheba records from the 1970s also noted that many refugees had "absconded" over the years for unknown reasons. Some of them probably repatriated, while others may have moved to self-settle elsewhere in Zambia.

The most common reason given by scheme-settled refugees in 1989 for their desire to repatriate was: "This (Zambia) is not my country." When asked to explain why they thought that Zambia was not their country, the refugees mentioned their treatment (name-calling and exclusion) by villagers and townsmen in Solwezi District. Scheme-settled refugees also noted frequently, in this regard, their unhappiness with needing to obtain travel permits. Generally, the refugees need to ask permission from the government's administrator of Meheba, and then receive a written travel permit

148

from him, before they can legally leave the scheme to visit, work, or even go to market.

Another reason given by the scheme-settled refugees for their desire to repatriate was the anticipation that economic conditions in Angola would be better than those in Zambia. The comparison was made at two levels: Local and national. People in Meheba and in Chavuma (both self-settled refugees and hosts) mentioned that the depopulation of rural Angola because of the war meant that: (a) there were many fish in the streams, (b) there were many game animals to hunt, and (c) there were many fertile areas to farm. These local-level economic factors were commonly cited as reasons why some refugees had already repatriated over the years, and why some refugees and hosts continued to travel into Angola during these war years. The worsening national economic conditions in Zambia also played a part in refugee dissatisfaction, as well as that of host villagers. People talked about the high prices for many goods (especially clothes) and the unavailability of others. For example, blankets, salt, sugar, powdered milk, and cooking oil were not available in Zambia during the period of May to August. There was a limited amount of cross-border trade in the Chavuma area in 1989, even with the continuing warfare. The trade was mostly in food items, dried game meat from Angola being exchanged for flour from Zambia. Earlier in the 1980s, when there was no warfare in the nearby border area, and the border was open for trade, Chavuma people remembered the low prices and ready availability of clothes brought in from Angola.

DEPENDENCY AND FEAR

The study also was designed to discover psychological differences in the two refugee populations. Two important differences were found. Scheme-settled refugees were more dependent, and self-settled refugees were more fearful.

Scheme-settled refugees exhibited more dependency (or less self-reliance) in their answers to the question about repatriation. While self-settled refugees clearly stated their desire to stay in Zambia, refugees in Meheba usually assumed that the government would make a decision about their repatriation, and that they would comply: "The government has the power" (jingolo jya fulumende). When an informant was asked whether he or she wanted to repatriate after the war was over, the most common response in the scheme was: "If the government tells me to go, I will go." The interviewer then had to explain carefully that the informant should suppose that the government really wants to know what the informant personally wants to do. This was almost always followed by a moment of silence, after which it became evident that the informant had never really thought that he or she has the freedom to decide. Saying that the scheme-settled refugees show dependency in their answers to the question about repatriation does not mean that the refugees have become psychologically (or learned to be) helpless. They may simply have learned the rational limits of their personal power in relation to the government.

Self-settled refugees, on the other hand, were found to be apprehensive about exposing their identity as refugees. They were worried that they would be picked up by the government and taken to Meheba. As noted elsewhere, the national law on refugees states that all refugees must live in schemes, and the government has conducted a number of sweeps over the years to round up self-settled refugees. Some refugees had been rounded up in Chavuma and taken to Meheba, where they were interviewed for this study, and others had moved away from Chavuma to escape the sweeps. There was a pervasive atmosphere of fear in the villages during the period of interviewing. Even hosts were afraid to mention that they had been born in Angola because they might be labelled as refugees and taken away. This pervasive fear likely resulted in some distortion of the data when refugees (and hosts) were lying. Generally, even though the self-settled refugees are completely integrated into Zambia and have Zambian identity cards, refugees are still worried about being dislocated again and losing their village identity and independence.

CONCLUSIONS, RECOMMENDATIONS, AND ISSUES OF EMPOWERMENT

"Which refugees are better off?" is not a simple question, because well-being is a multidimensional construct. Scheme-settled refugees were found to be materially better off in 1989 than self-settled refugees, but self-settled refugees were found to be more integrated and "at home." Overall, many scheme-settled Angolans remain "refugees" after more than 20 years in Zambia, whereas self-settled Angolans are no longer "refugees" in their eyes or in the eyes of their local hosts. Instead, self-settled refugees are now "poor rural Zambians." Therefore, the long-term consequences of the two settlement strategies are, in the most general and simplest terms, that self-settled refugees are now poor de facto Zambians, while the scheme-settled are richer, but still Angolan refugees. One mode of settlement has provided and promotes material benefits in schemes. The other mode of settlement promotes socio-political integration in villages.

My conclusions focus on integration rather than on material wealth because the former is a durable solution, and thus of special importance in any discussion of refugees. The status of refugee is deprived of many rights and privileges,[8] so people are fortunate when they can drop that status. Because they are integrated and enjoy more local social support, the self-settled refugees are more powerful and self-controlled than the scheme-settled.

However, this is not necessarily a matter of self-settlement empowering these refugees.

Certain arguments about empowerment seem to rest on the assumption that refugees lose all their power by becoming refugees, so any power they possess during settlement or resettlement must be due to empowerment. By contrast, I think that the loss of power is a variable. What seems to have happened in this case of Angolan refugees is that self-settlement allowed refugees to conserve more of their original (i.e., pre-flight) power because village life maximized "the transfer or maintenance of previous rank, status, and prestige . . . . [T]he refugee continues to live in a place where his or her experience, skills, and acquired knowledge may be put to use to rebuild."[9] Self-settlement did not force, or represent, such a major loss of power.

The scheme-settled could use many of their acquired skills and experience as well, but they were affected negatively by two significant structural factors that undercut their self-control: (a) the refugees were moved among strangers when the scheme was moved from Zambezi (a Luvale-speaking) District to Solwezi (a Kaonde-speaking) District, and (b) the scheme-settled were never allowed by the government--the administrators of the scheme--to forget that they were temporary visitors, at the mercy of the Zambian government.

However, I cannot be unduly optimistic about such self-settlement. Although the self-settled refugees are locally integrated, they are not legally integrated, which severely limits their self-control. Zambian law states that all refugees remain refugees; there is no provision for refugees to become citizens. Therefore, the self-settled refugees who are de facto Zambians, and who all possess Zambian identity cards, cannot become de jure Zambians. Similarly, the half of the scheme-settled refugees who wish to remain in Zambia do not now have that legal option.

As a result of this study, I have recommended that the Zambian government revise Chapter 112, the Refugees Control Act, of the Zambian legal code, to: (a) permit refugees to acquire citizenship after a period of residency in Zambia, and (b) to permit an alternative settlement option (self-settlement) for those refugees who are qualified (in terms of kinship, or other personal or social resources). These changes would allow self-settled (and other well-integrated) refugees to become de jure as well as de facto Zambians and would allow the existence of a dual system in which both scheme-settlement and self-settlement are permitted. I have also recommended that the government issue a public proclamation of amnesty to the long-term, self-settled refugees in the North Western and Western provinces. This would allow these people to become citizens (or to keep their Zambian registration cards) in spite of their earlier contravention of the Refugees Control Act, and would reduce the atmosphere of fear and insecurity in the villages.

This study also has generated important questions for further research and policy discussion. How representative of other long-term African refugee settlement situations are these Zambian findings? Who benefits from promoting a mode of settlement that encourages people to remain strangers? Which is better, a mode of settlement that promotes material benefits, or one that promotes integration--a durable solution? How could the procedures followed in Zambia be modified to improve the consequences of both modes? Is there a mode of settlement (or a manner of administering settlements) that combines the material and socio-political benefits of these two modes? What are the implications for governmental and international interventions in refugee aid?[10] Each of these questions, when thoroughly pursued, also will shed light on processes of empowerment.[11]

NOTES

[1]I thank the following for their financial support of the project: The Canadian International Development Research Centre, the John D. and Catherine T. MacArthur Foundation, the United Nations Research Institute for Social Development (UNRISD), and the University of Florida. This research was part of a larger, multidisciplinary project involving people from the University of Zambia and the University of Florida. This chapter only reports on the research conducted by the author. The overall research project is coordinated with other refugee studies being conducted by UNRISD, which disseminates the analyses to policy-makers through the United Nations system. As policy-oriented material, it is intended to benefit Zambian, other African, and non-African policy-makers who deal with refugee affairs. An earlier version of this chapter was published as an UNRISD discussion paper (Hansen 1990).

[2]Among the most important sources on the debate are T.F. Betts, "Spontaneous Settlement of Rural Refugees in Africa" (1980) and "Spontaneous Settlement of Rural Refugees in Africa, Part II: Tanzania (1981)," both manuscripts resulting from the Research Project Responding to the Recommendation on Rural Refugees, Sub-section (f), of Committee 'B' of the Conference on the Situation of Refugees in Africa, held in Arusha, Tanzania in May, 1979 (commissioned by Euro Action-ACORD). Other documents include two by R. Chambers, "Rural Refugees in Africa: What the Eye Does Not See," Disasters 3: 381-392, 1979, and "Hidden Losers? The Impact of Rural Refugees and Refugee Programmes on Poorer Hosts," International Migration Review 20: 245-263, 1986. See also G. Kibraeb, African Refugees: Reflections on the African Refugee Problem (Trenton, NJ: Africa World Press, 1985). My own work includes "Refugee Dynamics: Angolans in Zambia 1966 to 1972," International Migration Review 15:

152

175-194, 1981, and "Self-Settled Rural Refugees in Africa: The Case of Angolans in Zambian Villages," in Involuntary Migration and Resettlement: The Problems and Responses of Dislocated Peoples, A. Hansen and A. Oliver-Smith, eds. (Boulder, CO: Westview Press, 1982).

[3]Ibid., Hansen 1982, p. 33.

[4]A. Hansen, "African Refugees: Defining and Defending Their Human Rights," in Human Rights and Governance in Africa, R. Cohen, G. Hyden, and W. Nagen, eds. (Gainesville, FL: University Presses of Florida, 1992).

[5]Some data are still being processed. Later publications will have slightly different numbers and be more sophisticated statistically.

[6]The statistics presented here reflect gross cash incomes, i.e., the costs of doing business or buying goods for later resale have not been subtracted from the gross receipts. Currency exchange rates in 1989 were 15 Zambian Kwacha (ZK) to one U.S. dollar.

[7]The question-and-answer method is well understood, but the use of the model ladder requires some explanation. The interviewer shows the informant the ladder and states that a newcomer (ungeji, which means both newcomer and stranger) to the area starts on the first rung. The newcomer starts there because he or she has no home nor fields; he or she is just beginning to build a house and to plant fields. Over the years some people go up the ladder, some stay in the same place, and some fall off. Then the interviewer asks where the informant places himself or herself, and why the informant thinks he or she belongs on that rung.

[8]See note 4, above.

[9]See note 3, above.

[10]Other useful and relatively recent references include P. Freund and K. Kalumba, "The Social and Economic Condition of Refugees and Displaced Persons in the Mwinilunga, Zambezi, Kabompo and Solwezi Districts of Zambia's North-Western Province: Census of Refugees and Displaced Persons in the Four Districts," Community Health Research Reports, No. 9 (Lusaka: University of Zambia, 1983); A. Hansen, "Once the Running Stops: Assimilation of Angolan Refugees into Zambian Border Villages," Disasters 3: 369-374, 1979, and "Managing Refugees: Zambia's Response to Angolan Refugees 1967 to 1977," Disasters 3: 375-380, 1979; A. Hansen, "Refugee Self-Settlement Versus Settlement on Government Schemes: The Long-Term Consequences for Security, Integration, and Economic Development of Angolan Refugees (1966-1989) in Zambia," Discussion Paper, No. 17 (Geneva: United

Nations Research Institute for Social Development, 1990); and A.P. Wood, Agricultural Needs and Food Security in Refugee Affected Areas of Senanga-West, Zambia (Lusaka: United Nations High Commissioner for Refugees, 1984).

[11]Issues of empowerment and dependency elsewhere in Africa are covered in B.E. Harrell-Bond, "Ugandan Refugees in the Sudan, Part III: Administration in Planned Rural Settlements," Universities Field Staff International (UFSI) Reports, No. 50, 1982, and in her book Imposing Aid: Emergency Assistance to Refugees (London: Oxford University Press, 1986). In a somewhat different context, another reference of importance is H.A. Williams, "Families in Refugee Camps," Human Organization 49: 100-109, 1990.

THE UNHCR AND THE INTERNATIONAL REFUGEE PROTECTION SYSTEM: RESOURCES AND RESPONSES

Patricia J. Campbell
Debra Kreisberg-Voss
Joy Sobrepeña
University of Denver

INTRODUCTION

Refugee flow traditionally has been associated solely with the concept of fear of political persecution. Causes of contemporary refugee movement, however, derive from a variety of sources. The complex, interactive forces which now generate refugee flows impact the implementation of assistance and protection by the international community. Today, analysts find that political, social, and economic factors coalesce to stimulate flight.[1] As pressures from the large inflows of refugees[2] erode the humanitarian spirit and economic resources of receiving states (i.e., nations), policy makers become more responsive to the costs of assistance than to the needs of those seeking asylum. The continued vulnerability of refugees under these circumstances is the central concern of this chapter.

A spirit of cooperation and willingness to embrace those people in flight is the necessary basis for an effective international refugee protection system. As it exists today, this system consists of a body of international law which establishes standards and guidelines for the treatment of refugees, and a network of national and international governmental and non-governmental organizations (IGOs and NGOs), individual governments, and the refugees themselves. A key component of this system is the Office of the United Nations High Commissioner for Refugees (UNHCR), which endeavors to implement not only temporary protection and assistance measures, but seeks to secure durable solutions for refugee populations.

Despite the pursuit of these goals, many refugees remain at risk--still vulnerable to threats to their personal security and well-being. The crux of the problem lies in attempting to achieve durable solutions (see also Basok, Hansen, and Otis, this volume). A durable solution cannot mean indefinite maintenance and care for refugees.[3] It requires their incorporation into society through acculturation and economic integration. Incorporation can only be achieved when the refugees themselves are enabled to have a meaningful role in the determination of their futures. In short, a truly durable solution is dependent on refugee empowerment. The current refugee protection system, however, does not facilitate or promote this empowerment.

Once making the decision to leave the country, refugees are often deprived of life choices. They are forced to accept only what the international community is willing to offer. We believe that the current conception of durable solutions as formulated by the UNHCR is thus deficient.

The ability of the UNHCR to sucessfully implement durable solutions is influenced by several factors: (a) the organization's relationship to other actors in the international system, (b) the availability of resources both in the refugee-receiving country and to the UNHCR, and (c) the political will and perceptions of the refugee-receiving society (which we term environmental factors). These factors combine to both facilitate and impede the UNHCR's ability to fulfill its mandate--to protect refugees and to find durable solutions to refugee producing-situations-- within the context of the overall refugee system.

FACTORS THAT IMPACT THE REFUGEE PROTECTION SYSTEM

The Structure of the UNHCR: The UNHCR was established in 1950 by the United Nations General Assembly. Although originally set up as a temporary organization, the UNHCR today unofficially has become a permanent part of the United Nations apparatus.[4] It is charged by the General Assembly to "provide international protection" for refugees and to seek out "durable solutions" to their plight. The UNHCR mandate lists these solutions as voluntary repatriation, integration into the country of first asylum, and resettlement in a third country of asylum.[5] Efforts to achieve such solutions involve the coordination of UNHCR activity with governments and a variety of intermediary operating organizations.

The UNHCR defines refugees in terms of the 1951 U.N. Convention Relating to the Status of Refugees and its 1967 Protocol.[6] However, the UNHCR can provide assistance to "non-Convention" refugees (including drought victims and internally displaced persons) through the extension of its good offices with the approval of the General Assembly. The agency can assist refugees only after a formal request is made by the refugee-receiving state.

All administrative funding is provided by the General Assembly. Funding requests for material assistance and any other programs also must be channeled through the General Assembly. Requests are initiated only for existing refugee situations and emergency relief. All funding is strictly voluntary.

The implementation of a program of assistance is initiated through a formal agreement between the UNHCR and the refugee-receiving state. The host government is primarily responsible for the functioning of refugee camps and settlements, with the UNHCR serving in a consultative role. Third-party agreements often are made with voluntary agencies to facilitate refugee care and protection. Thus international law and the United Nations provide the structural framework that gives the agency authority to act on refugee issues. Implementation of specific programs is reliant on host government and third-party agreements wherein the UNHCR plays a predominantly coordinating role.

Resources: Accessibility of resources impacts the entire refugee process from generation through emergency assistance and finally durable solutions. First, access to resources (or lack thereof) is partially linked to the generation of refugee flows. Second, the responsiveness of asylum countries to flows is conditioned by their ability to provide resources to asylum seekers. In general, resources are limited. Most refugees are from developing countries and over 90 percent of them will stay in developing countries either by resettling in their first country of asylum or repatriating to their homeland.[7] UNHCR funding merely supplements the meager budgets of these receiving nations in their efforts to deal with the refugee population. The average annual budget for the UNHCR during the late 1980s was under $500 million. Funds currently are directed toward numerous programs of emergency assistance and durable solutions. In 1989 the UNHCR was faced with 80 percent more refugees than in 1980, but expenditures for that same period for the organization rose by only 15 percent.[8] This constraint has been compounded by a lack of cooperation from governments. Restrictions put on aid given to the organization also make it difficult for the agency to accomplish its goals. For example, Japan insists that its contributions should target only Indochinese refugees.[9] How this budget is allocated among refugee receiving countries can affect the level of protection refugees receive. We assess this in each part of the durable solutions section of this chapter, below.

Environmental Factors: Because resources are scarce, political will to deal compassionately and responsibly with refugee issues has abated. States desiring to reduce refugee flows have implemented policies which attempt to dissuade individuals seeking refuge. Government policies have sought to reduce obligations to protect refugees and to justify rejecting asylum claims. This has been evident in efforts to implement the three classical durable solutions to the refugee crisis laid out by the UNHCR mandate.

Social, economic, and political concerns of nations have resulted in more restrictive policies. The backlog of asylum applicants has adversely affected the image of asylum seekers by creating the impression that the refugee problem is an endless one.[10] Moreover, competing demands for admission have made it difficult for the public and policy makers to separate refugee issues from larger immigration issues. The ability of states and international governmental organizations to respond positively to refugee problems depends primarily on a favorable climate of public opinion. This has a noticeable impact on the shaping of governmental policies. The inverse relationship between the growing number of refugees and the increasing restrictiveness of admission policies by sovereign nations is taking on crisis proportions. With so many refugees remaining at risk, we believe the realization of durable solutions in a climate of growing resource scarcity is doubtful.

DURABLE SOLUTIONS

<u>Repatriation:</u> Most countries support voluntary repatriation as the most desirable durable solution. Yet, there is no formal consensus on the means of achieving it. This is the area where the UNHCR, the international community, and individual governments have the greatest limitations of authority, influence, and resources.[11]

In order for repatriation to occur, the UNHCR must negotiate with the refugee's country of origin, the refugee receiving country, and the refugee. These components are essential to the repatriation process. Yet limitations exist for each component. The country of origin must agree to accept the refugees, the refugee-receiving country must agree to the terms of any agreement so as not to be accused of forceably repatriating refugees, the UNHCR must agree that repatriation is in the best interest of these persons, and the refugees themselves must agree to be repatriated. This negotiating process requires political will on the part of the countries involved to seek out solutions which are most beneficial to the refugees. The UNHCR often acts as the negotiator, which is why the non-political nature of the organization is crucial to successful repatriation efforts. Resources required for repatriation include maintenance of refugees while repatriation is being negotiated, the necessary transportation and support services needed to get them home, and assistance with reintegration upon arrival.

The key to successful repatriation is that the process must be non-compulsory; refugees must voluntarily decide to return to their country of origin. Voluntary repatriation should occur only when the situation in the country of origin has changed to the point where causes of flight are no longer present, or are diminished to the point where refugees themselves believe that they can safely return. This is consistent with the concept of non-refoulement which prohibits the forced return of refugees to life-threatening situations in the countries from which they have fled.

There have been instances of successful repatriation. Repatriation appeared to be an effective means of addressing significant refugee movements after World War II. Many European refugees were successfully returned to their homelands. This set a precedent for future initiatives.

During the late 1950s and 1960s the rise of liberation movements threatened colonial rulers, in turn causing governments to employ policies of persecution resulting in refugee flight. As liberation movements began to succeed and decolonization lifted the threat of political persecution, refugees began returning home in large numbers.[12] UNHCR assistance was critical in the return of a large number of these individuals. Early successes with voluntary repatriation, such as 200,000 Algerians in 1962 and 194,000 Sudanese in 1972-73,[13] for example, gave hope that this method would provide the best means to achieving an end to the refugee dilemma. The ability to choose to repatriate allowed the refugees a chance to participate in their own future. It was a step toward empowerment.

The period of decolonization saw processes similar to those in post-war Europe. After the war in Europe many refugees could safely return to their homeland because the cause of flight, the war and associated political persecution, had been eliminated. The removal of colonial powers, as well as the end of the wars of liberation, enabled many refugees to return as well. In both types of scenario, the causes for flight were relatively clear. Once those were no longer present repatriation became the logical solution.

Unfortunately, the majority of today's refugee flows stem from more complex and unclear scenarios. During 1991 and 1992 alone, nowhere was this more clear than in the former Soviet Union, the former Yugoslavia, and the Horn of Africa. Underdevelopment and/or economic disintegration played significant roles, and could not easily be distinguished from political factors. Yet the majority of today's refugees are from--and remain within--the developing nations. While certain specific factors are similar to those seen in post-war Europe, the systemic interplay of forces is quite different.

Decolonization did not end the flows of refugees. In fact, decolonization revealed the deep and far-reaching consequences of colonization. The economic, political, and social chaos left behind by the colonizers proved to be a breeding ground for future conflicts, competition over domestic resources, civil strife, and warfare--stimulating further outpourings of refugees.[14] These diverse causes, and turbulent politico-economic systems, have called into question repatriation as a durable solution.

Recently the UNHCR's emphasis on voluntary repatriation has come under review. Repatriation efforts have been accused of being everything from overzealous to completely inhumane and illegal.[15] Yet, host countries with scarce resources already strained often wish to promote repatriation and reintegration. Pressure on the UNHCR by these host governments to shift assistance to repatriation raises the possibility that refugees may be returned to their homelands prematurely, into situations which may not have changed enough to ensure their safety. When this happens the needs of the refugees often become a secondary concern. Repatriation under these conditions undermines both the spirit and the intent of the UNHCR mandate. The refugees also are at risk since the element of choice is severely constrained.

Most threatening to refugees is the implementation of policies of refoulement or forced repatriation. Because many receiving countries believe their own economies cannot withstand the influx of refugees, they may opt for policies of forced repatriation.[16] The UNHCR's capacity to protect these individuals is limited because the receiving states retain the right of granting asylum. In order to maintain a presence in such areas and to provide at least some assistance, the UNHCR has deemed it necessary to help some of these countries with the use of mandatory repatriation.[17] A recent example has been the demand by Hong Kong for the mandatory repatriation of Vietnamese "boat people." In this case the UNHCR as well as Britain agreed to "take a tougher line and push mandatory repatriation."[18] This was ironic, since refoulement is illegal under international refugee law and mandatory repatriation contradicts the UNHCR's own mandate. The international outcry in the Hong Kong case resulted in cessation of the repatriation.

Breaches of the principle of non-refoulement are seen increasingly. For example, refugees are turned away at points of entry after only a perfunctory examination of their asylum requests. The increasingly common practice of admitting asylum seekers on a temporary basis has limited the number of would-be refugees from securing political asylum, and in so doing goes against basic precepts of international law. This has occurred in the United States with Haitian refugees.

The prompt designation of refugee status is key to preventing the forcible repatriation of those seeking asylum. Asylum seekers who are not designated as refugees can be treated as economic migrants, and as seen in the Central American - Mexican - U.S. corridor, this can result in refusal of entry or expulsion. If they remain, they enter the category of illegal immigrant, thus subject to detention and deportation.[19] Another example is the screening policy employed in Thailand. It is designed supposedly to separate refugees from economic migrants. Those who are "screened in" are put into refugee camps to await resettlement and those who are "screened out" are put in detention centers until they are forcefully repatriated. Another of the authors represented in this volume, Vang Pobzeb, tackled this problem as it pertains to Hmong refugees in his 1992 visit to S.E. Asia.

Alternative means have been used to prevent refugees from reaching a first country of asylum. In the South China Sea, for example, boat loads of refugees from Vietnam often have been prevented from landing in potential countries of asylum like Indonesia, being "pushed back" into the sea where they become vulnerable to pirate attacks and the vagaries of nature. For example, in September of 1990, fifteen Vietnamese died after being at sea for months. Of the thirty ships which passed them, only one gave them food and water.[20]   According to the U.S. Committee for Refugees, "[t]he UNHCR estimates that pirates caused the disappearance of more than 1,300 refugees, abducted several hundred others, and killed and raped nearly 800 and 1,100 respectively during a six and one-half year period ending June 30, 1987."[21]   Despite the law of the sea which states that a ship must come to the aid of another ship in distress, countless vessels pass these refugee boats without offering to help.

In reality, the pushback initiatives in Southeast Asia are nothing more than an implicit policy of forcible repatriation.   Within the last two years the United States more formally adopted a policy of pushback in its interdiction of ships believed to be carrying Haitian asylum seekers.[22]   The policy came under intense scrutiny in 1992.

Because of the perceived threat and potential resource drain raised by mass arrivals of Laotian refugees in 1981, Thailand initiated a policy of "humane deterrence" under which refugees were placed in austere camps and denied the chance to seek resettlement.[23]   Conditions in the camps are miserable.   Reports have been made that camp residents have been exploited and conscripted for manual labor.[24]   Camps resembling prisons with deplorable conditions are maintained in order to restrict resource reallocation and ultimately to prevent more refugees from arriving.   One camp in Hong Kong was declared by the UNHCR as "unfit for human habitation."[25] Vietnamese families are forced to live in small cardboard cubicles in buildings that are no more than warehouses.   The psychological impact of these conditions upon the refugees, according to one Oxfam observer, has been "to lose touch with normal life" and has contributed to a sense of "mental deadness."[26]   Such practices and camp conditions are communicated by governments to other potential refugees, in the hope that this will deter further influxes.[27]

In countries where the political situation actually has improved, economic considerations regarding resource scarcity continue to affect voluntary repatriation attempts. Prior to the collapse of the Somalian government, this was the case with Ethiopians returning from that country. According to the UNHCR, financial constraints have led to slowdowns in voluntary repatriation attempts.[28]   The same has been the case for a two-way repatriation project between Angola and Zaire[29] (see also Hansen, this volume).   Sudden reintegration of a large number of refugees into a country increasingly choked by resource limitations can cause increased economic, political and social tensions.   As the pressures caused by dwindling resources escalate, there is increasing pressure to stop refugee flows altogether by whatever means necessary.   From a systems perspective, it can be said that a negative, mutually-reinforcing feedback process has been created.   Voluntary repatriation becomes an unlikely durable solution.

Repatriation often includes a promise of aid by the UNHCR for up to one year in order to help with the reintegration process.[30]   The UNHCR's options are limited.   It cannot intervene on a truly system-wide basis; simple repatriation becomes its immediate goal.   Once achieved the agency's official responsibility ends and the local government's begins.   The one-year aid situation can come to be misused or abused by the local government if its economic situation is severe enough.

   This is because developing countries are often desperate for any possible economic assistance.   Such nations may be willing to welcome home refugees if aid from the UNHCR is forthcoming, and if a way can be found to manipulate that aid.   In such instances, seen in Africa and elsewhere, refugees become tools for implicit national economic policies that contravene international refugee law.

   Integration: The purpose of the integration process is to assist the refugee in becoming self-sufficient in the country of asylum.[31]   Yet the countries receiving the heaviest refugee flows are listed as being among the least developed by the United Nations and are ill-prepared to bear the shock of mass refugee arrivals.   As previously stressed, these countries have extremely limited resources; to provide for their own citizens is difficult enough.   The resource demands that newly established "integration communities" put on them can be unbearable.[32]   Again a negative, mutually-reinforcing feedback process becomes apparent, because (as most recently exemplified in the Horn of Africa), these countries also become unable to meet the basic requirements of security, protection, and human rights for the refugees.

   Basic standards of human rights obligations of states towards refugees are derived and find their force in customary law.   This law indicates the content of the minimum obligations which control and direct the treatment by states of aliens living under the protection of that state.   The Convention lists rights such as nondiscrimination, the right to security against refoulement, the right to residency and reentry, the right to engage in wage-earning employment, and the rights to education, welfare/social security, and administrative assistance.   These are fundamental rights to which all refugees, once granted asylum, are entitled.

   With these standards as guides, rural integration (the focus of most UNHCR integration projects) becomes aimed at helping "the refugee attain a level of self-sufficiency comparable to that of the local population."[33]   Therefore, efforts to promote refugee self-sufficiency become increasingly aimed at achieving a more general economic impact.[34]   This policy has created friction between residents of the host country and refugees.   The local population itself is not always self-sufficient due to scarce resources.   Large amounts of aid brought in to help refugees can lead to resentment and even violence.   The UNHCR has made attempts to ensure that the living standards of refugees do not contrast too sharply with those of the local population, but this is difficult in situations such as Somalia and Sudan where local residents themselves are suffering. Governments often exacerbate such situations by engaging in (or making no attempt to prevent) discrimination against and mal-treatment of refugees. Both government officials and the local populace in Sudan, for example, have been accused of property confiscation, torture, false imprisonment, murder, and rape.[35] These factors make integration a durable solution of limited applicability.

In Africa, strained resources have been one of the main sources of conflict between refugees and residents of local communities. This has been somewhat less of a problem in Eastern Europe, Latin America, the Caribbean, and Southeast Asia. Such strains cause problems at integration sites as they become so overtaxed that rural integration development strategies have no real chance to succeed. Once a settlement has been established it is not uncommon to find new arrivals being sent there without consideration as to whether the local environment can sustain them.[36]

If UNHCR integration schemes fail, it often is because of inappropriate planning and preparation. Appraisals of the lands designated to serve as the sites for integration camps may have been conducted poorly. An influx of people into an ecologically fragile area can virtually guarantee the failure of the plan, as well as having the potential to create hostilities between locals and refugees. With increasing numbers of people competing for limited resources, more people are being forced to farm marginal areas. The damage wrought on the environment can be long-lasting and, in some cases, irreversible. The UNHCR does not have the ability nor the authority to police such camps and resettlement sites in order to prevent these types of consequences.

While economic self-sufficiency of refugees is the immediate goal of integration, the overarching goal of UNHCR assistance is the achievement of durable solutions tied to durable protection. Protection is political. In the case of Africa, integration as a means to durable protection has been even harder to achieve than economic integration.[37] Many African states stop short of granting full citizenship to those who seek asylum. Effective integration does not actually occur, leaving the refugees unprotected. Without full participation, empowerment becomes impossible. From a systems perspective, it can be said that the UNHCR finds itself in the paradoxical situation of promoting a structure for which it cannot assure the intended function.

The UNHCR's mandate limits its ability to acquire material assistance. This forces the organization to seek solutions through the international legal system and consultation with the local governments involved.[38] Long-term planning for integration sites is extremely important in order to maximize their potential, as is the empowerment of refugee leaders to help in developing the socio-economic possibilities of the sites once settled. Material assistance often must be "leveraged," a process which has numerous positive and negative ramifications. Resource control becomes a central issue.

There are other considerations and constraints which confront the UNHCR regarding integration policies. The location of integration sites is very important. Placing camps and settlement sites close to the border of the country from which the refugees have fled can make people on both sides of the border more vulnerable. The invasion of Rwanda by Rwandan refugees living in Uganda is a recent example.[39]

Another consideration is that of ethnicity. The UNHCR recognizes that ethnicity should be taken into account as integration schemes are developed but should not be used to justify integration. Integration schemes for Somalis fleeing to Djibouti in the late 1980s took this into account; a large percentage of Djibouti's residents are ethnic Somalis. Refugees from Somalia in 1988 found family and clan members in Djibouti to help them, thus enhancing integration efforts. The ethnic Somalis living in Djibouti were willing to share their limited resources with the Somalian refugees.[40] However, this also has created problems. Djibouti has only a moderate resource base and the integration process further strained the local economy. Djibouti's fragile environment also has been extensively damaged due to excessive resource demands by the refugees and their kin.

Other considerations that should be--but unfortunately have not been adequately been--taken into account when the UNHCR has set up integration schemes are: (a) accessibility of the settlement for the most effective delivery of food and other supplies, (b) comparative cost effectiveness, (c) location of local markets in relation to the camps, (d) adequacy of water supplies, (e) appropriate means for delivering health care and education, (f) accurate evaluations of environmental and social impact assessments regarding the number of refugees who can be productively absorbed into the settlement, and (g) the adequacy of the land for the types of agriculture to be practiced.

In order to effectively address these issues, refugees must be sufficiently involved in the assessment and implementation process to ensure that they have a stake in the success of the project. Stakeholders must be empowered. Such involvement also is essential to minimize the boredom, lethargy, and depression which may result from spending long periods of time without engaging in activities perceived to be useful.[41] With involvement comes some measure of control (see Basok, this volume), yet some specialists have ignored this as relief and integration measures are being initiated. Too often refugees are objectified and do not have the opportunity to play a role in the designing of their future.

The UNHCR can only facilitate integration up to a point. If the refugee population is kept in isolation from the general population, development of the settlement will be unlikely (see Hansen, this volume). Chances for the refugees' continued vulnerability and dependence on the UNHCR will be increased.

As with the rural refugee, the urban refugee also faces problems in attempting to integrate. Finding employment in cities with already-high unemployment rates is difficult. Obtaining adequate housing is a problem. For those with education this may be somewhat easier. The question of "brain drain" arises as host countries often are more willing to enable the integration of those with needed skills, yet few such persons have been readily identifiable in most of the current large-scale refugee movements. Urban refugees also face other of the well-known barriers to integration including language, religion, ethnicity, and political discrimination, as well as the relative lack of both formal and informal support systems.

Several strategies have emerged in order to lessen the burden on some of these countries. One example is zonal development, whereby the whole zone where the refugees are to be settled becomes the focus of developmental aid. This promotes integration between the refugees and the local populace because the focus of attention is systemic, emphasizing the socio-political and economic environment within which both local residents and refugees interact. Unfortunately, the question of unequal development on a broader scale emerges, as more resources are committed to that zone than others in the region. The result is that the country's overall economic development can become skewed.[42]

In summary, on paper integration strategies have a great deal of merit. Actual successes have been limited by the fact that integration requires large amounts of material assistance, long-term commitments by all parties involved, and extensive planning and post-implementation evaluation. The UNHCR is constrained in its ability to acquire the necessary resources. The fact that it often is perceived as being a "temporary player" makes long-term planning difficult. For reasons mentioned above, host countries themselves often are unwilling to accommodate such schemes. The current refugee system does not allow for--nor adequately meet the needs of--integration as an effective durable solution.

Resettlement: Refugee resettlement into a third country is another option in dealing with the refugee dilemma. It is implemented when repatriation and integration are not feasible. Yet, despite its wide-spread use, it remains the least desirable solution for many reasons.

From the refugees point of view, their determination and aspirations to eventually return to their homelands become less realistic--less feasible--the further away they are moved. Receiving nations espouse a series of reasons for resettlement's undesirability. The increased diversity in new refugee arrival groups requires an expansion of resources to meet a broader range of ethnic and cultural needs. Even in relatively wealthy nations like the United

States, Canada, and France, available resources must be shared or their distribution patterns restructured for use by new arrivals. Transferring resources from already established refugee communities which have gained special commitments through public and private support mechanisms is politically and socially difficult. Furthermore, new groups (such as the Kurds arriving in the U.S. in 1992) often lack an already existing community to receive them.[43]

Although international legal standards define who is a refugee, the UNHCR remains dependent on sovereign nations for the actual granting of asylum. The role of state in the international system remains central. Today immigration authorities often are more concerned with domestic legislation, regulations, and political considerations in making these decisions. Economic and social concerns take center stage--humanitarian issues are increasingly being pushed to the side. The high cost of government assistance programs for refugees--well over $500 million in the U.S. in 1991-- coupled with difficulty in educating and housing new arrivals continues to result in the failure of some refugees to become self-sufficient. This ultimately forces them to rely on welfare. In the state of California, where the welfare dependency rate is exceptionally high, refugees and other immigrants are accused of being the source of social and economic problems.

Future refugee admissions will be based on previous social and economic performances. In view of all these reasons, third country resettlement solutions remain incomplete, remedial, and transient.[44]

The relationship between refugees and community residents has a significant impact on the acculturation of these new immigrants.[45] Prevailing xenophobic attitudes and behaviors in countries of resettlement undermine support for progressive national policies toward refugee admission.[46] This has been evident in Germany during the 1990s. Restructured admission policies reflect the perceived need to maintain social and economic stability in the receiving countries. Sovereign states maintain the right to use their discretion as to who is allowed to enter. In this sense, global levels of commitment to international standards of protection increasingly depend upon local levels of commitment to these principles.[47]

To achieve successful resettlement in a third country, its government must play a stronger role, thus (in one sense paradoxically) limiting the capacity for UNHCR involvement. By contrast, resettlement in a country of first refuge permits a more active role for the UNHCR. The procedure for third country resettlement of refugees is closely regulated and occurs under three-party agreements usually drawn up by the UNHCR, the country of first asylum, and the resettlement country. A well-known example is that involving this agency, Sudan, and the United States. Other than facilitating communication between parties and providing some material and travel assistance, the UNHCR has minimal participation in the actual resettlement itself. The protection of refugees thus is left primarily under the jurisdiction of the host country. When facilitation of social and political acculturation by the host government is inadequate, this process usually receives the help of private voluntary organizations (PVOs) and non-governmental organizations (NGOs). As noted previously in another context, the refugee is often considered the object of--rather than a participant in--the process.

A new climate of tighter restrictions in the Euro-American sphere has led to finer legal and policy-related distinctions for different groups of asylum seekers, with refugee status therefore being granted to fewer persons in several of these countries. Despite the universal tone of most immigration policies a majority of the developed nations have increased their use of administrative mechanisms which give preference to certain nationalities and those with certain skills. Truly equitable policies simply do not exist. The UNHCR's efforts are further constrained.

RULE OF "LEAVE TO REMAIN": The administrative rule or mechanism of "Leave to Remain" (LTR) is an element of many countries' domestic refugee policy, regardless of the particular name it is given. The granting to an asylum seeker (who has been denied formal asylum) the right to remain on a temporary basis is within the discretion of most immigration authorities. When applied to those who can make a legitimate claim to refugee status, this action bends immigration rules, thus effectively denying asylum seekers of asylum rights.[48]

Although these "refugees" are allowed to remain in the country, they are not accorded the same privileges as "convention refugees." For example, they are not given conventional travel documents, and are expected to renew their passports at own nations' embassies which many applicants are unwilling to do for fear of retribution. LTR status is granted on a year-to-year basis, often for a period of four years maximum. Any time during this period, if authorities feel conditions are suitable for the applicants to return to their country, the status of LTR can be withdrawn.

The mechanism of LTR was originally established as a humanitarian gesture. If nothing else, it enabled a refugee to buy time. The problem is that the disjunction between rules that the Convention has laid out to help refugees and the way in which they are being interpreted by states works against refugees. The mechanism of LTR is too often used to deny conventional refugees, especially those from coup-ridden countries, the privileges of refugee status.

The use of LTR calls for government officials to differentiate between persons having no compelling reasons for not returning to their countries and people who actually have well-founded fears of persecution. Individual discretion on the part of officials often comes to play too great a role, as personal knowledge, political pressure, racial prejudice, and even momentary moods can influence the outcome. This type of discretion becomes a potential instrument of corruption if used as a guise to reduce the number of permanent refugee admissions. Used in this way, LTR breaches the Convention.

Appropriately applied, Leave to Remain implies that an applicant must not only have a well-founded fear of persecution but that the situation that has produced such fear must be permanent rather than temporary. With LTR immigration authorities have assumed the responsibility for determining the "balance of probabilities" of persecution of an individual. They also presume the role of informed political forecasters by evaluating the nature and probable outcome of the political situation in the homeland from which a refugee is fleeing. Thus allegations that LTR is more often used according to the political priorities of governments than to meeting the needs of the applicants have emerged.[49] To the credit of the U.S., in 1992 it took preliminary measures which may enable it to redress this imbalance.

RULE OF "FIRST COUNTRY OF ASYLUM": Another mechanism to limit refugee flows to resettlement countries is the rule of "First Country of Asylum." It states that refugee status will cease to be the right of applicants if they have received protection in another country other than their own. Theoretically, upon fleeing a country refugees are expected to seek asylum in the first country through which they pass.

Yet some states do not take into consideration the conditions in the first country, at minimum, whether that country is prepared to offer asylum or whether it is a party to the Convention. Refugees therefore can be left in a state of limbo--unable to return to the theoretical first country of asylum and unable to obtain asylum in the country in which they now find themselves. In 1992 this happened to refugees fleeing Bosnia. This is known as the "refugee-in-orbit syndrome."[50]

At a broader level, the absence of agreement between states on the responsibility in such cases can cause partial collapse of the larger resettlement system. This illustrates how refugee protection can be undermined by states' self-interest. "Asylum," according to Grant and Martin, "should not be refused by a contracting state solely on the grounds that it could be sought from another state."[51]

The "catch-22" of this process is that no country is compelled to fulfill its obligations under the Convention until actual asylum has been granted. Thus persons who have been detained in a country for any reason, regardless of whether they found actual protection, are deemed to have enjoyed the benefits of asylum elsewhere. Normally refugee status is conferred after asylum has been granted and thus forcible repatriation can occur with refugees who otherwise are theoretically eligible for Convention status.

In summary, restrictive policies employed by resettlement countries make refugees vulnerable in key ways: (a) they may remain "in orbit" indefinitely without protection from any state, (b) within countries of resettlement, they may remain vulnerable to civil and human rights abuses as long as host governments do not accord them the privileges of citizenship, and (c) they may be detained indefinitely in countries of first asylum without being integrated into society. The latter is the fate of many Indochinese refugees. An estimated three-fourths of refugees living in camps in the late 1980s had been doing so for at least five years.[52]

The UNHCR is unable to directly influence domestic policies and can only resort to publicly rebuking a country whose policies and/or practices grossly undermine the refugee protection system. Yet the organization understandably is reluctant to do this because it is so heavily dependent upon state cooperation in order to resettle refugees. At worst, a public rebuke could lead to the termination of the country's financial commitment to the U.N.

EMPOWERMENT

Although the term empowerment only recently has been applied to the refugee situation, as noted in the introductory chapter it long has been used regarding indigenous peoples and grassroots development. In this more traditional sense, empowerment has been used to illustrate the transition of a group from a situation in which its members were powerless, to a situation in which they possess at least moderate authority or power. Empowerment thus describes the process of people moving from a condition in which they lack the element of choice and participatory control over their own destiny, to a condition in which the capacity to gain choice and participation in key social, political, and economic activities is actualized.

Resources and Empowerment: Durable solutions are only truly achieved when refugees are empowered. Given the current world situation with regard to resource scarcity, as detailed above, the viability of both the goal and the means to empowerment come under question.

Building upon what has been presented, voluntary repatriation theoretically would be an important path to empowerment. However, in actuality it is becoming increasingly impractical due to the nature of political strife and resource scarcity in developing nations. Perceived national self-interests regarding strategic military, political, and economic issues are increasingly incompatible with the voluntary return of refugees to their homelands. In situations where repatriation does become possible after several years, refugees find themselves to have become dependent on others. Dependency is extraordinarily difficult to terminate.

While voluntary repatriation allows refugees some decision-making power, at least as far as which country will

169

provide permanent residence, mandatory or forced repatriation deprives them of such an option. Any participation in decisions regarding their own future will only come about much later, and likely make but limited impacts.

For those eventually able to repatriate, reintegration often is a difficult process. Where resources are limited, efforts to reestablish a productive life--including housing, employment, and health care--can take years to achieve, if accomplished at all. Empowerment is difficult to achieve without flux (i.e., systems flexibility at the local level). It is virtually impossible to achieve when primary attention must be riveted on basic survival.

First country of asylum/local integration solutions raise questions about the appropriateness of traditional forms of refugee assistance. The impact of long-staying refugee populations on already limited resources within countries of integration can have serious repercussions on the country's long-term development plans. Competition for resources, as previously stressed, can lead to serious damage to the environment. Officials of many of these countries increasingly have come to believe that new refugee arrivals put the local population at greater risk, and that the continued local resettlement of refugees will encourage a never-ending flow. These fears in turn can lead to the suppression of types of refugee assistance that might otherwise be effective in facilitating empowerment opportunities.

For integration to succeed as a durable solution, refugees must become relatively self-sufficient. With the majority of today's refugees remaining in developing nations whose own indigenous populations are struggling, the likelihood of integration succeeding is slim. Dependency upon external sources, including the precarious resources of the UNHCR, will continue.

Third country resettlement, while the least desirable from one perspective, ironically is among the most desirable from another. While also constrained, resources in developed, industrialized countries have been brought to bear in alleviating the refugee plight. Resource redistribution has taken place. Perhaps three million refugees have been resettled in such countries during the last decade. In the U.S., fiscal resources have been used to create employment opportunities (see DeVoe, this volume), to establish training programs (see Adkins and Sample, this volume), and to assist Mutual Assistance Associations (see Mortland, this volume). With such programs come the possibility of facilitative empowerment. Ironically this is empowerment outside the refugee's homeland, empowerment which may lead to enhanced acculturation and adaptation within the host country, but seldom to eventual return.

Xenophobia and Empowerment: Within the developed countries, the empowerment process must attempt to overcome xenophobic attitudes on the part of the citizenry. In some ways xenophobia can be a greater barrier than that of resource scarcity, as the current situation in Germany attests. The high cost of resettlement programs, while in the fiscal sense being relatively affordable, exacerbates these attitudes on the part of the public. This in turn influences policy makers. One result is an increasing restrictionism in admission policies.

Xenophobia has two interactive psychological dimensions. One involves the actor (i.e., local resident), the other the reactor (i.e., refugee). Linguistic barriers can be made to loom even more ominously. Job insecurity can be exacerbated. Pathways to the attainment of self-respect and pride can be damaged. Information regarding access to community resources can be suppressed, or be perceived by refugees to be inaccessible. Xenophobia thwarts the free flow of information.

Overall, the difficulty of applying the three durable solutions discussed in this chapter in a world of increasing resource scarcity and political divisiveness suggests that the international community and its member nations will have to find alternative ways to increase their understanding and their capacity to cope with the continuing refugee crisis. Certain social scientists have said that policy must be a guideline for the allocation of scarce resources.[53] The allocation and accessibility of resources determine the quality of life of all individuals--it is the human dimension of policy, the outcome of the human experience.[54] Today's policy solutions continue to fall drastically sort.

CONCLUSIONS AND COURSES OF ACTION

Since its inception, the UNHCR has attempted to protect refugees and to achieve durable solutions to refugee situations. Operating as part of the international refugee system, the organization has confronted opportunities as well as constraints in its attempts to be effective. The opportunities are highlighted here.

The UNHCR's unique contribution to refugee care and protection is its access to the international community. Being part of the United Nations system has provided a forum for the agency to plead the refugee case. For example, the funding procedure has forced the General Assembly to formally acknowledge several particularly sensitive refugee-producing situations.

Potential exists for close cooperation between the UNHCR and various other U.N. organizations and/or programs. Operation Lifeline, which has brought food to thousands (many of whom are refugees), serves to illustrate this potential. Another example is the close cooperation between the World Food Programme, the Red Cross Societies, other voluntary organizations and NGOs, and the UNHCR. This allowed the UNHCR to launch an assistance program which provided $15 million in emergency assistance to Africa.[55]

The organization's ability to work with other organizations and programs is not limited to those tied to the U.N. The UNHCR has worked closely with the OAU, for example, to set up assistance programs, to hold conferences, and to resolve disputes which involve African refugees. The UNHCR also has worked unilaterally with certain NGOs. A great opportunity exists for the agency to develop more links with organizations such as those delivering aid in the Horn of Africa, thus broadening its resource base--particularly in regard to information. For example, our contacts imply that, in Somalia in 1992, the organization CARE had more up-to-date information than the UNHCR field office regarding preferable food distribution mechanisms.

One reason the organization has achieved a relatively high level of respect in the international community is its conscious, ongoing struggle to remain non-political. Its ability to negotiate solutions in highly charged political situations has helped to establish a level of trust between the UNHCR and the international community.

In attempting to fulfill its obligation to protect refugees, the UNHCR has been a strong advocate for the establishment of international legal protective mechanisms. These mechanisms provide a framework within which the UNHCR as well as other organizations, working within the overall refugee system, can operate. Legal instruments are an essential step in securing protection for refugees. They establish a standard level of acceptable behavior by which governments as well as certain intergovernmental and non-governmental agencies can be judged. These instruments complement those advocated by rights organizations such as the New York-based Lawyers Committee for Human Rights.

Some positive UNHCR impacts come about indirectly. While the UNHCR has been instrumental in helping establish legal protective mechanisms, it should be reemphasized that the organization is not empowered to force compliance. As a result, abuses of these legal mechanisms do occur. Witness the abuses of the first country of asylum rule discussed earlier. By states pursuing self-interests, the UNHCR can become a victim of the very mechanisms which it helped to establish. Yet indirectly, the outcries by non-UNHCR-based supporters of refugees victimized by these abuses can trigger other forms of action (e.g., among NGOs).

Many countries have attempted to prove their commitment to refugee issues by being signatories to refugee conventions and protocols. However, these have not always been followed up with financial commitments. The UNHCR's resettlement successes can provide modest amounts of indirect "finance-inducing leverage" in such situations, in some instances attracting private donors for country- or ethnic-specific causes.

In the final analysis, state-specific immigration and asylum laws are a powerful way to institutionalize the principles surrounding the offering of safety, security, and shelter to strangers in need. The global community, spurred by the UNHCR, must do everything possible to continue efforts to ensure that states grant refugees asylum, protect them against refoulement, and treat all migrating peoples in accordance with the most basic, recognized standards of human rights.[56]

The UNHCR serves as a catalyst (as well as lightning rod) for the entire refugee system. The system set up for the protection of refugees is reliant upon complex interaction and interdependence. The system demands open channels of both formal and informal communication--coupled with cross-culturally sensitive understanding--operative in a climate in which resource transfer, sharing, allocation, and access are stressed. A primary function of the UNHCR must be to encourage this type of interaction, coupled with commitment to the building and nurturing of collaborative multi-organizational relationships.

We believe that the following courses of action are both appropriate and possible:

* The UNHCR should be made an official, permanent organization of the United Nations. (Its current status is the equivalent of "unofficial, permanent.") Seeking durable solutions to continuing refugee crises while retaining the current status is contradictory.

* While still continuing to solicit voluntary and emergency funding, a permanent refugee fund should become instituted through the U.N. budgetary process. Contributions should be made mandatory for all member states. This would allow for long-term planning and would enable the UNHCR to pursue preventive as well as corrective measures. In terms of visibility, this guarantee of resources would signify a commitment by the world community to the refugee problem.

* Research efforts promoted by the UNHCR must continue to analyze the root causes of refugee flows. These efforts should also continue to focus on how to improve assistance mechanisms and how to further delineate what constitute truly workable durable solutions.

* A priority of the UNHCR in the 1990s must be to firmly establish the fundamental right of asylum. Objective criteria must be promoted more ardently, by which refugee status can be conferred--therefore eliminating the potential for discriminatory/capricious applications of refugee law and asylum procedures. These criteria must be based on principles of human rights protection.

* An international standard for what constitutes "minimum material welfare for refugees" needs to be established, with guidance provided by the UNHCR. Guidelines must specify what constitutes appropriate shelter, adequate amounts and types of food, and other basic needs.

173

These must be accompanied by effective means of implementation and monitoring.[57]

* The UNHCR must take advantage of opportunities to work
  with other organizations, especially NGOs and PVOs.
  Relationships with regional organizations such as the
  OAU, while politically sensitive, can be very beneficial. Ties to United Nations agencies like UNICEF
  can be useful. Interorganizational information exchange is essential. Such linkages also can encourage
  the donation of funds from alternative sources.

* The UNHCR should expand its efforts for voluntary repatriation. By working collaboratively with the governments in host countries, reintegration efforts also
  will be enhanced. Reintegration can benefit from UNHCR
  services.

* Where countries of first asylum are themselves impover-
  ished, and where conditions for repatriation remain
  dubious, the UNHCR should continue to promote resettlement in third countries of asylum. In concert with
  this, efforts must be made to encourage non-traditional
  resettlement countries in the first world to share in
  the protection of refugees and in the resolution of
  their situations.

* For resettlement to be a durable solution, substantial
  effort and commitment are needed to facilitate acculturation and the long-term economic and political
  integration of refugees. The UNHCR should promote this
  through the dissemination of culturally relevant information to host governments.

* In all durable solutions, the refugees themselves must
  play more significant roles. The UNHCR must continue
  to push for this. Empowerment must be facilitated.

NOTES

[1]For example, L. Gordenker, in Refugees in International
Politics (New York: Columbia University Press, 1987),
stresses the intermingling of political, economic, and
social factors in the generation of contemporary refugee
flows. A. Zolberg, in "The Formation of New States as a
Refugee-Generating Process" (Refugees in World Politics, ed.
by E.G. Ferris, New York: Praeger, 1985, pp. 26-42) draws
the connection between underdevelopment and the formation of
authoritarian states which insitutionalize political persecution, causing refugee flows.

[2]Today there are an estimated 17 million refugees worldwide,
as noted in Refugees (Jan. 1992), No. 88, p. 46.

[3]B. Stein, "Durable Solutions for Developing Country Refugees," _International Migration Review_ 20: 264-282, 1986.

[4]Ibid.

[5]Ibid.

[6]According to the 1951 U.N. Convention Relating to the Status of Refugees, a refugee is defined as a person who "owing to well-founded fear of being persecuted for reasons of race, religion, nationality, membership of a particular social group or political opinion, is outside the country of his nationality and is unable or, owing to such fear, is unwilling to avail himself of the protection of that country."

[7]Ford Foundation, _Refugees and Migrants: Problems and Program Responses_ (New York: Ford Foundation, 1983).

[8]This information is reported in an editorial entitled "Needs and Resources," _Refugees_ (June 1990), No. 76, p. 5.

[9]See V.O. Sutter, _The Indochinese Refugee Dilemma_ (Baton Rouge: Lousiana State University, 1990), p. 200.

[10]W.R. Smyser, "Refugees: A Never-ending Story," _Foreign Affairs_ 64: 154-168, 1985.

[11]See note 3, above.

[12]See note 3, above.

[13]T. Hodges, "Africa's Refugee Crisis," _Africa Report_ (Jan./ Feb. 1984), Nos. 29-30, pp. 4-11.

[14]See note 7, above.

[15]See Stein (note 3, above) for a discussion of Ethiopian refugees from Djibouti and the debate which arose over accusations that aid would be cut off to those who refused to repatriate. See also G.S. Goodwin-Gill, "Voluntary Repatriation: Legal and Policy Issues," in G. Loescher and L. Monahan, eds., _Refugees and International Relations_ (Oxford: Oxford University Press, 1989, pp. 255-292), for a discussion of this in terms of conditions in countries of return, with the "coercion" and "encouragement" techniques used. Sutter, in _The Indochinese Refugee Dilemma_ (see note 9, above), points to a lack of protests from the UNHCR regarding forced repatriation by Thailand of Cambodians.

[16]See S. Tefft, "Vietnamese Boat People Face Uneasy Trip Home," _Christian Science Monitor_ (Nov. 30, 1990), p. 3.

[17]Sutter (see note 9, above) discusses the UNHCR's attempt to fulfill its mandate in light of constraints put upon the organization in Southeast Asia.

[18]See note 16, above.

[19]T. Howland, "A Comparative Analysis of the Changing Definition of a Refugee," Journal of Human Rights 5: 49-50, 1987.

[20]This information is reported in the "Newsflash" column, Refugees (Nov. 1990), No. 80, p. 6.

[21]U.S. Committee for Refugees, Uncertain Harbors: The Plight of Vietnamese Boat People (Washington, DC: U.S. Committee for Refugees, 1987).

[22]Gordenker, note 1 above, pp. 158-160.

[23]U.S. Committee For Refugees, In Harms Way: Refugees from Laos (Washington, DC: U.S. Committee for Refugees, 1986).

[24]Lawyers Committee for Human Rights, Forced Back and Forgotten: The Human Rights of Laotian Asylum Seekers in Thailand (New York: Lawyers Committee for Human Rights, 1989).

[25]Lawyers Committee for Human Rights, Inhumane Deterrence: The Treatment of Vietnamese Boat People in Hong Kong (New York: Lawyers Committee for Human Rights, 1989).

[26]Ibid.

[27]Gordenker, note 1 above, pp. 158-160.

[28]See note 8, above.

[29]This information is reported in a commentary entitled "Africa: A Continent in Crisis," Refugees (Dec. 1990), No. 81, p. 11.

[30]Stein, note 3 above, p. 269.

[31]See S. Pittman, "A Comparative Survey of Two Decades of International Assistance to Refugees in Africa," Africa Today 31: 49, 1984.

[32]J. Crisp, "The High Price of Hospitality," Refugees (Nov. 1990), No. 80, p. 20.

[33]Economic and Social Council Report of the UNHCR, May 9, 1989, p. 19, paragraph 86.

[34]Ibid., p. 18, paragraph 80.

[35] B.E. Harrell-Bond and R. Dunbar-Ortiz, "Africa Rights Monitor: Who Protects the Human Rights of Refugees?" _Africa Today_ 32: 71-78, 1985.

[36] T.F. Betts, "Evolution and Promotion of the Integrated Rural Development Approach to Refugee Policy in Africa," _Africa Today_ 31: 7-24, 1984.

[37] See note 31, above.

[38] See note 36, above.

[39] P.J. Campbell, "Africa in Brief, Rwanda/Burundi: Ethnic Violence Revisited," _Africa Today_ 37: 73, 1990. For further discussion see T. Basok, "Welcome Some and Reject Others: Constraints and Interests Influencing Costa Rican Policy on Refugees," _International Migration Review_ 24: 724-725, 1990.

[40] T. Skari, "Djibouti: A Reluctant Haven," _Refugees_ (Jan. 1990), No. 72, p. 24.

[41] See Betts, note 36 above, pp. 21-22.

[42] See note 40, above.

[43] Although not discussing the Kurds, a pertinent overview is provided by R.L. Bach, "Third Country Resettlement," in G. Loescher and L. Monahan, eds., _Refugees and International Relations_ (Oxford: Oxford University Press, 1989, pp. 313-332).

[44] Ibid.

[45] According to J.W. Berry and his colleagues, acculturation is the "culture change that results from continuous first-hand contact between two distinct cultural groups." See J.W. Berry, U. Kim, T. Minde, and D. Mok, "Comparative Studies of Acculturative Stress," _International Migration Review_ 21: 491-511, 1987.

[46] G.S. Goodwin-Gill, _The Refugee in International Law_ (Oxford: Clarendon Press, 1983).

[47] D. Kreisberg (nee Kreisberg-Voss), "The Political Nature of Refugee Recognition," a senior thesis submitted to the European Center in London, Friends World College, May 1985.

[48] See note 46, above.

[49] See note 47, above.

[50] G. Melander, _Refugees in Orbit_ (Geneva: IUSE, 1978).

[51]L. Grant and I. Martin, _Immigration Law and Practice_ (London: Copden Trust, 1982).

[52]B. Stein as referenced in H. Adelman, "Refuge or Asylum: A Philosophical Perspective," _Journal of Refugee Studies_ 1: 8, 1988.

[53]P.W. Van Arsdale, "New Immigrants to Colorado: Impact of the Amnesty Program." Lecture presented to the Society for International Development, Denver, Colorado, October 25, 1989.

[54]D. Kreisberg-Voss, J. Sobrepeña, and P.W. Van Arsdale, "Immigration Reform and Barriers to Immigrant Integration: Enhancing Acculturation by Impacting U.S. Policy," in G.W. Shepherd, Jr. and D. Penna, eds., _Racism and the Underclass: State Policy and Discrimination Against Minorities_ (New York: Greenwood Press, 1991).

[55]See note 29, above.

[56]This information is reported in an editorial entitled "Reaffirming the Spirit of International Solidarity," _Refugees_ (Oct. 1986), No. 34, p. 5.

[57]J. Seaman, "Assistance: The System Breaks Down," _Refugees_ (Dec. 1990), No. 81, p. 13.

PART IV
CONCLUSION

TOWARD UNDERSTANDING THE REFUGEE DILEMMA: MIGRATION THEORY AND PRINCIPLES OF EMPOWERMENT

Olusegun A. Daramola
Timothy U. Mozia
University of Denver

In this chapter, we provide a brief review of refugee problems which builds upon information provided by the other authors in this book. The conceptual issues of internal and international migration, voluntary and involuntary displacement, and the implications of these for self-reliance and empowerment are examined. Where necessary, certain key points are exemplified by our own research on the Horn of Africa.

THEORETICAL FRAMEWORK OF ANALYSIS

Migration is here defined in the broadest sense, as population movements within and across national boundaries. It involves temporary or permanent relocation. Migrants themselves, as well as areas or countries of origin and destination, are the central features of analysis. Migration is an enduring feature of the prehistory and history of humankind. Individuals, families, and at times, whole communities have moved from one geographic area to another in search of better political, social, and/or economic living conditions. This has made the study of migration of increasing interest to researchers representing numerous disciplines such as anthropology, ecology, political science, history, and geography.

However, the study of migration has been bedeviled by definitional and methodological problems.[1] It has been difficult to achieve precise understandings of human relocations especially given uncertainties regarding the motivations which propel people to move.

While international migration historically has been the focus of much research, in recent decades internal migration (rural-rural, rural-urban, urban-urban, and urban-rural) has begun to attract more attention, especially in light of its demographic significance. For example, how migration affects population growth, ethnic differences in migrant streams, and the impact of migration on other characteristics of individuals and receiving societies, are yielding broader understandings of over-all societal transformations. A major question then becomes how to forge a marriage between pertinent theoretical approaches relating to migration, and the practical implications of societal transformations that are the inevitable sequels of migra-

tion. In this regard, we highlight two related issues:
Internal and international migration, and voluntary and
involuntary migration. Their implications for self-reliance
and empowerment are assessed in the latter part of this
chapter.

INTERNAL AND INTERNATIONAL MIGRATION

Much literature recently has been devoted to the
development of theoretical perspectives with which to
explain and evaluate the phenomenon of migration.[2] Internal
migration has received its share of attention. Internal
migration refers to the movement of people within specifically defined geographic boundaries or frontiers. Such
movements, at least theoretically, do not have to confront
restrictions imposed by legal processes. On the other hand,
international migration is conceptualized as population
movement across and beyond national borders or frontiers.
Given the frequently espoused principle of state sovereignty, it is no surprise that such population movements
inevitably confront an array of legal restrictions and constraints as these pertain to exit from the sending country
and entry, residence, and adjustment to the receiving
country (see Hansen, this volume).

The causes of such population movements are many and
diverse. They range from natural disasters such as
earthquakes, droughts, and floods, to political insta-
bilities and domestic upheavals. Additionally, economic
considerations also have continued to assume a position of
importance in discussions of internal and international
migration.[3] Internal migration takes place, in large part,
in response to structural disequilibrium and economic imbal-
ances among the various sectors of a country. The dominant
tendency has been for movements associated with income-
generating opportunities, usually of the rural to urban
type. However, as correctly pointed out by Adepoju, one can
expect "a substantial flow" of intra-rural migration in
cases where efforts are made by governments to develop the
agriculture industry in rural areas.[4] At the same time,
much international migration also can be attributed to gaps
in socio-economic development between the Developed and Less
Developed Countries. Migration streams flow from the latter
to the former as people seek better economic opportunities.
Certain theorists also have gone further, to hypothesize
that such migration flows could be expected to decrease
considerably with increased investments in the sending
countries.[5]

Another crucial issue germane to a better understanding
of migration streams relates to open and/or improper border
demarcations, especially in Less Developed Countries. Systems theorists find this of particular interest, as "open"
and "closed" systems are considered. For example, on the
attainment of independence, African countries, as exem-

plified in OAU resolutions, vowed to maintain the existing borders arbitrarily carved out for them by the colonial powers. In some cases, this had the effect of splitting people of similar ethnic and cultural heritage into different countries, while in others, lumping together in one country people of diverse cultures and value systems. Ethiopia, Somalia, and Sudan are differing but vivid cases in point. Added to this is the porous nature of most of these borders. It hardly occasions any surprise that international migration has been seen by some theorists as a mere extension of internal migration in the Horn of Africa and elsewhere.[6] Border crossing is done with relative frequency, even ease.

An additional issue concerns "wave" or group migration, with features common to both internal and international migration. This occurs among homogenous communities which migrate in groups or waves mostly for political or economic reasons, as with nomads in Sudan,[7] or for reasons relating to natural disasters in the home area.

These are but a few of the most important conceptual and theoretical issues to be considered in discussions of internal and international migration. Others are covered (e.g.) by Jones, Zaharlick and Brainard, and Hansen and Oliver-Smith.[8]

IMPLICATIONS FOR REFUGEE ANALYSIS

Refugee flows can be analyzed against the backdrop of the internal and international migration issues sketched above. In general, certain of the factors responsible for migration streams between nations also have been partly responsible for refugee streams. These include wars, civil strife, and other political disturbances, with the repressive rule of leaders such as Mengistu in Ethiopia (through May of 1991) generating a significant part of the refugee exodus through human rights violations. Famine and drought variously have contributed to both economic migrant and political refugee creation. The Horn of Africa, for example, recently has been ravaged by severe cases of drought and famine, a situation which has contributed to the creation of Ethiopian refugees who have fled to Somalia, Djibouti, and the Sudan, and contributed to the dissolution of the central government in Somalia. The 1962 Ethiopian annexation of Eritrea, the 1977-1978 Ogaden war, and the 1991-1992 inter-clan clashes in Somalia are vivid examples of the impact of internal strife on the creation of refugees.[9]

Evidence of the interplay of internal migration and refugee creation factors are reflected in the resettlement and "villagization" schemes prevalent in Ethiopia under former president Mengistu. Resettlement referred to the planned moving of large numbers of people from areas where land theoretically could no longer support them, to areas where land purportedly was underused. As noted by Ruiz, "more than 800,000 people were so forcibly moved in the mid-1980s before the international outcry over the brutality of the program's implementation led the government to halt it temporarily".[10] A similar situation emerged from the government's villagization scheme, which forcibly moved peasants from their scattered farms into new, more centralized villages.

International migration borne out of economic considerations also interplays with, and at times confounds, the analysis of refugee flows. In the Horn the Djibouti government claims that the country is a magnet for so-called economic migrants from Somalia and Ethiopia. Political considerations are downplayed. South Africa makes a similar claim for the laborers from Botswana, Lesotho, and Swaziland.[11] In the literature, there is little dispute regarding the fact that developed countries have, especially in the 1980s and 1990s, also had to deal with the increasing influx of migrants coming for economic reasons. This same set of factors also has contributed to internal and international migration streams in the Middle East and Central America.

The implications for refugee analysis are clear. Researchers must build upon existing "economic understandings" of internal and international migration, to appropriately include "political understandings." Refugees may be defined by various governments as a type of "political migrant," but in actuality an interplay of economic and political factors often propels them.

VOLUNTARY AND INVOLUNTARY MOVEMENTS

Cross-cutting our understanding of migration theory is our understanding of the distinctions that can be drawn between voluntary and involuntary migration (or displacement), either in internal or international contexts, as well as the analysis of related policy issues.

We share the view of Heisel, that the major cause of voluntary movement of populations between and within national borders in recent years is rooted in the initial and rapidly growing disparity in development among states.[12] While it also can exhibit social, political, and ethnic or cultural dimensions, voluntary migration often derives from economic factors tied to the migrant's desire to improve his or her economic status.

In sharp contrast, involuntary movements within and across national borders are rooted primarily in non-economic factors. They derive basically from political and religious factors as well as droughts, famine, and natural disasters. In the Horn of Africa, for example, the forced movement of persons owing to the resettlement and villagization policies in Ethiopia were classic examples of involuntary migration. So also is the forced repatriation of refugees from

Djibouti. Similar factors characterize involuntary population movements in other parts of the world. Vivid cases
in point are Hmong refugees and the Kurds in Iraq, both discussed in detail in this volume by Vang Pobzeb and Pauletta
Otis, respectively. Political instability and involuntary
migration often are closely linked.

The linkages between conceptual and operational or
applied issues arising from theories of internal/
international and voluntary/involuntary migration and the
analysis and understanding of refugee flows, briefly high-
lighted here, are inextricable. It remains to go a step
further to consider the implications of these linkages for
self-reliance and empowerment for the refugees under consideration in this book.

PRINCIPLES OF SELF-RELIANCE AND EMPOWERMENT

Most countries are ill prepared to bear the economic
and infrastructural burden imposed upon them by refugee
arrivals. Coping with the refugee burden is not only a
matter of meeting the needs of the displaced, but also of
ensuring that the local mechanisms and institutions designed
to support the citizens of the host countries do not crack
under the strain. Because of this, countries such as the
United States and Canada place strong emphasis on the
attainment of early self-sufficiency, self-reliance, and
economic independence for refugees. For them, one principle
of self-reliance can be assurance of lasting and fundamental
labor and employment programs which rest principally on the
identification of appropriate resources, use of indigenous
talents, and training/ESL opportunities (see Adkins and
Sample, this volume). Realistic expectations of socio-
economic independence must accompany such initiatives.

The patterns of migration streams identified in this
chapter have direct bearings on the realization of these
objectives. For one thing, it could be argued by some
(especially for the Less Developed Countries) that the relative ease with which internal/international migrations have
been carried out actually eliminates bureaucratic obstacles
which would otherwise have to be faced by refugees. Thus,
according to this logic, rather than concern themselves with
the problem of overcoming stringent immigration problems,
refugees are freed to devote more energy and time to enterprises designed for the achievement of self-sufficiency and
self-empowerment. However, we believe that this perspective
is flawed. For one, it fails to take account of the counterproductive socio-psychological effects of involuntary
migration on refugees. Again witness, for example, the
outcry generated by the 1980s policies of resettlement and
villagization in Ethiopia. We firmly believe that the
achievement of self-reliance is directly contingent upon the
socio-psychological state of the refugees and the cooperation evidenced by the host countries. A principle linking

185

self-reliance and empowerment is confidence, itself tied to socio-psychological well-being.

We share the optimism of others regarding the tenacity and resilience of refugees (see Van Arsdale, this volume). These are qualities and mind-sets which can be translated into positive behaviors in the quest for self-reliance and empowerment (see Basok, this volume). However, the practical situation confronting refugees is often one which would seem to restrain the conversion of this quality in proactive directions. Many refugees from Sudan, Ethiopia, Iran, Iraq, Turkey, and Angola, to name but a few, tend to perceive their sojourns in their various countries of asylum as transient--even though many of them have lived there for years. While on the one hand, this could be viewed as a kind of "overly optimistic empowerment," preparing them for possible voluntary repatriation, on the other hand it realistically creates a constant dilemma with refugees unable or unwilling to improve their conditions in the host country. The translation of resiliency into the ability to attain self-sufficiency is hampered.

Where refugees have attempted to convert their resilience into concrete action geared towards economic independence, the structure of the host country's economy often has acted as a hindrance (see DeVoe, this volume). The bureaucracy can seem complex, with difficult-to-fathom agendas (see Mortland, this volume). High refugee unemployment and underemployment rates are inevitable consequences of this. Many become dependent on seasonal and casual wage-labor. A large percentage of the refugees in Africa are dependent on wage employment in the agricultural sector. Even during good harvest years, a general lack of other forms of employment forces laborers in this sector into several months of unemployment or underemployment annually. To further exacerbate the situation, there is a general lack of legislation regarding refugees in the agricultural sector that has been developed in such countries. This has had the effect of exposing laborers to exploitation which, in turn, has served to increase their poverty.

The obstacles in the way of attaining self-sufficiency extend beyond the socio-psychological state of the refugees themselves or structural/economic shortcomings in their host countries. As suggested by Gorman, several other obstacles arise. These include the inability of donors to provide adequate additional assistance, the inability of host countries to absorb this assistance effectively, the inability of refugee development agencies and ministries to coordinate their activities effectively, and the inadequate capacity of the international system to maintain the momentum of refugee aid and development initiatives in light of overwhelming pressures worldwide.[13] This perspective has been reinforced with particular force by Harrell-Bond in her analysis of the impact of aid-giving agencies for camp-bound refugees in Sudan. She asserts in no uncertain terms that these agencies in fact have had a counterproductive effect on the refugees for whom aid is intended. Inter- and intra-agency rivalries, quests for personal aggrandizement, and preoccupation with scoring "political points" have been rife.[14] Slim effort has been made by these agencies to fully understand the complexities of the problems faced by camp-bound refugees, or to facilitate the empowerment process. Refugees neither have been given a means of expressing their opinions nor given even partial control of their own affairs, despite the efforts of some agencies to initiate refugee counselling services. Being out of touch with such realities, aid designed to see refugees through difficult times often has failed to have the desired impact. This problem has considerably undermined those agency accomplishments that have occurred. It is little wonder that the search for self-reliance and economic independence has, at best, remained a mirage for many. Indeed, some feel safer with remittances sent to them by relatives abroad, no matter how meager these amounts might be.

One of the most basic principles of empowerment is control, the opportunity to take charge of one's own destiny. As exemplified in foreign refugee camps or domestic resettlement agencies, this could be manifested in the opportunity to control or substantively assist with the distribution of resources. Self-reliance flows from this, although it is not to be equated with empowerment. Similarly, self-sufficiency flows from this, although it is not to be equated with empowerment either (see McSpadden, this volume).

CONCLUSIONS

Following the world-wide economic downturns experienced in the 1980s, a general atmosphere of hostility swamped migrants and refugees in many receiving countries. Residents felt threatened by their presence and the employment competition they seemed to present. Some, such as Gulf Coast Vietnamese in the U.S., became scapegoats for various economic problems being experienced by local residents.

It will be necessary for international organizations like the UN and regional bodies like the OAU (in the case of the Horn of Africa) to coordinate efforts to resolve refugee problems (see Campbell, Kreisberg-Voss, and Sobrepeña, this volume). It is instructive to take stock of the OAU's expansion of the original definition of refugee in a manner enabling it to deal with a wider category of displaced person. It also is worth noting the spirit of cooperation between the UNHCR and UNDP as earlier seen in southern Sudan. We believe it is essential to reiterate the importance of inter- and intra-agency cooperation; a positive institutional environment must be created for empowerment to have the possibility of occurring.

However, it would be wrong to assume that only external factors have roles to play in seeking an amelioration, and possibly an end, to the suffering of refugees. The governments of the various refugee-sending countries also have vital roles to play. As made clear during 1992 in the former Yugoslavia, they must cease violating the basic human rights of their citizens. Many refugees are fleeing the abusive policies of such governments. The use of force to implement controversial resettlement and villagization programs in such far-flung locations as Romania and Ethiopia has been widely condemned. The practice by which some governments inflate their refugee population figures in order to increase aid given by donor countries and agencies also has been condemned. Through practices such as this, as seen in 1992 in Somalia, aid is diverted to non-refugees and used to buoy up decaying national economies. The governments of developed countries also must work to avert antipathy--even xenophobic reactionism--towards refugees in their midst, while adopting measures enabling refugees to develop their economic potentials to the fullest. The unified Germany is a case in point. This will contribute to the creation of internal environments conducive to empowerment.

Refugees are a human tragedy at its most fundamental level, a tragedy usually created by people. The issues must be resolved by people, with refugees themselves playing key roles.

NOTES

[1] C. Stern, "Some Methodological Notes on the Study of Human Migration," in International Migration Today: Emerging Issues, Vol. 2, C. Stahl, ed. (Brussels: UNESCO Publications, 1988). See also G.W. Haag, ed., Interregional Migration: Dynamic Theory and Comparative Analysis (New York: Springer Verlag, 1988); and W. Peterson, "A General Typology of Migration," American Sociological Review 23: 256-266, 1958.

[2] M.M. Kritz, C.B. Keely, and S.M. Tomasi, eds., Global Trends in Migration: Theory and Research on International Population Movements (New York: Center for Migration Studies, 1981); International Migration Today: Emerging Issues, Vol. 1, R. Appleyard, ed., and Vol. 2, C. Stahl, ed. (Brussels: UNESCO Publications, 1988).

[3] R. Lucas, "International Migration: Economic Causes, Consequences and Evaluation," in M.M. Kritz, et al., eds. (see note 2, above).

[4] A. Adepoju, "Links Between Internal and International Migration: The African Situation," in C. Stahl, ed., pp. 34-35 (see note 2, above).

188

[5]See Stern, note 1 above, pp. 28-33.

[6]For details concerning this assumption, see Adepoju (note 4, above).

[7]P.W. Van Arsdale, "The Ecology of Survival in Sudan's Periphery: Short-Term Tactics and Long-Term Strategies," _Africa Today_ 36: 65-78, 1989.

[8]G.W. Jones, ed., _Demographic Transition in Asia_ (Singapore: Maruzen Asia, 1984); A. Zaharlick and J. Brainerd, "Demographic Characteristics, Ethnicity, and the Resettlement of Southeast Asian Refugees in the United States," _Urban Anthropology_ 16: 327-372, 1987; and A. Hansen and A. Oliver-Smith, eds., _Forced Migration and Resettlement: The Problems and Responses of Displaced Peoples_ (Boulder, CO: Westview, 1982).

[9]A general discussion of several of these crises is found in "Beyond the Headlines: Refugees in the Horn of Africa," Issue Paper (Washington, DC: U.S. Committee for Refugees, 1988). Most of the research for this issue paper was conducted by H. Ruiz.

[10]Ibid., p. 2.

[11]For background information, see Adepoju, in C. Stahl, ed. (see note 4, above).

[12]D.F. Heisel, "Theories of International Migration," in _International Migration in the Arab World_ (Beirut: United Nations Economic Commission for Western Asia, 1982).

[13]R.F. Gorman, "Coping with Africa's Refugee Burden: A Time for Solutions," Working Paper (Geneva: UNITAR, 1987). Certain of these issues also are covered in Campbell, Kreisberg-Voss, and Sobrepeña (this volume).

[14]B.E. Harrell-Bond, _Imposing Aid: Emergency Assistance to Refugees_ (Oxford: Oxford University Press, 1986).